COACHABLE

COACHABLE

How the Greatest Performers Reach Their Highest Potential

RIC BUCHER

AVERY
an imprint of Penguin Random House
New York

AVERY
an imprint of Penguin Random House LLC
1745 Broadway, New York, NY 10019
penguinrandomhouse.com

Copyright © 2026 by Ric Bucher Productions, LLC
Penguin Random House values and supports copyright. Copyright fuels creativity, encourages diverse voices, promotes free speech, and creates a vibrant culture. Thank you for buying an authorized edition of this book and for complying with copyright laws by not reproducing, scanning, or distributing any part of it in any form without permission. You are supporting writers and allowing Penguin Random House to continue to publish books for every reader. Please note that no part of this book may be used or reproduced in any manner for the purpose of training artificial intelligence technologies or systems.

Avery with colophon is a trademark of Penguin Random House LLC

Most Avery books are available at a discount when purchased in quantity for sales promotions or corporate use. Special editions, which include personalized covers, excerpts, and corporate imprints, can be created when purchased in large quantities. For more information, please e-mail specialmarkets@penguinrandomhouse.com. Your local bookstore can also assist with discounted bulk purchases using the Penguin Random House corporate Business-to-Business program. For assistance in locating a participating retailer, e-mail B2B@penguinrandomhouse.com.

Book design by Angie Boutin

Library of Congress Cataloging-in-Publication data is on file.

Hardcover ISBN: 9780593853030
eBook ISBN: 9780593853054

Printed in the United States of America
3rd Printing

The authorized representative in the EU for product safety and compliance is Penguin Random House Ireland, Morrison Chambers, 32 Nassau Street, Dublin D02 YH68, Ireland, https://eu-contact.penguin.ie.

For Helga Bucher, my biggest cheerleader,

and Mathias Bucher, a.k.a. Coach

CONTENTS

COACHABLE

INTRODUCTION

THIS IS, BY ALL APPEARANCES, A BOOK ABOUT SPORTS. IT IS NOT.

It is about people of various genders and generations who, independently, adopted one common trait they consider indispensable to their subsequent success: the ability to synthesize who and what they wanted to be with someone else's vision of who and what they could be through a mutually embraced idea of how to get there. They were all, in a word, coachable.

That is not a concept exclusive to sports or athletes.

This book is organized around the ten "truths" of being coachable, with each truth illustrated by an athlete's full story and their road to reaching their highest potential. I chose to illustrate the value of being coachable through a variety of athletes, rather than a variety of professions—athlete, musician, business executive, astronaut, politician, etc.—for a couple of reasons. One, because if there is a universal language, it is not Esperanto; it is sports. No matter what profession we ultimately pursue, at some point we were all enthralled with a sport, whether playing or watching. And two, to truly show the dynamics that make someone coachable, I needed to dig into the events and experiences that shaped my subjects at an early age—events and experiences that weren't always flattering. My long career covering sports and the relationships I've built have earned me the necessary trust to do that.

As a kid, I didn't dream of writing a book about the value of being coachable. Like a lot of us, I dreamed of being a professional athlete, a dream I surrendered when I was accepted into an Ivy League school; as the first person in my family to go to college, I felt I owed it to my parents to shift my focus from the pitch to the classroom. I still made Dartmouth's varsity soccer team as a walk-on freshman, but I played more out of pure love for the sport than pursuing a future career. Having always had a creative bent—I had played trumpet and piano, drawn cartoon strips, and written short stories and poems since grade school—I always fancied myself as a performer or creator of some kind. When I landed an internship with *Sports Illustrated* the summer before my senior year, it offered the chance to splice my sports dream with my artistic one. Working with the writers and editors at *SI*, I saw for the first time that sports were a sneaky way of writing about life lessons. Every sports story in some way is about facing an obstacle and overcoming it or being inextricably changed by it. Sportswriting gave me the chance to identify formulas for success and present them in a way everyone could appreciate and understand.

I now know that my experiences as an athlete—including the sobering reality that I would not reach as high as I had hoped—shaped, inspired, and informed everything I've done ever since. As a sportswriter, I was most interested in the life experiences and relationships of the athletes and coaches before they reached the pinnacles of their sports, particularly those experiences and relationships beyond the locker room or field of play. Part of it was to understand what they had that I didn't; part of it was to identify their formulas for success and see if they would work equally well on my nonathletic goals.

I am happy to report that those formulas do. They are, it turns out, the most valuable intangibles an athlete can extract from playing a sport. Author and motivational speaker Simon Sinek crafted a parable about two road signs: one that read VICTORY and pointed in one direction, and another pointing in another direction that read FULFILLMENT. The value of victory, in short, is reaching a specific goal or destination, a moment of standing at the top of the mountain as the crowd cheers and confetti falls. Fulfillment is all about what is gained—and shared—on the way to the summit. What this book suggests is that victory and fulfillment can both be realized treading the same path; victory, however, is a roadside car wash, while fulfillment is a lifetime AAA card. Monumental victories are part of every performer's story in this book, but they were mere mile markers on the way to fulfillment, which is what they truly cherish. Equally important to them were the places they crashed on the journey because they are now convinced the victories would not have been realized without them.

While this book is about more than sports, there is a coachability crisis in American sports today. Far too many young athletes and their families today are all about victory when it comes to what they hope to gain from playing a sport. That has led to their dreams being exploited by anyone dangling exposure and connections to land an athletic scholarship (and, now, a name-image-likeness bonus). There's nothing wrong with aspiring to earn an athletic scholarship or an NIL (name, image, likeness) deal, but making it the be-all and end-all as soon as a kid shows any degree of aptitude creates a host of repercussions. Besides, if a Division I or Division II free ride and a few extra bucks are the lone measure of success, the vast majority of athletes (and their families) will have wasted considerable time and money and be sorely disappointed with the results of their efforts. I'm reminded of legendary NFL quarterback Aaron Rodgers, who, in the aftermath of achieving his lifelong dream of winning a Super Bowl, thought, *Is that all there is?*

"I was like, 'Did I aim at the wrong thing, or did I spend too much time thinking about stuff that ultimately doesn't give you true happiness?'" he said in the Netflix documentary *Aaron Rodgers: Enigma*. Anyone who has achieved anything noteworthy is sure to tell you that the final product—be it a Vince Lombardi Trophy or inventing a bagless vacuum cleaner—is not what they treasure; it's what they discovered along the way.

James Dyson, a billionaire thanks to his invention of the aforementioned vacuum cleaner that bears his name, took as much satisfaction out of inventing the Contrarotator, a washing machine. It was, essentially, a commercial bust, but it worked exactly the way Dyson had hoped.

"That it was not necessarily a commercial success came secondary to the pursuit of solving the problem," he told the BBC. "That is what I really enjoy. Failure is the best medicine—as long as you learn something."

The reality: everyone has a gift or special talent. Identifying it, encouraging it, and, perhaps most important, challenging it determines whether it's ever fully developed. One of the common threads among the athletes in this book is that they were strengthened by *not* being favored, not playing on the "A" team right away. That prompted them to build muscle *and* character, which came to serve them later on. It saddens me seeing the confused and despondent look on an athlete's face (and the disappointed or even angry look on their parents' faces) when they fall short of reaching a certain objective, whether it be starting on their high school team or getting a free ride in college or playing professionally—especially since I've been around sports long enough to see it coming, akin to watching a car crash unfold in slow motion. Having watched that scenario play out over and over again, I've often thought to myself, *If only they knew . . .*

This book is my invitation to know.

I had the great privilege to befriend three-time NBA champion B. J. Armstrong through my work covering the NBA, which in turn gave me insight into one of his teammates, the greatest basketball player I've ever seen, Michael Jordan. B.J. was the first to bring to my attention what Jordan claimed was the secret to his success. It wasn't the body control that earned him the nickname "Black Cat" or the athleticism that allowed him to glide through the air as if suspended on some invisible wire. None of that. Not his pterodactyl wingspan, either—arms that seemed to engulf opponents and earned him nine first team All-Defensive Team awards and a Defensive Player of the Year award, something generally reserved for shot-blocking and rebounding big men. Nor his hands, so massive and nimble he could palm a basketball with either one like a grapefruit. Nor his foot speed—4.4 seconds in the forty-yard dash as a college sophomore—that made it impossible for defenders to stay between him and the basket short of knocking him to the ground.

The aforementioned gifts all served as the raw material for being a six-time NBA champion and five-time league MVP—an award now named the Michael Jordan Trophy—but they weren't what separated him from all the other uniquely blessed NBA stars.

The secret to his success? "I was coachable," he said.

I know, I know. It seems preposterous that someone as

physically gifted, savvy, and ferociously competitive as Jordan would credit his coachability as his No. 1 asset. Isn't that for role players or someone just trying to make the team? Someone not blessed with an extraordinary physique? At the very least, it contains a level of humility that seems out of character for any athlete of Jordan's magnitude; it's an admission that he needed help, a guide to reach the summit. It flies in the face of the fierce image we have of him—and most other champion-level performers—with that give-me-the-ball-and-get-out-of-the-way steely gaze. But his admission doesn't discount those physical gifts and mental temperament; he's simply saying that he could not have exploited them to their fullest capacity had he not *also* been coachable. Jordan is extremely proud of the fact that he didn't always win, didn't always succeed, so much so that he made a commercial about all the game-winning shots he missed. He has gone out of his way to remind the world that he had to learn a lot of hard lessons on his way to the top, because he is proud of the resilience and effort that went into learning them. He is comfortable acknowledging his failures because they were the building blocks to his success. He also came to understand that no single game, no single objective, defines success or failure. It's about taking on the challenge in the moment, learning from it, and seeking insight on how to perform better the next time.

Tom Brady, the seven-time Super Bowl–winning quarterback, talks a lot about the obstacles he had to overcome and making the most of his limited opportunities. That isn't just out of pride; that's how he developed the tools that led to his later success. Mental tools that go far beyond accurately throwing a football or reading a defense. At one point I considered making both Jordan and Brady part of this book, but their achievements are so extraordinary, it might take some convincing that you, too, reader, can be like Mike or Tom. Their extraordinary fame also has resulted in them being guarded about their personal lives and relationships, and dissecting those relationships is essential to understanding how and why they were coachable. So, instead, I selected a more relatable array of athletes who attained their own lofty achievements by developing into the best versions of themselves—on and off the field or court—and were willing to give the intimate details on how they did it.

No matter their gender, generation, or sport, all of them—along with countless others that I interviewed and consulted—attribute their success in doing that to being coachable.

So what, exactly, does that mean? It is an oft-used word, but it does not have a universal meaning. Everyone I spoke with could offer a definition, but none of them were exactly alike. I gave you mine already: synthesizing your vision of who and what you *want* to be with someone else's vision of who and what you *can* be by collaborating to realize that shared vision.

Looking back at my athletic career, I wish I had been more coachable, more earnest about seeking perspective on what I did and didn't do well and how to improve. It requires a combination of confidence and humility; I was long on the confidence, short on the humility. I was a tireless worker, but I know now my energy and focus could've been channeled in a much more effective way. If I had been able to see the big picture, to truly understand all that I could learn from acknowledging and addressing my weaknesses, I am sure I would've pursued my goals in a much healthier way, for both myself and those around me. The price for having to be forced into realizing the value of being coachable is wondering what could have been if I'd only had that realization sooner. In hindsight, it's hardly a shock that I replicated that approach early on in my professional career. I am painfully aware of how having a knack for doing something well can be a crutch or inhibitor to development. We stick to our strengths because we don't want anyone to see our weaknesses, not knowing that we're setting ourselves up to have those weaknesses revealed but not by our choosing.

In writing this book, what was truly gratifying is that almost everyone I asked to participate and share their story was passionate about doing so. It wasn't just that they felt incredibly blessed for having learned to be coachable and wanted to pay forward that discovery; they are also painfully aware, as I am, that the value of being coachable is sorely misunderstood and undervalued in today's world. They have seen, as I have, the rampant hucksterism that has misled parents and athletes alike—not only about what it takes to be successful but how success truly should be defined. Or what the true purpose of playing a sport should be. Those I spoke with—athletes and their parents—also had the simple desire to share secrets they wish they had known sooner. The all-time great coaches who responded were equally eager to share a coach's responsibility when entrusted with someone who is willing to be coached.

When I texted Richard Jefferson, the seventeen-year NBA veteran, champion, and member of ESPN/ABC's No. 1 NBA broadcast team, that I wanted his thoughts about my intention to write a book about the value of being coachable, my phone buzzed fifteen seconds later. If you've spent any time with current or former professional athletes, you can appreciate just how extraordinary a response like that is.

"It's an amazing idea for a book and I believe you'll do it well," he gushed. "This will be a must-read for coaches, for parents, for athletes. Being coachable is maybe the most important thing an athlete could ever have."

I can only hope that I proved him right. And that, after reading it, you will agree.

TRUTH 1

Giving In Is Not Giving Up: Steve Young

AS CONTRADICTORY AS IT MAY SOUND, STEVE YOUNG MIGHT NOT have ever been an NFL quarterback, much less one inducted into its Hall of Fame, had he not accepted his college coach's advice to stop playing the position.

A three-sport high school athlete in Greenwich, Connecticut, Young had an array of offers but ultimately chose Brigham Young University. Part of it was being Mormon and the great-great-grandson of Joseph Young, older brother to the school's namesake, Brigham. Part of it, as someone who had never spent a night outside of his parents' house, was the comfort of knowing that, despite being on the other side of the country, he had a safety net of friends and family near BYU's Provo, Utah, campus. But the biggest part? BYU's reputation for producing NFL quarterbacks. Young, with a poster of Roger Staubach on his bedroom wall, dreamed of being one of them.

What he didn't know until he arrived on campus was that he was one of four incoming quarterbacks and there were already four upper-class QBs on the roster. When he saw his name at the bottom of the list, "I thought for sure it had to be alphabetical," he said. "No way there were seven guys in front of me."

What he also didn't know was that offensive coordinator Doug Scovil had disdain for left-handed quarterbacks–and Young was the only lefty among the eight. If Scovil had had his way, Young might not have been on the list at all.

"He told me directly, 'I won't coach lefties,'" Young recalled Scovil saying after a week of summer camp. "I'm like, 'Oh, really?' I didn't even know. I thought, 'Is that legal?'"

It wasn't just the hand that Young threw with that prompted Scovil's lack of interest. Young had backdoored his way to Provo. BYU, by and large, didn't scout the East Coast for talent at that time. A member of the Youngs' church happened to be BYU head coach LaVell Edwards's college roommate at Utah State. The friend had watched plenty of Young's high school games and convinced Edwards to visit the Youngs while he was in New York with starting quarterback Jim McMahon for a Heisman Trophy promotional event. Edwards invited Young to take his fifth and final official recruiting visit to Provo and that sealed the deal.

For Young, anyway. Scovil, not having recruited him, practically acted as if Young weren't there, especially after his first practice. He had no experience as a drop-back passer, and it showed. In his very first BYU quarterback drill, a three-step drop, he fell on his butt and fumbled the ball. And despite being an outstanding pitcher in baseball and a point guard in basketball, as well as the star quarterback for the Greenwich High

Cardinals, Young did not throw a football particularly hard or accurately. What made him special? Freakish speed and agility. At the time, that made him highly coveted by a host of collegiate offenses built around quarterbacks who could hand the ball off to a running back going one way or keep it and go in the other direction. Quarterbacks who can pass and run are in vogue now in both college and the NFL, but back then the skill sets prized at the amateur and pro levels were distinctly different. College coaches saw the passing game as a risky proposition for eighteen-to-twenty-one-year-olds to get right—the quarterback having to throw it in the right place at the right time and the receiver having to be in the right place at the right time—in contrast to the simplicity of a quarterback tucking the ball into a running back's belly or tucking it into his own. Passing also presented infinitely more risk of losing possession altogether via interception. The heightened level of play in the NFL, on the other hand, required teams to be more offensively balanced. There was also the entertainment factor: the passing game was just generally more exciting, and NFL teams didn't have the built-in fan base of students and alums.

All of which is why Young could be highly coveted by a vast majority of respected Division I programs and an afterthought at BYU.

"Anybody that was running any kind of option offense at the time was like, 'Yeah, let's get this guy,'" Young said. "North Carolina, Virginia, every school up and down the East Coast. I was recruited all over the place for that."

That's where Young's fixation on BYU went beyond his faith or family history. He saw himself playing in the NFL, which meant proving he also could be a stand-tall-in-the-pocket passer. At the time, LaVell Edwards ran one of the few college programs that featured a pass-heavy offense and looked for quarterbacks to fit it.

"It was one of two or three in the whole country that was a throw-first offense," Young said. "There were no designed runs. There were no options. There was nothing. We were dropping back and throwing it. And in that way, it was the greatest place for me to be to prepare to play pro football. My intent, from the very beginning, was that I was going to be a classic drop-back quarterback who could run."

There was just that one hitch: Scovil didn't share his vision and Young had seven names above his on the depth chart. His ability as a run-option quarterback, though, did have its usefulness. Since most of BYU's opponents featured mobile quarterbacks, it earned him a starring role on the scout team. The downside: as the eighth-string QB, he was viewed as expendable, which meant the defense was free to tackle him with as much force as they would an opponent. Hence the scout team's moniker: the Hamburger Squad.

"I'm in summer camp and I'm lost in a sea of quarterbacks," Young said. "I'm running the scout team and I'm getting pummeled by Kyle Whittingham [son of Fred Whittingham, the defensive coordinator] and the defensive guys who were too stupid to know that I wasn't actually the Wyoming quarterback. I was just getting smashed. No one knew my name. No one knew anything."

If he was going to be ground beef, Young reasoned that he should at least do it in games that actually mattered. Operating a run-option offense at an East Coast school suddenly seemed far more appealing. He was fully aware that North Carolina, one of the schools that came after him hard, had told him he'd start as a freshman. He floated the idea of going back to Greenwich to reconsider his options to LaGrande "Grit" Young, his father.

"Dad, let me come back and let's refigure it," Steve said.

LeGrande, a former BYU fullback and Manhattan corporate attorney whose no-nonsense approach and indomitable spirit prompted the nickname, had an immediate answer for his oldest of five kids.

"No, that time is gone," he said matter-of-factly. "You can do whatever you want, but you can't come home. I don't live with quitters. I'm not living with you. You made your decision. You've got to fight through it."

Kimberly Shaffer, a professor of sports and exercise sciences at Barry University in Miami Shores, Florida, who has lent her expertise to a variety of teams, athletic programs, and athletes, applauded Grit's stance.

"So much of how we approach challenges is shaped in our younger years," she said. "That's when those habits are ingrained—our work ethic, the way that we view success, our ability to give up or quit when things get hard. It sounds so trivial, but it starts when the three-year-old is running and loses a race and just wants to go inside, and Mom and Dad are like, 'Okay!' No, it's not okay. Losing a race is okay. Going inside to hide, instead of talking about why the race was lost or the secret to running faster or racing again, is not okay. Parents can foster the right kind of environment. We can't expect our kids or anyone else to have a growth mindset and approach failure as 'What do I learn from it?' unless we teach that from a young age. The ability to approach things that are going to intentionally make you struggle, instead of just going for the thing that you're good at, is a growth mindset."

Grit knew something about perseverance in general and as a BYU football player in particular. He had grown up in Provo and played football at Brigham Young High. When his high school coach moved over to BYU to coach the freshman team, he extended walk-on offers to Grit and two of his teammates. Grit was the only one to make the team. He sat out his sophomore season with a knee injury and then went on a two-year mission. When he returned, BYU had a new head coach and Grit had to try out as a walk-on all over again—and again made the roster. By his senior year he was a starter.

Steve wanted to learn how to be an NFL quarterback. Grit wanted Steve to learn how to persevere. "That was just the way I was made," Grit said. "I was intent on getting through and winning the job, and I knew that's how I wanted my kids to be, too."

Being rejected by Scovil had to be doubly hard for Steve because of Scovil's reputation as an offensive wizard and quarterback-coaching savant credited with developing a list of highly regarded NFL quarterbacks, including Steve's idol, Staubach. Young, whose 4.4 time in the forty-yard dash made him the fastest player on the team, took out his frustration by trying to embarrass the starting defense in intrasquad scrimmages. He was so effective at mimicking Wyoming's Wishbone offense for the scout team that at one point a senior offensive lineman who doubled as JV coach, Andy Reid—yes, *that* Andy Reid, the Kansas City Chiefs head coach who developed three-time Super Bowl champion quarterback Patrick Mahomes—couldn't help himself.

"Steve Young is so good at the Wishbone, he's abusing our varsity defense!" Reid exclaimed one day.

Reid threatened to make it the JV team's full-time offense. He made it the primary plan for a JV road game against the University of Nevada–Las Vegas, where the artificial turf was so molten that the bottom of Young's cleats melted. But Young convinced Reid to make it the exception, not the rule, because it would only reinforce the idea that he was not made for a pass-oriented offense. "Holy hell, no," Young said to Reid when he floated the idea of making him the full-time JV starter if he was willing to run the Wishbone. "I'm trying to make the [varsity] squad!"

Despite having played collegiate football, Grit didn't involve himself in how his son played the game.

"My dad wasn't a tiger parent," Young said. "He was all about picking something you really wanted to do and then sticking with it. His big thing was you just don't quit. But what I was going to do and how I did it, he wasn't focused on that at all."

That left it up to Young to figure out his dilemma. Although the practice squad players were routinely dismissed early, he made a point of arriving at practice before anybody else and being the last to leave. Once his Hamburger Squad duties were done, he dedicated himself to watching everything that McMahon did–down to how he gripped and threw a football. He almost immediately noticed something different about McMahon's throwing motion from his own.

"Jim McMahon was a nutball, a crazy guy," Young said. "Everyone knows that; it's well-documented. But his throwing motion was as technically sound as any quarterback I ever saw. And that's why watching him was the perfect thing to have happen for me. Jim was a righty, and I'm lefty, so I'm staring at him in the mirror, essentially, and I saw his arm come down. I'm like, 'Wait a second. I don't throw it like that.' And seeing that, I started to mess with it and it was as if the heavens opened. I mean, literally, suddenly I had this unknown talent that was unlocked. I'd fought throwing the ball up until then. I couldn't throw it hard; my arm hurt when I did throw it. I wasn't doing it right. And then, all of a sudden, I got this little turn of the key by getting my hand inside, like throwing a screwball in baseball. Getting my shoulder and arm behind the ball suddenly gave me all this power. And then my accuracy went skyrocketing. I could put it anywhere. And so, by the time the fall ended, here I was with this newfound incredible talent that I didn't know I had. But because I threw with my left arm, they've decided I should play safety. I was like, 'Geez . . .'"

Between his value as a run-option QB and his newfound ability to throw a football with power and accuracy, Young was named junior varsity MVP. When Edwards called him into his office at the end of the regular season, Young hoped it was to hear he would be traveling with the varsity team to the Holiday Bowl as a reward.

Instead, Edwards told him he was too great an athlete not to be on the field and would be moving to the defensive side of the ball. He meant it as a compliment. Young took it as a punch in the gut. When Christmas vacation arrived, he went home planning not to return to Provo. He knew Grit was serious about not letting him move back to Greenwich, so he filled out and submitted the documents to go on a two-year mission on behalf of the Church of Jesus Christ of Latter-day Saints. (The Mormon Church strongly encourages all of its followers to do so once they turn eighteen.) If he couldn't be trusted to run a spread offense, maybe he needed to turn his attention to spreading the word about his faith.

"I wasn't going to come back to school," Young said. "I was going to just go on a mission."

The Mormon faith suggests that its followers pray and fast before making any big decision. Young did exactly that. He reflected on the terms missionaries were required to follow at the time. They could be sent to any place in the world and were only allowed to contact their families on Christmas and Mother's Day. For an extreme homebody, that was terrifying. He sat down with Grit and told him he thought returning to Provo was the better choice. At Grit's suggestion, he met with their local bishop and told him of his decision. The bishop surprised him by sharing that he'd had a vision Steve was going to tell him that. He also said he'd had a premonition that he, the bishop, would be compelled to endorse it.

"Between his dad's perspective and going to a school like

BYU that encourages going on a mission and adopting a completely different identity than athlete, Steve was forced to have more than one," Shaffer said. "All of that is humbling–and developing humility, as counterintuitive as it might sound, is the best performance technique you can have. Because you're going to succeed in performing if you can somehow reduce the importance of your sport in your mind."

Right before Steve returned to school, Grit sat down with him one more time. "What do you want to do?" he asked.

"I still want to play quarterback."

Grit was tough, but he was also empathetic. As bleak as the situation appeared thanks to Edwards's plan and Scovil's attitude, telling his son to stick it out felt akin to telling him to beat his head against an impenetrable wall. They agreed Steve should give it one more shot, and if nothing changed, they could revisit the subject at the end of the school year.

Young returned to school and dutifully worked out with the team's incumbent star safety, Tom Holmoe, learning the art of backpedaling and covering receivers. It killed him to look across the way and see the quarterbacks going through their passing drills. Then, only days after the spring semester began, it was announced that Scovil had accepted the head coaching job at San Diego State. It was all the glimmer of hope Young needed. He continued working out with Holmoe but started throwing on his own, perfecting that dreaded three-step drop and firing into a net at one end of the field house.

"In research we talk a lot about harmonious passion and obsessive passion," said Shaffer. "Oftentimes athletes feel that, to be successful, they need this obsessive passion, this unrelenting work ethic. But the obsessive passion leads to burnout and anxiety. Doing it out of this place of 'I have to do this because I need to be the best' will drive an athlete into the ground. Harmonious passion is 'I'm truly doing this because I just love this game' or 'I want to do it and I don't care what anybody else says.' There is an intrinsic-versus-extrinsic motivation that drives it and how it's necessarily cultivated. His dad had no interest in what Steve might accomplish as a football player; he just always asked about his process. That allowed Steve to keep pursuing his dream of being an NFL quarterback out of love for throwing a football rather than from the pressure that he'd be a failure if he never became one."

Edwards spent the winter on the recruiting trail, but Ted Tollner, Scovil's replacement as the offensive coordinator and quarterbacks coach, made a habit of strolling through the field house while the respective units were working out. He couldn't help but notice the young defensive back all by himself, taking snaps from an imaginary center and hucking passes with surprisingly good form and velocity day after day.

"It was an awkward time because we couldn't coach," Tollner said. "You were limited on the number of days you could work with players during the offseason, so I wasn't actually coaching him, initially; I was just observing him. But that's how I got to know him."

Tollner was aware of the plan to move Young over to defense, but because it had been made before he arrived, he didn't know why. He assumed it was because Young wanted to get on the field and knew he could by playing safety.

Tollner also was aware of how excited Fred Whittingham was about Young's potential as a defensive back after watching him run circles around his defense as the scout team quarterback. As the new guy on the staff, he had no desire to create discord within the coaching staff by laying claim to an eighth-string quarterback. But he couldn't ignore what he saw watching Young throw.

"I thought we were getting away from the idea of him being a quarterback too early," Tollner said. "What I really liked, more than anything, was his accuracy and his release. It was a quick release. There had to be some little minor refinements, but the work we had to do was with his feet. His background was all scramble movement stuff, and we were basically a pocket-passing team."

One day Tollner finally called Young into his office. "Hey, we are moving you to safety," he said.

Young's head dropped. "Yeah," he said. "I know."

Tollner scrunched his brow. It was not the reaction he had expected. Having been impressed with the way Young fired passes to imaginary receivers in the field house, he asked, "*Why* are we moving you to safety?"

Young told him about Scovil's anti-lefty stance.

"Well, that's ridiculous," Tollner said. "Based on what I think and look for in a quarterback, you have the skills and, by working at it, could be special as a quarterback. But I don't want to try to change LaVell's mind by getting in his ear if you want to start next season. Jim's our quarterback. But I do think you have a future as a quarterback and you've got a lot of years left."

Hearing that Tollner would be willing to go to bat for him felt to Young like the heavens were opening up a second time.

"He got excited about that," Tollner recalled, chuckling. "I did, too, because I really believed he could be special. We had another kid, a good kid, who was supposed to be the next quarterback, but I didn't see near the potential."

Edwards was willing to reconsider the decision after Tollner had him take a stroll through the field house to see Young throw.

"LaVell was very tactful and respectful of his coaches," Tollner said. "He said, 'Let me think about it before we decide. And let me talk to Fred.' I knew Fred wouldn't be happy. He wanted [Young] as a safety."

LaVell proposed a compromise. "Let's give him the first

two weeks of spring ball at quarterback," he told his two coordinators. "Then we'll see where we are."

Unlike his first snap as a BYU quarterback, Young took a crisp three-step drop, stood tall, and fired a pinpoint pass. "I started spring ball just wanting them to put the ball in my hands," Young said. "I could just rip it and my accuracy was fricking crazy to me. I could just throw it wherever you wanted. You could put a finger up, and I'd hit it. Once that happened, all I wanted to do was throw the ball."

After the two-week trial, Edwards agreed to give Young two more weeks. At the end of the four-week spring ball season, he had leapfrogged six of the seven quarterbacks in front of him. He was so impressive that even Whittingham had to admit BYU would be better served by keeping him at QB.

"Once we started giving Steve a chance to show what he could do, Fred stopped negotiating to move him to defense," Tollner said.

And once that happened, LaVell said, "Okay, we're on the right track here."

Forty years later, Young still gets emotional thinking about that turn of events. "It was an amazing thing," he said, a catch in his throat. "It changed my life. At the end of those four weeks I was backing up Jim McMahon and off we went."

Well, not exactly. Young had the arm strength and accuracy to be in charge of the BYU aerial attack, but he still had to develop the technique and patience to move around in the pocket and explore every passing option.

"We still wanted him to be able to scramble," Tollner said. "We just didn't want him to panic and bail early. As soon as there was one little defensive-colored uniform in his face, his instincts were to tuck it and run. We needed him to be able to slide and adjust in the pocket and go through the progressions of our offense."

Tollner made it clear to Young that he and LaVell didn't want to eliminate his strengths but merely to augment them to take advantage of the BYU system. His scrambling skills were valuable; when and how he used them was what had to be refined.

"You're a natural at the movement part of the game, Steve," Tollner said. "I can see why you moved because you made plays. When you got out of the pocket, you always made something good happen. We don't want to lose that; we just want to get you to where you understand how to go through progressions of reads in the pocket and put the rhythm of your feet and your hands together."

Young stepped into the starting role after McMahon graduated, and the year in waiting paid off royally. He led the Western Athletic Conference in passing yards, completions, and completion percentage. He was even better his senior year, setting an NCAA record for accuracy with a 71.3 completion percentage and being named Quarterback of the Year. Tollner stayed true to his word and still took advantage of his foot speed, going so far as to cap his collegiate career by using him as a receiver to catch the winning touchdown in a 21–17 win over Missouri in the Holiday Bowl.

The former eighth-string quarterback was now poised to be the No. 1 choice in not one but two professional football leagues. The fledgling eighteen-team United States Football League had just formed and was beginning play in the spring of 1984. At the same time, the NFL's Cincinnati Bengals held the No. 1 pick and, despite already having an All-Pro quarterback in Ken Anderson, intended to use it on Young in the league's April draft.

As rosy as all that sounds, Young faced nearly as many daunting, unforeseen circumstances in his professional career as he did that first year at BYU. It all went sideways when he chose going to the USFL with a better chance to start over, most likely being a backup in the NFL with the Bengals. Three years later he found himself in a familiar situation: having to prove he deserved to be the backup to a great quarterback, this time to the San Francisco 49ers' Joe Montana.

Grit, reflecting on his son's knack for landing in difficult situations, told him one day, "You know what? I think you like third and 10."

Steve protested. "I do not like third and 10."

"Yeah," Grit said, smiling. "I think you do."

If nothing else, Steve certainly became comfortable facing third-and-10 circumstances. None of his subsequent success would've been possible if he had dodged his biggest weakness, which was an inability to throw a football with power and precision. The decisions he made all along the way, from returning to BYU for his second semester to working as Montana's understudy, hinged on Young accepting who he was—and wasn't—and putting in the work to become who he wanted to be.

"Being coachable," he said, "is fundamentally about self-improvement. I want to get better and I'm willing to go backward to go forward. I was once asked a question: 'Do you want to find out how good you can be?' I'm like, 'Well, yeah, of course I do.' And the person asking me the question said, 'Well, you might not be as good as you hoped and it might not be what you think. Are you ready for that?' Quit victimizing yourself and trying to find all the faults of everyone around you. Go on the quest to see how good you can get and be open to the fact that you might not be as good as you'd hoped."

Grit played a part in his son learning that lesson that first year in Provo.

"If he would've said, 'Hey, yeah, they're screwing you, come home,' who knows what I would've done?" Steve said. "So it was definitely influential. That was his thing: Just don't fricking quit."

Grit also believed in expanding odds: Shoot for the moon all you want, but just in case the rocket ship doesn't launch, equip it with wheels so you have some kind of transportation. When Steve was still in high school, he shared that he wanted to be the next Staubach. Grit said, "That's good, but that has about a 1 percent chance of happening. That's the dream. Everyone should have a dream. But what's the plan? What has an 80 percent chance of happening? Give me your plan."

Steve eventually came back with an answer: "I'm going to go to college, and then I'll go to law school and I'll probably be a lawyer like you, Dad."

Grit nodded. "That's a plan. I think there's an 80 percent chance you can do that one. Go after the 1 percent idea. Live your dream. But have a dream and a plan."

After Steve signed his first professional contract with the LA Express, he suggested to Grit that the 1 percent dream had come true and there was no longer any need for a plan. The $40 million deal was the richest in sports history at the time. The bulk of it was deferred, but it assured Young of being wealthy into his sixties. Grit shook his head. Financial security as a twenty-something wasn't a meaningful life goal; finding a way to be a useful member of society was.

"The average pro career is three years," he said. "You have the rest of your life. What are you going to do with it?"

Grit had reason to be cautious. One day Grit asked one of his BYU teammates, an offensive guard from Los Angeles, what he had been doing before he came to BYU. "I was working as a handyman in a gas station," the teammate said. Ten years later, Grit took a business trip to Canada and his client invited him to attend a Canadian Football League game featuring the BC

Lions. Lo and behold, he saw that same former teammate's name in the program. They met afterward and the guard said he was ready to retire.

"What are you going to do now?" Grit asked.

"I'll go back to pumping gas, I guess," he said.

The shock of that stuck with Grit. "I saw so many guys that had opportunities in college and didn't better themselves and ended up with no job," he said. "I had those pictures in mind when I was trying to lead Steve to not be that kind of person."

Shaffer suggested every parent should picture their son or daughter facing that prospect.

"I love that his dad wasn't reinforcing his sports identity," she said. "That is actually a healthier way to do it. The No. 1 issue we see with athletes when they retire or they have to step away is because they've only dumped their energy into their 'I'm an athlete' cup and not anywhere else. When that sport inevitably goes away, they go through a lot of psychological issues–not necessarily clinical but simply internal questions like 'Who am I? And what do I do now? I've done this thing my whole life and now what's next?'"

That doesn't happen just with athletes. Today, more than ever, technology is constantly shifting the landscape in every field at an amazing rate; constantly evolving, developing new skills, and being prepared to pivot are essential. The rudiment to doing that is seeking counsel and honest appraisal, and exploring options before they need to be exercised. The basic principle is the same: *Synthesize who and what we want to be with someone else's vision of who and what we can be*. That is not a static concept but a fluid one.

Steve promised Grit to continue working toward a law degree. As it turned out, careers with fledgling pro football teams are not safe bets. The Express folded after two seasons and the owner claimed bankruptcy. The NFL held a supplemental draft for teams to choose college seniors who already had signed with a USFL or Canadian Football League team; veterans in those rival leagues like Young who might be interested in making the jump were eligible as well.

Not only did the $40 million evaporate with the team's demise, the USFL demanded $1.2 million to release Young from any further obligations to the league. He paid it and the Buccaneers made him the supplemental draft's No. 1 pick, projecting him as the backup to Steve DeBerg. While it gained him entry to a more stable league, he was joining one of its perennial doormats. After DeBerg lost eleven of the first twelve games, Young took over as the starter for the final five, going 1-4. The next season he became the full-time starter, but the Bucs suffered another 2-14 season, costing head coach Leeman Bennett his job. His replacement, Ray Perkins, shared Scovil's belief that lefties should not be quarterbacks and promptly traded Young to the San Francisco 49ers.

That put Young behind one of the all-time great quarterbacks in NFL history, Montana. While head coach Bill Walsh inserted Young into games for a series here and there to catch defenses off guard, Young had to wait four full seasons before the 49ers dealt Montana to the Kansas City Chiefs and made him the full-time starter. At that point Young thought Grit might finally agree that the dream had become substantial enough to abandon the plan.

"Dad, now it's a career," Steve said.

Grit once again took issue with his perspective. "So you retire at thirty-five," he said. "Then what? Are you going to sit out in front of a car dealership and shake hands?"

Young already had been part of two Super Bowl championship teams and was now positioned to win a third as the starting quarterback. He would be named league MVP twice and a Pro Bowl selection nine times. But he stuck to the plan, grinding out seven semesters to earn a BYU law degree. On one occasion it meant flying into Provo to attend class and argue a brief the day after a Super Bowl victory parade.

"I don't know that I'd ever want to do that again," he said. "We go to the Super Bowl, the next day we go to the parade, and the next day I'm in class being berated because it's the Socratic method. You walk in, there's the case of the day, and then the first thing the professor says is 'Mr. Young, could you please give us a brief on . . .' Everyone laughed and thought it was funny. But then it was game on. Two days earlier I had been in the Super Bowl and it meant nothing."

Continuing to set future goals rather than dwell on past accomplishments or current comfort prompted Young to tap into the technology industry that had just begun taking root around the team's Santa Clara practice facility. Who wouldn't want to share their business plan or offer an early investment opportunity in exchange for rubbing elbows with a Super Bowl–winning quarterback? And how many Super Bowl–winning quarterbacks were well-versed enough in the fine print of contracts and lawyer-speak to be able to differentiate between a 1 percent Silicon Valley dream and an 80 percent plan?

Having successfully completed the plan and realized the dream, Young teased Grit when he turned ninety.

"What's the dream and the plan, Dad?" Steve said.

"The plan is to reach one hundred," Grit said. "The dream is one hundred and ten."

YOUNG IS LIVING PROOF THAT situations rarely remain static and opportunities are everywhere; we just aren't always aware of them. Was Young lucky? In that Scovil was hired away by the Aztecs, yes. But Scovil leaving wouldn't have mattered if Young hadn't resolutely kept working on himself by studying McMahon, adopting his throwing mechanics, and then continuing to hone his form in the field house for Tollner to discover the freshman safety with the quick feet and cannon arm. It wasn't easy; it required believing that somehow it would pay off without knowing how. Just as his dad had to believe instilling in Steve the value of perseverance would one day pay off as well.

Changes are constantly occurring, not just from season to season, but game to game and practice to practice. Coaches (or bosses) leave or get fired, players transfer or get injured (or colleagues go to another company), game plans (or business strategies) are altered. How ready are you to fill a need if it arises? What do you need to do to be ready? Whatever the current situation may be, it is certain you know more about it than any other one you might be considering. Had Young's dad supported transferring to North Carolina, Steve would not have had the opportunity to study McMahon's throwing form and transform his own, which completely changed his trajectory as a quarterback. The Tar Heels would have encouraged him to keep scrambling, which would have severely limited his chance of ever playing a meaningful role in the NFL. Had Young not accepted being Montana's understudy, recognizing that he had someone in Walsh who not only believed in him but could mold him into the pocket-passing quarterback he always aspired to be, he might have forced his way out of the Bay Area and squandered the business opportunities that subsequently set him up for life.

TRUTH 2

A Fixed Flaw Is a Fountain of Faith: Stephen Curry

FORMER DAVIDSON COLLEGE BASKETBALL COACH BOB MCKILLOP recognized a special quality in Stephen Curry the very first time he saw him—as a center fielder and shortstop for the 10U Charlotte Heat baseball team.

McKillop wasn't some crazed recruiter trying to get the jump on every other college basketball coach in the country. He was just another dad, eating fast food, sleeping on lumpy motel mattresses, and getting coated with infield dust while fulfilling his youngest son Brendan's desire to play baseball. Brendan McKillop was the Heat second baseman. The McKillops—Bob and his wife Cathy, Brendan, Matt, and Kerrin—spent almost every weekend with the Currys—Stephen and his parents, Dell and Sonya—traipsing from one North Carolina baseball complex to the next, covered in the same infield dust, staying in the same three-star hotels and eating at the same chain restaurants.

"That's how I got to know Steph," McKillop said.

At the time, there was no reason to believe Steph would have the requisite size or skill to play collegiate basketball, much less become a two-time NBA MVP and four-time champion. Steph was one of the smallest, skinniest players on the team. You'd never guess he was the son of a standout collegiate volleyball player (Sonya) and one of the NBA's best long-range shooters (Dell). But there were subtle indicators of a unique athleticism, potentially more valuable than size and strength.

"His hand-eye coordination was extraordinary and I'm a big believer in turning your hips," McKillop said. "I think the great athletes can turn their hips really well, and he had that capacity to step on first and make that turn to second base or round the bag at second and get back to force a throw. Or throwing a ball in from center field, the hip turn in the catch-step-and-throw motion, turning his hips as he's swinging at a ball, seeing the ball as it comes out of the pitcher's hand, all those things that make great baseball players. As a ten-year-old, he was far advanced, and it was because of his hips and hand-eye coordination."

But what really set Steph apart, from McKillop's perspective, was his capacity to quickly absorb information.

"He has fast-twitch eye muscles and fast-twitch ear muscles," McKillop said. "He hears what you're saying and you might think that's not that big of a deal. My goodness gracious! The ability to listen is one of the key components to being a leader. His eyes are much like his ears. He doesn't just see where the ball is; he sees where the ball is going to be. He doesn't see where his defender is; he sees where his defender is going to be."

All of it resulting in a kinetic chain that gives Steph an edge in any given situation. His ability to hear what is being asked of him, see the opening to do it, and translate that information to his hips and feet is, McKillop said, "why he is the success that he is."

Curry has not lost a shred of that capacity over the years; if anything, he has sharpened it. Anyone who has spent time around a professional sports team talking to athletes is aware of the constant commotion in the usual interview settings, either on the practice court or in the locker room. There is music being played, other interviews and conversations being had, and various personnel roaming around, collecting or dispensing equipment. Curry has the ability to cut through all of that and home in on the person in front of him. It's as if he has an insatiable hunger for information and perspective in order to plot his next move. He is sometimes momentarily lost in thought, but only as he reflects and forms his response to whatever is being discussed. And whether it's in a room full of reporters, in a chaotic locker room, or, for the purposes of this book, one-on-one in an empty hotel ballroom near the end of a tumultuous season, Curry's concentration to absorb what is being said to him is palpable and unwavering.

Curry credited some of that to his innate humility resulting from believing in an entity, or power, greater than himself. He sees his life as one long quest for enlightenment in everything he does—as a basketball player, golfer, father, husband, and friend.

"My faith in God is a big part of it, because it's how I see the world," Curry said. "You're always growing and evolving. There's always lessons to be learned."

The first and maybe most instrumental: what you do best may not be good enough. Thanks to his extraordinary hand-eye coordination, even as a nine-year-old he could heave a basketball from long range into the basket with unusual consistency. But because of his diminutive size and strength, there wasn't much else he could do. So whether he was playing for his dad or someone else, he was only inserted in the game when the opposing team played zone defense, which is meant to discourage anything other than long-range shots.

"Skinny and rail thin" is how Curry described himself to *Cigar Aficionado*. "They called me the 'Zone Buster.' As soon as a team went to a 2-3 zone, they'd say, 'Put Steph in.' As soon as they went back to man-to-man, it was 'All right, come back to the bench.'"

Dell knew Steph had dreams of following in his footsteps as a collegiate and pro player. He also knew that, at Steph's size, he had no chance of playing beyond high school with a shot that could easily be blocked or discouraged. Still only five-foot-nine at the end of his sophomore year, Steph was anxious that he was a virtual unknown to the scouting services and not a single college or university had shown interest in recruiting him.

Rather than put him on a traveling AAU team where he might have the chance to play in front of scouts and college recruiters, Dell told him the harsh reality: he'd need to spend the summer focused entirely on developing a different way of shooting a basketball. Keep in mind, Steph was already having considerable success with the way he was shooting it, flaws and all. He was accurate enough from long range that as a sophomore he started on Charlotte Christian School's varsity team. But Dell knew a little something about making shots at the highest level, having finished a sixteen-year career as one of the NBA's top fifty in 3-point shooting percentage and a two-time All-Star 3-Point Contest winner.

He didn't mince words. "You want to play at the next level, son?" he told Steph. "Well, this is what has to happen."

As stubborn as Steph could sometimes be and as much as it

alarmed him that his dad was telling him his best attribute as a basketball player needed to be fixed, he abandoned his old form and began the process of developing a new one on their backyard basket. It started with form shooting in front of the rim, standing still, knees slightly bent, the ball in his right hand held shoulder high, as if he were a waiter with a serving tray. With his old form he could comfortably make shots from twenty feet away; now he was struggling to get the ball up and over the rim standing in its shadow.

"It was at least a month before he took a shot outside the paint," Dell said.

When he finally did, he found there was more work to be done. Transferring power from his legs and hips into his upper body and maintaining his new upper-body form was yet another hurdle.

"I had the identity that I was a great shooter; that was the one thing I could do," Stephen said. "My form, my comfort zone, my identity–all of it was taken away. Literally, for three months I couldn't make a shot outside the paint. I was frustrated the whole summer. Why was this not happening as fast as I thought it would?"

It felt awkward and humbling and there were plenty of days he stomped into the house ready to quit.

His parents, both having been high-level athletes and both having gone through similar challenges in developing skills or techniques to advance to the next level, took it in stride. For all the pride and joy Dell and Sonya took from watching their son play, they knew he couldn't simultaneously compete in games and fix something as fundamental as his shooting form. They were confident that one summer away from the AAU circuit, especially at this stage of his physical development, wasn't going to undermine his trajectory; exposure with such a fundamental flaw might actually be counterproductive. They could have shared Steph's anxiety about not being recruited and acquiesced, had him focus on other parts of his game and put the change in his shooting mechanics on the proverbial back burner. With his hand-eye coordination, he might have focused on ballhandling and hoped that he grew tall enough by his senior year to find a college program that would take him. Or found an AAU or high school coach who might feature him, anyway, because of his name. Instead, Dell showed him the form he needed, gave him feedback when he asked for it, and left it at that. He knew that if Steph was willing to go through the painful process of reconstructing his form, week by week, day by day, shot by shot, the trial-and-error process would pay off going forward, because he'd have a far more intimate understanding of how his mechanics needed to mesh to consistently make shots. Or what he needed to adjust when he didn't.

Besides, if he was truly passionate about the game, spending a summer with a ball in his hands in the North Carolina sunshine was not exactly hard labor. He had a choice and Sonya reminded him of that. If improving his shooting form required more work than he was willing to do, or he didn't believe it would pay off—or it simply didn't mean that much to him—Sonya shrugged and said, "Then stop and play something else."

Eventually, of course, the new form took hold. He could make two in a row, then three. The transfer of power became effortless, as did launching the ball from farther and farther away from the basket without having to contort his body. Much like Steve Young, he didn't need a dedicated coach or sophisticated training facility to make that discovery. Steph identified the basics by watching and talking to his dad and then incorporated them to fit how he was built. All of which unleashed Steph's hand-eye coordination in a new and even more masterful way. Now he could shoot from range and get off a shot in a split second. It wasn't textbook form, but the summer of trial and error allowed him to develop one that worked for him and, as he would discover, at any level.

As agonizing as that summer might have been, Steph is forever grateful that he went through it. Shifting focus elsewhere, or finding someone—a parent or a coach—to offer permission to do so is not just taking the easy way out; Stephen believes it's missing an opportunity to develop a toughness and resolve that will be valuable when faced by the next challenge. Which will assuredly come.

"You find a space with the most comfort just because you're never challenged," he said. "You're never in a situation where you feel vulnerable and you've got to work through that identity crisis. For me, there is a faith and patience that comes with being in those positions."

In the final weeks of the summer, the earlier frustration gave way to the excitement of returning to his high school team with a shot that was infinitely easier to take without getting it blocked. The new shooting style also streamlined his overall form, making it more easily repeatable, reducing the number of elements that could go wrong and therefore making it more efficient.

But the process did so much more than simply give Curry a shooting form that would work at any level of competition. It made him a clinical expert on the mechanics of shooting in general and his shot in particular. The trick shots that he routinely makes—sky-high underhanded scoops, falling-down one-handers off the glass—are a by-product. Starting behind the proverbial eight ball forced him to learn how to maneuver around one—a powerful lesson that has served him ever since. Eight balls haven't daunted him ever since.

Reconstructing something as fundamental and intrinsic to his identity as his shot also gave Steph the confidence that there was nothing in his game—or his life, for that matter—that he couldn't take apart and rebuild and make better.

"That summer I had to have the confidence and faith that I was going to reach the result that I wanted while not knowing how long it was going to take," he said. "You don't know what that road map actually looks like, what the experiences will be, how deep and dark it might get along the way. There's faith that comes with going through that, working toward that intended outcome of who I want to be. But that whole process, for me, requires having trust in myself to be able to solve whatever challenges are in front of me. But you also have to have the resources around you and the openness to say, 'Okay, I don't know everything, I don't have all the answers, but I'm curious.'"

A growth spurt that pushed Steph over six feet, plus his new shooting form, caught the attention of several mid-major schools, none more so than the local one, Davidson. But being a Wildcat wasn't Curry's dream; playing at Virginia Tech, where his mom and dad had competed and met, was. Despite the family legacy, the Hokies were not interested. That provided Davidson an opening, for no one understood the mentality of an overlooked underdog, or how motivating rejection could be, better than McKillop.

Born in the New York City borough of Queens, McKillop came up when the New York area produced a steady stream of outstanding high school basketball players, especially out of private Catholic schools and particularly point guards. He did not appear to be one of them; he loved the game, it seemed, more than it loved him. He was cut from the Chaminade High School varsity three times, finally making the squad as a backup point guard his senior year. Chaminade went 15-6 and finished second to its rival and national powerhouse, Archbishop Molloy, but, not surprisingly, springtime rolled around and McKillop had zero scholarship offers. He did have a few childhood friends who played for Archbishop Molloy, though, and that got him into a summer pickup run in the AM gym, which featured a healthy number of Division I alums home for the summer. AM coach Jack Curran, who made a habit of sauntering through the gym to check on his current players and say hello to the returning ones, had to be surprised to see Chaminade's backup point guard holding his own in such high-level competition.

One day Curran pulled McKillop aside and asked where he was playing in the fall. McKillop told him he didn't have any offers and planned to attend nearby Siena College—then a no-name school as far as basketball was concerned—on an academic scholarship. Curran had sway with college coaches thanks to AM's record of producing quality players under his guidance, and he arranged a tryout for McKillop at East Carolina University. "I'd never heard of it," McKillop said. "I wasn't even sure which state it was in." No matter. He displayed the toughness of a New York City cop's son, suffering a cut above his eye in the tryout, which required stitches. The ECU trainer stitched him up without any painkiller. On the way to the airport, coach Tom Quinn offered him a scholarship.

McKillop spent two years at ECU before the social unrest at the time, fueled by the Vietnam War and the Civil Rights Movement, made him homesick. He moved back to New York, got a job working construction, and made enough money to enroll at Hofstra University for the fall with no promise of playing basketball.

Lou Carnesecca, then coach and GM of the professional American Basketball Association's New York Nets and a New York Catholic school alum, offered McKillop a job as a counselor in his summer basketball camp, where high-level pickup games were once again part of the schedule and once again where McKillop showed out. Hofstra coach Paul Lynner saw him and offered him an athletic scholarship, allowing him to bank that construction money. McKillop played two seasons as Lynner's point guard and then earned a tryout with the

Philadelphia 76ers. He didn't make the final roster, but for a kid cut three times by his high school team, to be considered pro material was quite the accomplishment. McKillop attributes it to consistently understanding what his coach wanted done and figuring out how to do it.

"I was constantly in a situation in which I was not as talented as somebody else or judged to be not as talented as somebody else," McKillop said. "So I got the attention of the coach by listening and understanding what made him happy. That was a lesson I learned in the classroom. I was not a particularly bright student, but I was a high-achieving student because I had the capacity to listen to what was important to the teacher. And I transferred that onto the court or the field by trying to listen to what was important to the coach."

Taking that dual approach led to a dual career as a teacher and coach. Having made the most of his ability with that approach, McKillop looked for the same traits in the kids he recruited to Davidson.

"I watched the way a kid acted with his teammates," he said. "I watched if he looked his coach in the eye. The way he responded to a referee. What kind of focus did he have in practice? How did he walk down the hallway to class? How did he interact with his classmates? I watched whether or not he had a neatness about him. I'm convinced that sloppiness is a disease. A sloppy kid will be a sloppy player. Sloppiness is the opposite of details. Anyone that's not going to be a detailed kid is not going to be coachable."

That didn't mean McKillop wanted players who were robotic out of fear of making mistakes; he understood well enough that missed shots and mistakes were part of the game. It was how a player responded to a mistake or missed shot that was important. Nothing was more revealing about a player's character.

"In all my years at Davidson College, I never feared coaching against the team with more skill or more athleticism," McKillop said. "What I feared was coaching against a team who had better character than us. It's a simple statement, but it's a powerful statement. Steph had that character."

That's why a performance that might have convinced a lot of coaches to cross Curry off their list put him at the top of McKillop's.

"AAU tournament, July of 2005 in Las Vegas," McKillop said. "For anyone who hasn't been to one, they use gyms all over the city. And in any one gym there's the main court and then the auxiliary court. The main court has a thousand people watching, coaches from the SEC, Big East, ACC, all the big conferences. The auxiliary gym might have thirty people in it, mostly parents and a couple of coaches or scouts. Steph was not on a sneaker team, as in a circuit team sponsored by a shoe company. He was on a local AAU team coached by his dad. So he played in all the auxiliary gyms, never in the main gym, and he didn't get exposure to a lot of coaches. I did not lament that at all, because I didn't care what they thought."

McKillop made a beeline for the auxiliary court. He knew he had very little chance of landing any of the four- and five-star high school players on the main court. He'd seen plenty of Steph back in North Carolina, but he wanted to see him under these brighter lights—even if they weren't the brightest lights of the weekend.

"He was awful, absolutely awful," McKillop said. "Dribbled the ball off his foot, threw it out of bounds, fumbled passes, got beat defensively, missed shots, threw up air balls. But throughout that painful experience, he never relented as a great teammate or as a hard worker. He never pointed fingers at a teammate who maybe missed a pass. He didn't show emotion about shooting an air ball or a bad call by the ref. He never said anything.

He'd go to the huddle and look Dell right in the eye during the time-out. Dell is yelling at him and he never said anything. He sat on the bench when he was taken out of the game and he cheered his teammates; he greeted them when they came off the court. He showed character that far transcended his physical performance."

As McKillop walked out of the gym, he turned to his assistant coaches and said, "We need to get that guy. That is the conviction we want right there."

That conviction would serve Steph in more ways than one. Dell, understanding the timing and luck that goes into a player simply making it to the NBA, refrained from filling his son's head with grandiose ideas of what he could be. He already knew what his son's dream was and wanted to make sure that Steph never thought realizing that dream would define whether or not his dad considered him a success.

McKillop, though, was not afraid to tell Steph just how good he thought he could be–if he was willing to put in the work.

Although several higher-profile schools courted Curry at the last second, he believed in McKillop because McKillop not only believed in him but could articulate it in a way that made sense.

"I'm confident enough now to say Coach McKillop saw more potential in me than I ever could have imagined," Curry said. "And the way that he communicated it, it allowed him to be very hard and rough and harsh with me at times when I needed to hear it. And that was a process I've never forgotten."

McKillop did not coach him as a precious gem that had, by the oversight of Virginia Tech and bigger programs, landed in his lap. He coached him as if he was a rough stone that needed to be honed with a chisel and a hammer. The first day of practice, Curry overslept and was late; McKillop threw him out of the gym and told him to come back the next day, on time, if he wanted to be on the team.

"Any hard conversation was quick, direct, explicit, and I didn't have to ever, ever beat around the bush with him," said McKillop. "It started on day one. Back in those days, you couldn't have practice in September, but you could have three-man workouts. He overslept for his first one and showed up two minutes late and I threw him out. I didn't yell or scream or make him run. I didn't want a track team. I just threw him out. Next day he comes back for his second one. It was incredibly challenging, all basketball related, but it was relentless. Dribbling drills, shooting drills, cutting, screening, outletting the ball, defensive footwork. I am old-school and carry a handkerchief in my pocket. About halfway through, I pull out the handkerchief and wave it and say, 'Steph, you ready? Are you waving the white flag?' Every time he started sucking wind, I'd pull out the handkerchief and say, 'The white flag, Steph: Are you waving the white flag?' I dared him to surrender and he never did."

Even then, coaching Curry was a balancing act. His unique hand-eye coordination led him to occasionally try shots and passes that were beyond the imagination, let alone skills, of most players. Curry's character assured McKillop that his unconventionality was in pursuit of winning, not personal attention, and he'd seen him pull off enough How-did-he-do-that? plays going back to those dusty baseball diamonds to know their value. McKillop still stressed the importance of simple, high-percentage shots and textbook passes, but he did so with Steph in a lighthearted way.

"I used to call him 'Ichiro,'" McKillop said, referring to the former Major League Baseball player Ichiro Suzuki. "Remember Ichiro? What was he famous for? Singles. I'd jokingly call Steph 'Ichiro' because he was always trying to hit home runs and I wanted him to hit singles."

The Currys, despite all their experience with the game and high-level collegiate competition, never questioned McKillop's approach, directly or indirectly. They didn't interfere *because* of all that experience, well aware that nothing assures a team or player of falling short more than the discord or distraction that comes from the insertion of personal agendas.

"Dell and Sonya were rabid fans of Davidson basketball *and* Steph Curry, not Steph Curry," McKillop said. "They would sit there, believe it or not, without saying much during the game. If Steph shot an air ball, Sonya would be the one yelling out, 'Air ball!' It endeared her to the rest of the fans. Here's a mom not just cheering for her son. She was so honest with her assessment of what was going on out there."

Dell, who played both baseball and basketball at Virginia Tech and could have pursued a career in either sport, doesn't believe there is one right way to coach. He knew from personal experience that there is value for an athlete in learning how to handle different styles. Steph, his younger brother, Seth, and younger sister, Sydel, were all encouraged to play an array of sports growing up and did not play any of them year-round. Dell coached both Steph and Seth in their preteen years in basketball but then handed them over to a trainer—with one prerequisite.

"The trainer asked me what I wanted him to work on with them," Dell recalled. "I said, 'No, you do a workout with them and then come back and tell me what they need to work on, and I'll tell you if you're right.' Fortunately, he was."

Dell wanted his kids to understand that coaches can have vastly different styles of communication and all that matters is digesting the message and not being distracted by the delivery.

"I probably learned more about being coachable playing baseball and football than I did basketball and I only practiced with my high school football team," he said. "They recruited me to be the scout team quarterback. The football team was coached differently than any other team I'd been around and I gained perspective from that. My high school basketball coach, a big Christian man, never cursed once in his life. We had prayer before games. But the football coaches cursed. As a youngster, you've got to learn how to deal with both. Some coaches are harder than others, so all that plays a huge role."

Despite his elite level of understanding the game, the only time he ever discussed or suggested tactics or strategy with McKillop was when he was invited to do so. After Steph helped lead Davidson to the Elite Eight in the NCAA tournament his sophomore year, McKillop anticipated he would draw a heightened degree of attention. With senior point guard Jason Richards graduating, he also wanted to move Steph over from shooting guard. McKillop hoped Dell could illustrate on a whiteboard plays that could create shots for undersized point guards against defenses geared specifically to stop them.

Dell surprised McKillop by presenting ideas that weren't just designed to get Steph open but used the attention he'd draw to create opportunities for the rest of the team.

"Everything he said was so inclusive of what our team was all about," McKillop said. "Yeah, he was trying to help Steph, but he was more concerned about helping us. That was the only kind of X's-and-O's interaction we ever had. It was just eye-opening because it affirmed and validated why we recruited this kid in the first place. He had such great parents."

For the parents reading this, rest assured your interaction with a coach becomes part of their assessment of your child's ability and the coach's ability to work with them. There are coaches—two-time NCAA men's basketball champion Dan Hurley comes immediately to mind—who will cross a player off their recruiting list because they are convinced the parents of a prospect will make it impossible for them to realize their potential. Do your homework on a coach. Know how a player operates based not just on what any previous players or parents say about them but what parents and players who share your principles say—and then let them do their job. Besides, learning to forge a relationship with an authority figure and be their own advocate is one of the most valuable skills an athlete can acquire from playing a sport.

McKillop's willingness to develop a symbiotic relationship with his star player prepared Steph for a similar relationship as a pro with Golden State Warriors coach Steve Kerr.

Much like McKillop and Curry, Kerr knew the sting of being overlooked because of his limited physical attributes. After a recruiting visit to Gonzaga, in which he played in an informal scrimmage against senior and future NBA Hall of Fame point guard John Stockton, Gonzaga coach Dan Fitzgerald pulled him into his office.

"Hey, sorry, we're not going to offer you a scholarship," Fitzgerald said. "It might've been one thing if you were one step too slow, but you're kind of two steps too slow."

Kerr couldn't argue.

"That hurt," he said, "but John wiped the floor with me. Dan was being honest, and I didn't really blame him. I really wasn't that good at that point."

When Lute Olson took over a troubled University of Arizona program, he cleaned house late in the recruiting season and went to scout a summer league run in Long Beach with one last scholarship, looking for a sharpshooting backup point guard. Kerr, who lived in the Pacific Palisades, happened to be there and played well enough to land an offer.

"I didn't even visit the school," Kerr said. "I said yes before they could change their mind."

Kerr spent four years at Arizona before making it into the NBA as a second-round pick. He developed passable foot speed and carved out a fifteen-year career as a sure-handed guard with dependable accuracy from 3-point range (career 37 percent) and at the free-throw line (career 87.6) and a toughness that resulted in Michael Jordan infamously taking a swing at him. All of which allowed him to contribute to five championship teams (three with the Chicago Bulls, two with the San Antonio Spurs) and play for two Hall of Fame coaches, Phil Jackson and Gregg Popovich.

As soon as he was hired by the Warriors, he went to work cultivating a relationship with Curry beyond the court, arranging for the two of them to play a round of golf at the famous Pebble Beach course just south of the Bay Area, on the Monterey Peninsula. Curry was just coming off his first season as an All-Star and receiving All-NBA recognition (second team), but what excited Kerr the most, in light of all his NBA experience, was how Curry viewed being part of a team.

"We talked the whole time," Kerr said. "I got to know him as a person and I immediately thought, 'I hit the jackpot. I am the lucky coach who gets Steph Curry in his first job.' Our personalities are very similar. Our values are very similar in terms of family and perspective and joy. And I'm a very patient person. I'm a delegator. I'm not a dictator, and I observe. And so we hit it off from the beginning. I felt an immediate connection and I knew I better not screw this up because this guy's a unicorn."

He had learned firsthand from Jackson and Popovich the importance of developing relationships with players beyond their roles on the team. That part was relatively easy with Curry.

"Being coachable is, number one, accepting ideas and collaboration and Steph defines that," Kerr said. "I'm comfortable with him making suggestions, as he is with me, and we're both comfortable just finding the best solution, whatever that might be. It's not only important for the player to be coachable; it's important for the coach to be coachable, too. Maybe that's the difference in modern coaching compared to the old days. I believe the modern NBA coach has to collaborate. Another part of it is accepting that ideas could go wrong and then not blaming others after the fact. If you're in a true collaboration, you come up with an idea together, try it, and then you either celebrate it together or lament it together, but you don't go behind the scenes and say, 'Well, this guy made it.' And let's be honest: there's not many superstar players who don't do that. There has to be incredible self-awareness and security in oneself to reach that state. Very few people ever reach it in their lives in whatever they're doing, because we're all insecure by nature. We're human beings. It's even harder in modern culture with all the criticism and judgment. That's what makes Steph so unique: his ability to collaborate genuinely without judgment and with so much authenticity. His only goal is winning."

The challenge for Kerr with Curry was adapting to the high-risk, high-reward way in which Curry pursued that goal.

"What I learned quickly was that he was going to take some crazy shots," Kerr said. "It took me a while to change my mind on what was a good shot, what was a bad shot. From the beginning I'd never tell a guy, 'Hey, that was a bad shot,' because I believed in feeding guys' confidence. Then, on an off day, I might say, 'Hey, what do you think about looking to get this shot instead?'"

The testing of their relationship and moment of truth came a half dozen games into their first season together. The Warriors were 5-0 before getting molly whopped in Phoenix. Steph had been careless with the ball in the previous two wins, committing five turnovers in each, but he matched that combined total with ten against the Suns.

"Some of them were pure insanity," Kerr said. "He threw a left-handed hook pass along the baseline that hit the shot clock."

When the Warriors lost their next game by committing twenty turnovers at home against the San Antonio Spurs, Kerr told the team flatly, "We can't turn the ball over like that. If we keep the possession battle even, we'll win."

There is a power dynamic on NBA teams, just as there is in every business. In team meetings or huddles, superstars are judicious about how and when they cosign a coach's directive; they're not necessarily keen on empowering him or risking their autonomy in the eyes of their teammates. Kerr didn't direct his comment at Steph, who'd had only three of the twenty turnovers, but Curry responded as if he had done so. Presenting the idea that they were better than most of the teams in the league but couldn't show it unless they took care of the ball was simple but effective.

"That was the first time I saw how matter-of-fact he was about coaching," Kerr said. "He was like, 'Yeah, you're right. That makes sense.' And then we went on a run where we won sixteen in a row."

It wasn't just lip service from Curry. After averaging 4.5 turnovers through the first seven games, he averaged 2.8 over the winning streak.

It was Kerr's turn later in the season to adjust. In a March home game against the Los Angeles Clippers, Curry zigzagged in and out of the Clippers' defense before dribbling back behind the 3-point line. His equally sharpshooting teammate, Klay Thompson, was open eight feet away. His other teammate Draymond Green even pointed to Klay in case Steph didn't see him. Instead, Steph spun around and launched a 3-point shot. Kerr raised his outstretched arms with an anguished look on his face as if to say, "What are you doing?"

When the ball hit nothing but net, Kerr turned back toward his bench, hands clasped on top of his head, and laughed.

"That's the moment where I decided any shot Steph Curry

takes is a good shot," Kerr said. "If he gets the shot off, it's not a turnover. It's Steph Curry shooting a shot that's worth 3 points and he's shooting 44 percent on 3s. I had to shift my thinking because every coach I ever had, their voices were in my head, saying 'Bad shot, bad shot, bad shot.' That's where I had to be coachable as a coach. Where we ended up was 'Hey, shoot any shot you want. Let's just not do too much other crazy shit.'"

Curry acknowledged later that he went "on autopilot" and should have passed the ball. But the extraordinary license from Kerr prompted Curry to be obsessed with holding up his end of the bargain. After every game he could be found at his locker, running his finger along his box score line to the turnover column and grinning anytime he found a zero. "Clean sheet!" he'd say happily.

Such cooperation and adaptation to fit someone else's needs, especially by the two most powerful entities in the locker room, proved infectious. That season ended with the Warriors winning their first championship in forty years and Curry being named the league's Most Valuable Player. The Houston Rockets' James Harden finished second despite leading the league in total points by a wide margin—and possibly because he also led the league by an equally wide margin in total turnovers. A case could be made that Curry bested him for the award because of Kerr's early admonition and Curry's response, resulting in far more assists and far fewer turnovers—and eleven more wins than the Rockets.

Kerr and Curry have been careful to keep their communication lines open and their relationship sound ever since, fully aware that failing to do so can lead to misunderstandings, which can lead to division. After the Warriors suffered a loss by being particularly sloppy down the stretch, Curry said in the postgame press conference that he had to be better with his decisions and shot selection and that the team collectively had to be better organized and commit fewer mistakes. Kerr saw the remarks on the plane ride home and texted Steph that he agreed and promised to use the following week to get the team better organized.

Steph immediately fired off another text. *You saw that I took accountability first, right?* Steph wrote. *I wasn't throwing you under the bus.*

Kerr reassured him he hadn't taken it that way at all. *You took accountability, which you always do*, he texted back.

The entire exchange underscored for Kerr the premium Curry put on holding himself accountable and honoring their player-coach relationship. But also the importance of clear communication.

"His first concern was for me as his coach, feeling like he had criticized me," Kerr said. "That's who he is. His emotional intelligence is just off the charts. He is always thinking about his teammates, what guys need and how we can get the best out of them."

Curry's concern is born of humility.

"I've never felt like I have all the answers," he said. "So even to this day Coach Kerr would probably tell you that not much has changed with my demeanor when it comes to being able to take some criticism or some redirection and do something with it. And I feel like that's a great attribute to have, for sure. It's something I'm trying to teach my kids, because it is hard when you can find people to validate whoever you are, as you are. You can probably find the cheerleaders to say, 'This is good enough; you're good enough.' But there's a difference between where you are and where you're trying to go."

Curry has watched younger teammates hit a wall as pros because they were being treated for the first time as if they were not as good as they thought they were. "There were some rough interactions with some of them before they got to a point where they understood, 'Oh, okay, you're really trying to help me,'" Curry said. "But it was a process."

One that Curry was willing to help his teammates through because of–again–his humility. After the Warriors lost to the Toronto Raptors in the 2019 NBA Finals, their dynastic run of three championships in four years and five consecutive appearances in the finals appeared to be over. Two-time Finals MVP Kevin Durant elected to sign with the Brooklyn Nets as a free agent. Thompson, Curry's longtime backcourt mate whose own shooting prowess combined with Curry's earned them the unofficial title of best-shooting backcourt ever and the sobriquet the "Splash Brothers," had torn his ACL against the Raptors.

Four games into the following season, Curry broke his left hand. The Warriors would finish dead last in the Western Conference in a season that, for them, was mercifully ended a month and seventeen games early by the Covid pandemic. The following season was marginally better despite Thompson sustaining another season-ending injury, this time a torn Achilles tendon. Several new young, talented additions–Jordan Poole and Andrew Wiggins–had a chance to assimilate into the Warriors' system and style of play. Their 39-33 record was good enough to finish eighth in the fifteen-team Western Conference. Under the league's new play-in format, that earned them a showdown with the seventh-seeded defending champion Los Angeles Lakers. They fell short, 103–100, on a 3-pointer in the final minute by LeBron James, but still had a shot at the postseason if they could beat the Memphis Grizzlies two nights later on the Warriors' home floor. A heartbreaking 112–107 loss in overtime meant a healthy Steph Curry would be at home watching the playoffs for the first time in eight years.

Franchises generally don't win a championship, fall out of contention for two years, and then return to championship form with the same (older) nucleus. The hunger for another ring is dulled by the accolades and financial dividends that come with already being crowned. But the results of that long, seemingly dark tenth-grade summer inspired Curry to approach the 2021–22 season with a similar resolve. He couldn't be sure that, at thirty-two years old, surrounded by only a handful of players from the franchise's last championship run and Thompson still trying to regain his form, the Warriors had enough to win another title. But he was determined to find out by making the talent they had believe that they could.

To do that, he would have to be the best version of himself that they had ever seen.

"I was coming from a workout with him at a high school near his house late that summer," said Warriors assistant coach Bruce Fraser, the frost-bearded man fans see feeding passes to Curry as he warms up before every game and Curry's personal trainer when he is in the Bay Area. "That's when it hit me: he's chasing greatness. He knows he has another shot at this. He was going so hard, I thought he was going overboard, but I didn't say anything. It inspired me. It made me think about what more I could be doing. And you could feel it, day one, when he showed up at training camp. Our entire team could feel it."

The Warriors roared out of the gate, winning eighteen of their first twenty games, and this time avoided the play-in scenario, finishing as the third seed in the West. Curry snared the all-time 3-point-scoring title in December, a pursuit that weighed on him; while the record would validate all the work he had put into his shooting, he didn't want it to be a distraction from the team's goals. His humility came into play once again when he suffered a late-season knee injury that raised uncertainty about his effectiveness and availability for the team's first-round playoff battle with the Denver Nuggets.

Curry missed the last twelve regular-season games and it

took a minute for the Warriors to adjust, but they did, rolling into the Denver series on a five-game winning streak.

Curry was cleared to play by the team's medical staff and it was reported that he would start, but Kerr elected to bring his two-time league MVP off the bench. The move was equal parts surprising and understandable. It was surprising because a superstar player medically cleared invariably assumes their rightful place in the starting lineup, but it was understandable considering Curry had not played in nearly a month, and Kerr wanted to manage how much he played in the first half in case he needed to keep him on the floor late in the game. What Kerr did after the Warriors won, 123–107, was as surprising as Curry's performance (16 points in twenty-one minutes): he elected to keep his replacement, Jordan Poole, as the starter for game two as well. That resulted in another Warriors' win, this time with Curry exploding for 34 points in twenty-two minutes.

Curry not only didn't have a problem with the game two decision, he declined Kerr's offer to start game three. With the team winning and Poole playing well, Curry didn't want to disrupt the team's formula for success. The relationship between Kerr and Curry was so strong that Kerr leaned over at one point before game three and told Curry that if he worked really hard he might get to start a playoff game again. Curry subsequently ran around the next day's practice shouting at Kerr, "Look how hard I'm working, Coach! I know I can do this!" Only after the Warriors lost the fourth game of the series with Curry once again coming off the bench did Kerr insist on him being in the starting lineup, resulting in another 30-point performance from Curry and a series-clinching win.

"He was perfectly content coming off the bench," Kerr said. "That's Steph. What might have been a serious issue with other players turned into a complete joke for him where we're laughing at it."

Curry attributed that awareness to eavesdropping on his dad's conversations with teammates about how to handle sticky or potentially divisive situations. Those fast-twitch ears were apparently always working.

"From eight to thirteen years old I heard my dad and his teammates talking about their perspectives on how to handle stuff like that," he said. "It made me more comfortable being in that space. There is a way to tell people what you mean and how you feel without being emotional or loose with it. What am I trying to get out of this particular interaction, conversation, or interview? It's understanding that anything I say—right, wrong, or indifferent—will be used in some way, shape, or form. So I'm very thoughtful around that."

When the Warriors upset the Boston Celtics, recovering from a 2-1 deficit in the best-of-seven series thanks to a 43-point night by Curry to tie the series, flipping the momentum and inspiring a closing run of three consecutive wins, Curry reacted in a starkly different way than he had to the previous three championships. Instead of shouts of joy, he burst into tears, overwhelmed by what his faith in himself and those around him had accomplished.

"That '22 season, to me, was his greatest accomplishment on an individual level," Kerr said. "We were no longer the most talented team in the league, but he was the best player in the playoffs for two straight months and better than everybody he faced. He carried us. It was just so fitting that he won that title. I just felt like he, of all people, deserved it. It didn't just happen. He had to overcome the hand injury. There was the previous year's frustration of not making the playoffs. We didn't trade our draft picks for veterans who could have helped him. There were a lot of things that could have gotten him off-kilter, and he just put his head down and worked and won the championship. I think that's where the tears came from afterward. It was such an emotional load that he was carrying to get there. My favorite moment of watching Steph for all these years is that last moment in Boston. I knew what he had overcome to get there."

An extraordinary achievement can be interpreted by someone in one of two ways: they can see themselves as the maker, the one who did it, or they can see themselves as the fortunate recipient of gifts that made it possible. Some NBA players who grew up in tougher circumstances have suggested Curry has had an unfair advantage with a father who played in the NBA and the comfortable upbringing that an NBA salary can provide. Curry has never taken it as a shot at his personal capabilities because, one, he knows he has been blessed and, two, he knows that his success is built on making the most of those blessings.

"He knows he's been dealt an incredible hand," Kerr said. "He probably has the best hand-eye coordination of anybody on earth, and he doesn't ever forget that. Not only is that part God-given, but then he was born into this NBA existence where he could learn from his dad and watch his dad go through ups and downs. The table was set for him and then he seized it. But he never forgets the good fortune part of it."

Performers who take results as a measurement of their worth, rather than their actions, are more inclined to struggle in high-pressure situations. Professor Kimberly Shaffer suggested Curry's attitude of gratitude is the key to being so calm, cool, and collected with a game on the line.

"Research tells us that connecting gratitude to the process is extremely valuable," she said. "Gratitude combats the way our brain is naturally wired, which is to pick out the negative. Going back to our caveman days, every reaction was a stress response, fight or flight. Our brain became wired for survival. The stimulus was almost always life-threatening. So now when we get put in stress situations, our body reacts the same way, as if there's a bear chasing us. But it's not a bear. It's a basketball game that we're losing."

It is possible, she added, to change that primal response. But it doesn't happen overnight.

"We can rewire our brain to see those situations in a different light," she said. "Instead of thinking, 'Oh, man, we're losing,' and feeling all sorts of stress and pressure, we can change the thinking to 'How lucky am I to be playing basketball? How lucky am I to know that my team trusts me to have the ball in my hands in this last-minute situation?' as opposed to thinking, 'Holy shit, what do I do?' With kids, it can be as simple as asking them to name one thing they are grateful for before bed. But it happens over time. Hopefully, over an entire year of going to bed saying what you're grateful for, you learn to pick up the good in situations and stay away from the 'Oh, no!' reaction."

Curry reinforces that wiring at every opportunity. Notice when he or the Warriors are in a hole and there is a break in the action: Curry can be seen nodding his head with the slightest of smiles and a gleam in his eye. He's not focusing on how deep the hole is; he's envisioning the ladder to climb out of it.

"There's a tremendous sense of self-confidence and belief, and that comes from what he does every day," Kerr said. "He loves the process of it all. To him, everything is a gift. Life is a gift."

After collecting a treasure trove of accolades and far exceeding his hopes and dreams, Curry derives the most satisfaction from reflecting on the hardships and challenges—and, yes, tough summers trying to master something new—that made them possible.

"The trophies and the rings and all that are amazing to have and amazing experiences from the process working," he said. "But that's not the most fulfilling thing."

He paused and squinted, seeing images only he could see. "It's all the stuff that was the in-between."

BELIEVING THAT EVERYTHING IS GOING to be okay no matter what happens is crucial to being able to do our best in high-stress situations. To reach that state, though, requires applying that mindset in less stressful situations. The key is seeing every event, big or small, as practice and preparation so that we might perform better when the next one comes along. It also requires a belief that nothing happens by accident and that obstacles are meant to teach us something we have yet to learn—something that will expand our horizons and inform our subsequent choices. Steph has embodied those beliefs and is a testament to their power.

That faith has not only allowed him to navigate the ups and downs of his career but to deal with the foibles of his teammates in particular and the NBA in general with understanding and acceptance. He knows that a healthy relationship—with anyone—requires both sides to place their shared success ahead of their individual interest and that he is responsible for only one part of that equation. Steph has navigated a host of discordant circumstances involving teammates—Andrew Wiggins balking at receiving the league-mandated Covid vaccine and Draymond Green punching Jordan Poole are only two—by seeing them as opportunities to learn and grow. He also has accepted that not everyone sees the world the same way he does, which allows him to be grateful for every relationship that does work, rather than resent the ones that don't. This has given him the latitude to still value as a teammate Draymond, who acknowledged the damage done by the punch, and sympathize with Jordan, who couldn't get over the incident, resulting in his trade to the Washington Wizards.

THE PUBLIC SCRUTINY AND INTERNAL politics of the NBA—or any enterprise—can sour its constituents and prompt them to lose sight of the opportunity they have been granted. Former Warriors forward Andre Iguodala once said to me, "I still love basketball. But I hate playing in the NBA." I knew why he said it; the business aspect of the league can sometimes overshadow and sully the sport part of it. But that is looking at what the league has done to, rather than for, basketball—which includes providing Iguodala and most of its participants extraordinary wealth and platforms to expand their influence.

Curry has never allowed such cynicism or skepticism to take root. How? By recognizing that not getting what he wanted has, more than once, led to a bigger opportunity that simply wasn't visible at the moment. His dream of going to Virginia Tech didn't materialize, but he landed with a coach who equipped and inspired him to be something greater than even he imagined. Similarly, he hoped to be drafted by the New York Knicks and wound up instead with a Warriors organization that had been to the playoffs once in the previous fifteen seasons—and he now not only stands as a four-time champion and the greatest player in franchise history, but easily the most beloved person in the Bay Area's rich lineage of athletes. Not just because of what he has done, but how he has done it.

TRUTH 3

No One Knows Your Priorities Better Than You: Rose Zhang

THERE ARE PARENTS WHO INVOLVE THEMSELVES IN THEIR KIDS' athletic careers, and then there's Haibin (Henry) Zhang, father to young LPGA phenom Rose Zhang. He believed in the value of playing sports—not professionally, necessarily, but simply as a healthy hobby—and therefore had Rose and her older brother, Bill, try just about every one of them—soccer, swimming, basketball, badminton, tennis—as kids.

"He wanted me to do something, but I was very small and skinny," Rose said. "Not a lot of people believed I could be an athlete. You need some sort of advantage and I didn't have it."

Born and raised in the People's Republic of China, Henry had been a record-setting four-hundred-meter runner at his university and had taken up a variety of recreational sports as an adult. Golf was one of them. He was practicing his swing on the small patch of grass in the backyard of the family's California condominium in Irvine when nine-year-old Rose asked if she could try.

The 7-iron was practically her height. At first, he had her swing without a ball and gave her a couple of pointers, like how to keep her head still. Then he placed a golf ball in front of her and asked her to hit it. Henry's eyes widened when she hit the ball cleanly into the park behind their condo.

"I actually almost hit it out of the park," Rose said. "It felt natural. My dad realized this could be a game-changer for my life."

Henry still had a full-time job then, working as a product manager for Lotus, a Chinese-owned Japanese toy company. To keep from ruining the backyard lawn, he bought a turf mat and collected as many plastic water bottle caps as he could. He then positioned the mat about six yards from a retaining wall and dropped a handful of plastic caps at Rose's feet. "If you get the cap over the wall," he said, "then it means you hit a good shot. Try and hit as many outside of the yard as you can."

Rose loved the challenge. "I hit hundreds of bottle caps every day," she said. "That's all I did."

(Later, when the Covid pandemic resulted in the temporary closure of golf courses and facilities in California, Rose went back to the practice of hitting those plastic caps to keep her swing sharp. "It's the only way I could practice my loft," she said. "And you could hit them and see the spin. If it went right, you're like, 'Oh, okay, I pushed it.' Or whatever. It was my secret workout.")

By the time Rose was eleven, Henry would come home from work every day and find countless bottle caps on the other side of the wall. It convinced him to quit his job at Lotus and dedicate himself completely to Rose making the most of her talent as a golfer. Every day after school they'd head to the local driving range. Then he arranged for lessons. Then he entered her in local tournaments. He sometimes served as her caddy, offering her advice from the spectator gallery even if he wasn't carrying her bag. Her immediate success in the park behind their condominium was no fluke. She wasn't outright winning tournaments, but top-five finishes became routine fairly quickly, qualifying her for national tournaments. Henry escorted her to all of them.

He studied every aspect of her swing and closely watched her approach to every shot. Rather than instruct her, though, he would quiz her about why the ball went where it did or why she swung the club the way that she did. If he asked her a question, she had to have an answer.

In doing so, he instilled in Rose the idea of diagnosing results, especially if they weren't what she intended. She couldn't just take another swing and hope it produced a better outcome.

"It forced me to figure something out," she said. "Saying 'I don't know' meant to my dad that I wasn't working hard enough to find a solution. Ultimately, all those interactions with him taught me to take initiative of how I should go about my business when I'm practicing."

General golf etiquette is to leave a golfer alone as they contemplate and then set up for their next shot. Even broadcasters whisper a few select words or fall completely silent. Not Henry. Even if he was behind the ropes as a spectator, his reaction to everything Rose did was both visible and audible. Traditionalists were shocked by his running dialogue with his daughter, sometimes even as she stood over a putt. George Pinnell, Rose's coach for more than a decade, said most parents involve themselves watching their young golfers take a lesson, gauging how they're being coached and how they respond to that coaching. Not Henry. He'd sometimes leave Rose with George and return at the end of the lesson. Where he made his presence felt was on the course when she was competing. He prepared by studying every detail of a course beforehand and then kept a laser focus on every aspect of her swing and the result of every shot—and was not bashful about sharing what he knew and saw. It was akin to a boxing trainer standing on the ring apron, shouting at a fighter as they ducked and weaved and exchanged blows. Totally acceptable behavior in boxing. Not so much in golf. But as Pinnell saw it, as long as Rose took it in stride, he would do the same.

"I've never seen any father—and I know a lot of fathers—work harder or smarter than Henry does with Rose," said Pinnell. "Where he really gets involved is on the golf course, and that's where he gets his attention from, because he's involved in everything. He is watching from the sidelines. He knows every shot that she's going to make and everything about that shot. The only thing that he doesn't know is the lie, because he's not close enough to see it, but he knows what club she should be hitting. He knows the distances. He really does his homework. He knows as much as the tour caddies. Even back in the day when I played, I couldn't remember everything about all eighteen holes, what I got on the sixth, say, at the end of the round. I had to go look at my card. But not Henry. He remembers every shot, every putt."

Even now that Rose is a pro, Henry will compare notes with her caddy, Olly Brett, and ask pointed questions about club choices. All of that might sound like a supersized helicopter or snowplow parent, but Pinnell spoke about Henry's involvement as an unvarnished positive. Asked why, he said, "A four-letter word. R-O-S-E."

The distinction, Pinnell said, is threefold. One, Henry is feeding her information, not instructions. Two, the strong and loving bond between Henry and Rose, strengthened through countless hours together and endless conversations beyond when she has a club in her hands. And, three, Rose is not afraid to let Henry know when to give her space and Henry is fully responsive when she does.

"Henry is extraordinary and not conventional, that's for sure," Pinnell said. "Rose has her battles with him, but she is so protective of her dad, and her love for him and what he's done for her is so strong, she can get around all that. She's listened to Henry for so long and she knows him so well, she trusts him."

Understanding that Henry's heart is in the right place, and that sometimes he simply can't help himself, has gone a long way. Pinnell recalls one qualifying tournament early on where he observed Henry and Rose having a heated conversation as she walked down the fairway during a practice round. "He can be pretty emotional and high-strung," Pinnell said. "I was in a cart and they were walking, and I couldn't understand what he was saying but I could tell he was a little bit heated and she wasn't enjoying it."

At the next hole, Pinnell pulled Rose aside. "Would you like me to talk to your dad after the round?" he asked.

"Yeah," Rose said. "Would you?"

"Of course."

It was not a difficult conversation. "He was very open-minded and very accommodating," Pinnell said. "We probably talked for fifteen or twenty minutes. That probably happened three or four times." Rose was around fifteen when a similar incident occurred once again. This time, though, when Pinnell asked Rose if she wanted him to speak to her dad, she said, "No, I'll take care of it myself tonight."

Pinnell marked it as a turning point. "That's when she started to grow," he said. "She's dealt with Henry directly ever since."

What Rose mastered at a relatively early age is how to communicate openly and honestly with her coaches and parents about how they could best support her. That can be challenging for a parent or a coach to accept as an authority figure, but done by the athlete in a respectful and thoughtful way–backed by an explanation as to why that method of support would work best–it generally earns cooperation, at least on a trial basis. Rose didn't address it right away but later in the evening, when whatever emotions might have existed had a chance to cool. That is a tremendously mature approach. There is nothing harder to do than refrain from reacting in the moment and yet there is nothing more important for the health of a relationship. There is this, too: working relationships and terms should be fluid. A method can be tried, and if it doesn't work for one side or the other, adjustments and alternatives can be explored. The aim should always be to get everyone committed to the same means and goal.

The principles and influences at the heart of Rose's success mirror those of two other subjects in this book, Hall of Fame quarterback Steve Young and Golden State Warriors guard Stephen Curry. (Rose, coincidentally, sat next to Curry in awe for three hours at a dinner celebrating one of her NCAA golf titles at Stanford, talking more about their shared Christian faith than their shared love for golf. That forged a relationship that has resulted in Steph offering her counsel since she became a pro. "I said something about how it's hard not to lose yourself in the midst of everything," Rose recalled, "and he said, 'Yes, no matter what, don't lose yourself. Always remember who you are.' When someone says something, you want to see them live it out. And Steph is very intentional. Everything he says, he does.")

Like Steve and Steph, Rose accepted being challenged by her dad and bought into what he suggested. Like Steve and Steph, she developed the ability to digest instruction, no matter how it was delivered, and apply it or store it away. And, like Steve and Steph, she was selective about whose advice or insight she solicited.

"I don't like hearing conflicting voices," she said. "I don't like switching the people I'm working with. Unless it's absolutely necessary."

She learned to seek counsel from those close to her before making a decision, but it didn't mean blindly following whatever they said. She'd aggregate their input and then ultimately make the choice that felt right for her. Perhaps the biggest case in point: her decision to enroll at Stanford University.

With all of Rose's prolific success as an amateur, Henry was excited about the prospect of her turning pro, as were most of the Zhangs' friends and extended family. There is a general belief that if someone has the potential to play golf professionally, they should dive in as soon as possible—that the demands of working toward a degree, the NCAA limits on how much time college coaches can spend with their student-athletes, and the inferior competition are all counterproductive. I shared that belief at one point because I had competed against nationally known hotshot club soccer players who had outstanding years as college freshmen but were only marginally better four years later when they graduated. What I know now is that there are ancillary benefits and if a player truly wants to evolve, they can do so anywhere. But it requires setting specific standards and being intentional about building the proper incubator. There might've been a host of reasons why those hotshot club soccer players flatlined—the campus party life distracted them, they became complacent, their education shifted their focus—but it was not because maximizing their potential as an athlete and a student were incompatible. Mental and psychological growth is as integral to a performer's success as the development of their performance skills. But sometimes only the performer knows where they stand in each of those areas and what needs attention.

"A lot of people doubted me," Rose said. "Especially in the golf community. Even our family friends were like, 'You sure you want to go to college?' They asked my dad, 'Do you want

Rose to go to college? She has so much potential to earn money on the LPGA. And she's a girl: she doesn't have a lot of time in her career.' Because not a lot of people who go to college are en route to turning pro. That was very much the trend. You were either choosing college or you were choosing your professional career. I was like, 'Why can't I do both?' In my mind, if I don't want to turn pro, I don't want to turn pro. Is there an issue with that? I don't care how good I was in my junior golf career: it's so different from being a professional athlete. I have big respect for the people who don't go to college and just start their professional careers. But it was not for me."

It's understandable why outsiders might have thought otherwise. She was in eighth grade when she not only qualified to enter her first LPGA major, the 2018 ANA Inspiration, but was one of seventy-six golfers to make the cut and finished tied for sixtieth. *As an eighth grader.* A year later she entered the 2019 U.S. Women's Open, her first major, and finished tied for fifty-fifth. A year after that, she qualified for the 2020 ANA Inspiration and finished tied for eleventh. She clearly could handle competing against the best of the best under the brightest of lights.

But her sights weren't set on merely making money playing golf tournaments; she wanted to win them. And while she might have had all the physical tools to compete, those early pro tournaments—particularly the majors—gave her a glimpse of the mental challenge involved in flying around the country week after week, looking to beat the tour's best in Nelly Korda, Ko Jin-young, and Minjee Lee, all in their mid- or late twenties. Having no margin for error was mentally exhausting. She had the prescience to recognize that being a great amateur—even the world's best—could not compare to the challenge of beating opponents with years of experience over her, on and off the course. Her dominance as an amateur offered no guarantees that she could reach the same heights as a pro, that the challenges and demands went well beyond a sweet swing and club choices and reading lies.

"It was a good amount of intuition," she said. "When someone is at the top of their golf game, especially as a junior player, they tend to put themselves on a pedestal. They're like, 'Oh, I am the big dog in the game.' And the career, the profession, is very tempting. As an amateur I played ten majors and made the cut in all but two or three, and if you make the cut as a pro, you make money. But I was not prepared to go out on tour. I was worried about burning out. After every week of playing in a pro tournament, I'm like, 'This is tiring. This is hard.' And even though everyone thought that I was just floating around, chilling, being the best, it was not the case. You have to put a lot of perspective into making something your profession."

Rachel Hoogasian, a clinical assistant professor at Arizona State University specializing in multicultural counseling and sport and performance psychology, applauded Zhang for her honest self-appraisal.

"The root of it all is just being able to listen to yourself," Hoogasian said. "Do you actually enjoy your sport? Is it the hard practices or the travel that you're struggling with, or is it that you just don't enjoy competing anymore? If it's just those hard sessions, then it's a matter of working with a coach or trainer to manage some of the heavy loads, make them more fun, find a social component so there's a connection with others to get through those hard moments and get to the fruits of it."

Pinnell helped temper Henry's desire for Rose to go pro and supported her instincts. While she had the physical talent to compete with pros, the preparation and attention to detail required was something she still had to learn.

"It was very wise of her to go to college," Pinnell said. "We were down in Charleston in 2019 for the U.S. Open, but the week before, she had an AJGA tournament in Phoenix, the

Thunderbird Heather Farr Classic. It was an important tournament to her, but we had the U.S. Open that next week. And so I went in on Saturday to meet her there. I'm sitting there, waiting. She doesn't drift in until Tuesday about noon. That gave us a day and a half to get ready."

Mechanical issues forced Zhang to take a red-eye out of Phoenix to Charleston, which was hot and humid when she arrived, adding to her fatigue.

But Pinnell was not about to waste another day with the Open starting on Thursday.

"Come on, we've got to get on the course," he said as soon as he saw her on Tuesday afternoon. "We've got to get in at least nine [holes]."

After her first round did not go well, she looked at George and nodded. "Now I know why you needed me in here earlier."

Rose still managed to make the cut on Friday, leaving Henry more confident than ever that she was ready to go pro full-time. When he and George sat down for lunch in the Charleston clubhouse, he tried to enlist George to help him convince Rose to do just that.

"George," he said, "we've got to get Rose to turn pro!"

Pinnell laughed. "Henry, she's not anywhere ready to turn pro. And she knows that. She doesn't want to turn pro. You can dream about it because it will be there someday, but for now just leave her alone."

Pinnell had an ally in Stanford women's golf coach Anne Walker, who understood exactly what Rose had to gain from being on a college campus and how it was an important component to being a successful pro.

"We've had a lot of success here with self-discovery, and I believe that's really the only avenue when you're working with the very, very elite," Walker said. "They have already had a lot of success. I tell them, 'We're recruiting you because of who you are and what you've done. You've built the foundation of potentially the strongest house on the block, sometimes the strongest house in the neighborhood. But we have to keep building it. We know the foundation is rock-solid, but we have to build it all the way to the peak of the roof. So that's what we talk about, how each layer we put on, each brick that we lay, that keeps going, that doesn't stop."

Walker made sure Rose understood her growth at Stanford had little to do with how well she swung a club.

"Within her first couple of weeks of being on campus, I was very open with her," Walker said. "There was so little room for growth in her golf game at that point. Where the real room for growth was in her person. Just like someone goes to law school or med school or business school to be a lawyer or a doctor or a businessman, they all require learning how to act like a professional. She got it. She understood that once you jump over that line, [from] amateur to professional, there's no coming back. And she wanted to make sure when she said farewell to the amateur game and, in a way, her youth, that she felt good about that and had done all she wanted to do, gone to all the places she wanted to go, experienced all the things she wanted to experience."

If Rose had any doubts about putting her pro career on hold to have the experience of being away from her parents, living in a dorm, and making friends who didn't know or care anything about golf, it came by way of an Instagram message from Beatriz Stix-Brunell, a twenty-eight-year-old world-class ballet dancer who was now pursuing a Stanford degree. Stix-Brunell, a Miami-born New Yorker, was still in high school when she moved to London to join the Royal Ballet. She made her way to first soloist before deciding to apply to Stanford and retire from dancing. Just in case Rose was having any second thoughts, Stix-Brunell sent her a private message, the essence of which went something like this:

> *Hey, I just wanted to say how amazing it is, how great you're doing, and how glad I am that you came to Stanford. I started dancing at the Royal Albert Hall in London when I was fifteen. I had an amazing career, but I felt like I missed out. I'm a twenty-eight-year-old freshman, and I'm happy to be here, but I don't fit in. I feel like my youth is gone. Everyone else is eighteen and it's not the same. Golf will always be there. But this won't. That's why I'm so proud of you for doing this.*

Rose told Walker about the exchange. "Coach, this is why I came to Stanford," she said. "There are so many people here who are the absolute best at whatever they do. On campus I'm not Rose the golfer; I'm just Rose. People know I'm a top golfer, but they don't treat me different. They don't ask about my golf game. They're too busy telling me about some cool thing they did. I've never felt so motivated to continue to get better, to continue to excel, because I'm surrounded by minds, even though they're all in different fields, like mine."

Hoogasian understood firsthand the challenge Rose faced choosing a path different from the one her father and erstwhile coach had in mind. As the youngest of six kids and the only one interested in sports, her father, a high school football coach and former NFL lineman, devoted himself to coaching her in the discus and shot put.

"We didn't have a lot of money, so the focus was on getting a college degree through sports," Hoogasian said. "I did fairly well, qualifying for the Junior Olympics several times. But there was a lot of pressure."

By Rachel's junior year in high school, she was the last of the kids still living at home. The focus on Rachel earning an athletic scholarship intensified. Her dad learned about visualization and mindfulness techniques. For the shot put, he had sheets printed up that read "40 or Bust," referring to the goal he'd set for her—to throw a shot put forty feet—and posted them everywhere, even tucking one into her throwing-shoe bag.

"He was ahead of his time in that way," she said. "I'd lay down in the dark and he'd have me imagine myself in the ring, imagining the movements and doing them well and everything would be good."

But it was not a relaxing exercise and it only heightened the pressure to succeed. "I would win, but if I didn't get past my personal best or match it at every single meet, it would just be terrible," she said. "I'd be so disappointed in myself." Sensing that her dad was equally disappointed only made it worse.

It all came to a head at the Arizona state championship. "I was so choked up that my spinning technique got all loosey-goosey," she said. "A few of my throws didn't even make it within the boundaries. They were so off, they'd wind up in different places or even in the net behind me."

Hoogasian wanted to find a way to earn a college degree but she was done with the discus and the shot put. She met with her high school counselor and enrolled in classes that would count toward her high school degree and earn college credit.

"I had to convince myself and my dad that I wasn't running away from something out of fear, I was running toward an opportunity to get an education another way," she said. "I wound up earning an academic scholarship and I know my dad was very proud of that. He just didn't know that was an option."

Hoogasian's work in sports psychology has allowed her to understand why her dad's methods, advanced as they might have been, didn't work.

"It was so much about hyper-focus on perfection," she said. "Anything short of that just didn't register. I had taken on an identity where I was no longer Rachel; I was Rachel the athlete. When only one of those identities exists, there can be a whole lot of angst and distress. There's something psychologically and physiologically that happens within a person's body when they're in a high-stress situation and they don't have the psychological tools and emotional capacity to cope with them. And when a parent is also the coach, it feeds more into that athlete identity if the parent can't establish a clear difference between the roles of coach and parent."

Walker helped ease any concerns about Rose missing out on a pro career by promising her and Henry that she would not be allowed to continue to play golf for the Cardinal the second Walker sensed she had everything she needed to be her best at the next level.

"If you are ready, I will kick you out the door," Walker told her. "Because it's a small window in time. And I know it's something people can't see from the outside or from scores or trophies or results. But when your line as a person crosses with your golf line on the graph and they meet, and they're at the top of the bell curve, then I'm going to kick you out the door."

Rose laughed. "Really, Coach?" she asked.

"For real," Walker said. "Because you, Rose, are more important than you, Rose the golfer."

Sharing the same goal and perspective with Walker erased any potential conflict between her dedication to golf and the rest of her Stanford experience. Plenty of college athletes look to combine those two interests, but either their coach isn't involved beyond wanting the athlete to stay academically eligible or they don't approach what they're doing as a student—socially or academically—as performance preparation. The latter group may utilize their popularity or value as an athlete to get away with certain behavior rather than holding themselves to a higher standard to fuel their success down the line.

The surest sign that a coach-athlete relationship is built on the wrong principles is when one or the other expects special treatment.

"With top athletes, there's so many people in their circle," Walker said. "And a lot of them need something from that person or are relying on them, or they're getting their self-worth from that kid. For me to be like, 'Hey, I'm good. Stanford Golf was here before you, Stanford Golf will be here after you. We're super thrilled that you're here, but we're going to be okay.' I think that went a long way with her."

Rose also did not want her entire persona to be defined by golf and how well she played it. She was well aware of how many athletes had distinguished amateur careers and didn't pan out as pros, either because they didn't have the necessary social and psychological development and support or because they couldn't continue to expand their game to compete at the next level. Rose inherently knew, as the daughter of parents who moved to the other side of the world and forged lives in a culture completely different from their own, the lunacy of thinking there is one strict definition of success. That awareness didn't take away a single ounce of her desire to be the best golfer she could possibly be; it merely removed the straitjacket that golf, and only golf, would determine her fate.

"I was worried about putting so much expectation on my golf career and my golf identity that if anything happened to go wrong, if anything happened injury-wise, or if I lost my passion for the game, I'd have no purpose," she said. We are sitting at a table outside the Stanford Golf Center on a warm late Friday afternoon. She has finished practicing for the day but is still decked out in golf gear, ball marker clipped to the bill of her cap, golf bag standing a few feet away. The lush greenery of the Stanford course's first hole sits just beyond a rustic wooden fence. "College was my time to grow, to make mistakes, to seek a new world and find new perspective on life," she said. "To know who I really am. And there's no better platform than coming to Stanford, a school full of prestigious students, staff, coaches, and venues. I mean, you get the best of both worlds here."

Winning both the individual NCAA title and clinching the team title for Stanford as a freshman made her wonder if maybe it was time to make the leap. The fact that she had to ask herself the question if she was ready, if it was time, was an answer in itself. She didn't want to *think* she was ready. She wanted to *know* she was ready.

"I don't like to skip steps in my career," she said. "I went from basic local tournaments, to the Southern California Golf Association junior tour, to the JLPGA, and then to college. I felt that if I was able to play well in college, then I will know I'm ready for the next level. So my goal was to win a national championship. That was essentially what I was playing for. But even then I was like, bro, that one year could have been a fluke. I need to make sure that I am doing everything I can to prepare myself for the next level.

"Golf humbles you. It is the ultimate sport where, if you play well one day, you're probably not likely to play well the next day if you're not consistent. And that's always what I believed. I was always thinking, even if I am playing well this tournament, even if I am trending toward a really good direction in my golf game, I can't get ahead of myself. That's when you lose awareness of what you're doing. And that was the same mindset that I had with turning professional."

Pinnell, rather than thinking about the attention and promotional value he might garner for being the swing coach of an LPGA player, went to extraordinary lengths to support Rose's desire to go to Stanford. He arranged for a Chinese venture capitalist he knew who lived in Atherton, a tony neighborhood not far from the Stanford campus, to meet Rose and Henry and share with them the immense value of going to Stanford for a minimum of two years. The school would then allow her to return and finish her degree at any time in the future and it would endear her to the rest of the Stanford community more than if she showed up, checked off the NCAA title box, and left.

There was a point where Rose actually considered staying all four years and earning her Stanford degree before turning pro. But midway through her sophomore season she told the team it would be her last. She still planned to earn her degree, but she was ready, emotionally and psychologically, to join the tour.

There was, however, some unfinished business swinging a club as an amateur. The Augusta National Women's Amateur was the one jewel she had yet to capture.

"That was the only event she really didn't have on her résumé," Walker said. "She'd won every other amateur event. And she'd had a few shots at that Augusta event, but she hadn't gotten it done. There was pressure on her from all the media outlets saying, 'This is Rose Zhang's year, she's been number one in the world for three straight years, it's time.' It was coming at her from all roads. She knew that everyone expected her to win. She expected it, too. Anything less than a victory, in her mind, would've been not living up to her skill set."

Entering the final round, it appeared as if the box was already checked. No one had ever played the first two rounds of the tournament better. *Ever.* She set the tournament record for low score on day one with a 66 and then reset it on day two with a 65, good for a commanding 5-shot lead going into the final day.

It's important to note that the first two rounds were played at the Champions Retreat course in nearby Evans, Georgia. The last round is reserved for Augusta National, which is, as any golfer or golf fan knows, arguably the most fickle, unforgiving, and unique course in the world. Thick groves of towering Georgia pine trees line the fairways. The greens are as slick as a greased skillet, with undulations and drop-offs into surrounding hazards, sand, and water. Lots of water. An approach shot can be like landing a prop plane on a glacier: desired speed, angle of descent, and point of touchdown can vary depending on the pin placement. Because the surfaces are so hard and fast, there's no room for a miscalculation on distance or trajectory.

Or for feeling out of sorts with your swing. Zhang's first of the day, on her opening drive, landed up against the lip of the fairway bunker. That resulted in a double bogey, slicing 2 strokes off her lead right at the start. Three more bogeys ensued, offset by a single birdie, shrinking her overall score from 13 under par to 9 under. Storm clouds were gathering–figuratively for Zhang and literally for everyone on the course–as she finished the seventh hole. During the ensuing three-hour weather delay, she tinkered with how she was gripping her clubs and found the answer to her wonky swing.

Play resumed and Rose hung on to the lead–until the par-5 fifteenth hole. For pro-level golfers the green is reachable in two shots, but it's also a risky gambit: miss the green long or short and it will land in water, drawing a stroke penalty. Rose and Henry, serving as her caddy, had a long conversation about what to do. Despite a stiff wind in her face, Rose went for it–and paid the price, the ball landing in the water short of the green. That resulted in both a bogey and a dead tie with the University of Georgia's Jenny Bae.

That's how it stayed through the final three holes, forcing a sudden-death playoff between Zhang and Bae, who had just shot the day's low eighteen-hole score of 70. Zhang had just shot her worst score of the week, 76, and blown a 5-stroke lead. It took two playoff holes and Bae narrowly missing a long birdie putt on the first one, but Zhang pulled out the victory.

"The relief, you could see it visibly in her eyes," Walker said. The dramatic win and its significance resulted in a media frenzy. She stayed at Augusta to make an appearance with another Stanford alum synonymous with historic Augusta victories: Tiger Woods. She then jetted up to New York and appeared on *Good Morning America*. Then it was time to hurry back to Palo Alto to begin her NCAA title defense.

Walker told her to take some time off, that she didn't want to see Rose on the course or at the facility for a couple of days. When she arrived at her office the next morning, it was evident that Rose had not listened to her. A package of teddy bears and an attached note sat outside Walker's office door. The teddy bears were for Walker's daughters; the note thanked Walker for being at Augusta.

"I'm, like, are you kidding me?" Walker said. "That's Rose."

But there were still two more mountains to climb: validating her first individual title by winning it again and breaking Woods's record for total college tournament wins, twelve. She stood at ten wins with three tournaments left–the Pac-12 championship, the NCAA regionals, and the nationals. She breezed to the Pac-12 and regional titles, but it looked as if she might have to settle for tying Woods's record, because she found herself in the exact opposite circumstance as Augusta: rather than 5 strokes ahead, she reached the final round of the individual championship 5 strokes behind USC's Catherine Park with several other players bunched between them.

The Grayhawk Golf Club in Scottsdale, Arizona, isn't as imposing as Augusta, but its greens are relatively fast. Playing from behind didn't appear to faze Zhang the way blowing a lead at Augusta had done. She exuded a matter-of-fact confidence that even the broadcasters noticed. "The way she is playing, you feel she has the lead even though she is a couple strokes behind," one observed.

Walker knew that look well. She witnessed it the first time she ever saw Zhang play in person. Walker made a recruiting trip to Florida to watch a junior tournament that included Rose and several other young golfers she thought might be Stanford material. Rose was thirteen years old.

"I saw her on the ninth hole for the first time," Walker said. "I waited at the turn for her to come up, and she hit a 5-wood from the middle of the fairway, just terrible. It was so bad. It was kind of like a low, drop-kick, snap hook. And I was like, 'Okay, well, that's interesting.' And then she hit an all-world short-game chip with the very next shot. It was a very tricky, delicate, tough chip shot and she put it within two feet of the hole."

Walker was impressed that Zhang, at thirteen, could shed the disappointment and frustration over the poorly hit shot, as well as any anxiousness over the golf coach from one of her dream schools witnessing it, to execute the next shot perfectly. "It's the first time the Stanford head coach has walked up to see you hit a shot," Walker said. "Your mind is reeling. I knew she wanted to go to Stanford or one of the Southern California schools. I was standing on the cart path, even with her ball, about twenty-five yards away. We hadn't met but I had on my Stanford gear. She knew who I was. For her to be able to gather herself, a newly minted teenager, it was really pretty incredible. It was all I needed to see. I would come to learn that that was really Rose: that she was fairly unflappable no matter what had come on the shot before."

Or, in the case of the 2023 NCAA National Championship, the *rounds* before. Rose nearly birdied the first three holes of the day before scoring three of them over the next four holes. By the seventeenth, she had erased the deficit and staked a 1-stroke lead over Park and San Jose State's Lucia Lopez Ortega.

Not unlike the fifteenth at Augusta, Zhang had thoughts of attempting to reach the par-5 eighteenth green in two shots. Walker informed her she had a 1-stroke lead and suggested she protect it by taking a more conservative approach. Zhang took her advice, completed her seventh consecutive par, and got the comeback win.

Neither Rose nor anyone else needed any more proof that it was time to move to the next level.

"With my game trending in the direction that it was, especially with the attention on women's sports growing significantly bigger, if there was a time to take advantage of the momentum and challenge myself further, I had to turn pro," she said. "I announced it at the end of my sophomore year but everyone in the program already knew that it was my last year. And I still played well."

She was saying goodbye to being on the Stanford golf team but not to being a student. Working toward her degree remained part of the plan because she considered it an indispensable part of her growth as an all-around person, which was vital to becoming an all-around great professional golfer. Being on the Palo Alto campus surrounded by students and faculty who had goals far more globally impactful than making a twenty-foot putt also kept the ups and downs of golf in perspective.

"The value isn't about the actual paper [degree] itself," she said. "The value is the experiences involved in being a part of the school and being here and not only learning information but also challenging myself. You're not going to see more brilliant minds than here. And the special thing about Stanford is they're both good at academics, but they're really good at extracurricular activities. With that in mind, I felt like I could do so much in learning from these people. And some of my closest friends, I actually don't know how they do it. My goal is to hit a small ball into a small hole. And that's essentially what I do for a living."

But by finding, and collaborating with, coaches and mentors who shared her vision and principles, she discovered that putting that small ball into a small hole for a living required skills and knowledge beyond the simple physical ability to put a small ball into a small hole. If her coaches listened to her feedback, it was because she readily accepted and applied their instruction or suggestions first. If her parents respected her decisions, even when they didn't necessarily agree, it was because she was both thoughtful and respectful in how she made them. She took full ownership of not only where she wanted to go but how she wanted to get there. A note to parents: Be sure your child's dream is being pursued, not your own. To do otherwise plants the idea that your happiness and satisfaction supersedes theirs.

IN A TRULY HEALTHY RELATIONSHIP, the path to a goal is afforded as much value and importance as the goal itself, because there's never a guarantee that the goal will be reached. By giving equal weight to her personal growth and development and her ambitions as a golfer, Rose created an identity far richer and deeper than simply Rose Zhang, professional golfer. It not only provided her an alternate path should golf no longer offer one, for whatever reason; it actually made her a better competitor by giving her the emotional balance and perspective to handle the pressure of performing.

It also allowed her to take the approach to being in the LPGA of *I get to do this* rather than *I have to do this*. It's not a matter of being indifferent to pursuing excellence but having the awareness that the performer's identity is not defined by their success or failure. It's knowing that the sport—or any other occupation—is not *who they are* but simply *what they do*. Rose might've been able to accomplish that on her own, but it was infinitely easier that her coaches and parents shared her vision of who and what she wanted to be and how she planned to get there.

TRUTH 4

Who You Are, Not Where You Are, Will Decide What You Are: Fred VanVleet

AS FAR AS FREDDERICK VANVLEET IS CONCERNED, NOT MUCH HAS changed from his days growing up in Rockford, Illinois, sitting on the bench for his stepdad's AAU team, watching bigger, older, stronger players—including his brother, Darnell, and stepbrother, J.D.—and believing with all his heart that he should be in the game. He may be a little bigger, older, and stronger now, but he still finds himself having to prove, over and over again: *I'm better than you think I am.*

At the beginning, it was less about proving how good he was than about fairness. He was up at the crack of dawn every morning, right alongside J.D. and Darnell, lifting weights, playing full court one-on-one, and going through ball-handling and shooting drills. His skills were equal to, or better than, theirs. He was just as tough if not tougher. He was just a whole lot shorter and not quite as strong or fast–all of which was understandable since he was two years younger than J.D. and three years younger than Darnell.

That shouldn't have mattered, in Fred's eyes. As for anybody else on his team, the Rockford Five-0, he *knew* he was putting more time into his game than they were.

"It was humbling," he said. "We would go to tournaments and get our ass kicked and I wouldn't play. I knew I was better. I just wasn't physically ready. My stepdad was not wrong by saying that I was too small, but I felt I deserved to be out there."

A typical tweenager might have sat on the bench and sulked or grumbled or studied their fingernails, lost in a fog of disappointment. Not Fred. He channeled his frustration into having all his senses in overdrive, studying everything he might not be able to take in if he were playing, gleaning every bit of information that might give him an edge should his stepdad decide to put him on the floor. He was sharpening his metaphorical knives so that he could carve up the competition once he was given a chance.

"You can find different things to motivate you," Fred said. "It taught me how to watch a game and how to get better without playing. To learn from people's mistakes. To watch the other team on the bench and their coaches and the reactions and listen to what the parents are saying. Just being in tune with everything that's going on. I'm not playing, so I might as well just check on everything else that's going on. I learned a lot, and when it was my time to play, I had all this information."

A lot has changed for VanVleet since those early days; it's only his perspective and approach that hasn't. He starred at Auburn High School, leading a previously perennially losing program to a twenty-two-game winning streak and a third-place finish in the state tournament his senior year. He played four years at Wichita State, leading them to the first 31-0 regular-season record in NCAA history as a sophomore. He has spent more than a decade now in the NBA, twice the length of the average NBA career. He has been named an All-Star. He won championships with both the Toronto Raptors and their minor-league affiliate, Raptors 905. His first contract guaranteed him only $50,000; seven years later he signed the largest contract in NBA history for an undrafted player, $129 million over three years, with the Houston Rockets. Perhaps most impressive, the kid who couldn't get on the court is now rarely off of it. In Fred's second season in Houston, the Rockets had ten first-round draft picks—five among the top-five selections—yet Fred averaged far and away more minutes per game than anyone else on the roster.

Resentment over having to prove himself over and over again has morphed into appreciation—to the point that he wouldn't have had it any other way.

"I had to earn it every step of the way, from a character, personality, and playing standpoint," he said. "It builds you up to who you are as a man. I can't even imagine another world where it didn't go like this. I've made my living off of guys who have had everything handed to them. My whole mindset and approach to the game is different."

Fred was five years old when his father, Fredderick Darnell Manning, was shot and killed. For the next five years his mom, Susan VanVleet, worked multiple jobs to support the family; Darnell looked after Fred. Then Sue met Joe Danforth, a Rockford police officer, at a basketball tournament, where his two sons, J.D. and Tre, were also playing. Susan, Joe, and the four boys all eventually moved in together, but Fred was not enthralled with the idea of having a stepdad, particularly one that was a former soldier and career police officer.

"I told my mom she had to choose, me or him," Fred said.

"I threatened to run away. I was going to go live with my grandparents. I said she'd ruined my life. She told him about it. When he came home, he's like, 'You think you're going to run some shit around here?' So now I'm all disappointed that my mom went behind my back and told him what I said. That was my moment as a kid. I was like, 'All right, well, she ain't leaving him, so I better get comfortable.' I resented my mom because she was so much on his side. But she wanted a man to discipline us and put us in position to be successful later on in life. I always loved and respected him, but that took a little bit of adjusting for me as a ten-year-old kid. And then the older I got, the more I could appreciate the lessons that I was being taught."

The lessons were severe, almost primal. That's because Joe believed that life was severe, almost primal, and that, as a parent, his job was to prepare the four boys to face an unforgiving world. It's easy to see why someone who served as a detective in the Rockford gang unit would have that perspective. Located eighty-five miles northwest of Chicago, Rockford earned the nickname "Screw City" because it was one of the nation's biggest manufacturers of the metal fastener, but it was also an apt description of how it treated Black people and other minorities. When Fred was in grade school, the school district was court-ordered to make $252 million worth of upgrades after being found guilty of discriminating against minorities through shoddy facilities and educational standards. The Rockford unemployment rate for Black men at one point was the highest in the nation: nearly 30 percent. For most of the last thirty years, Rockford has been ranked among the top ten most dangerous cities in the United States.

The Army taught Joe how to fight in more ways than one. Out of boredom while stationed in Korea, he started boxing, competing at one point for the Army championship.

"I was in during the Brown Boot Army," he said, a reference to a harsher era in U.S. Army history and identified by a time when soldiers wore light brown boots rather than today's black ones. "I used to do some grueling shit. Running in combat boots and weighted vests and rucksacks. They'd cuss your ass out and beat your ass if you messed up. They phased that out in the late '90s, but I was in when it was some *Apocalypse Now* shit. That was a big part of my life. It was all I knew."

Once the boys got bigger, Joe utilized his boxing expertise. Their chores included having the house clean and in order when he came home. One day it wasn't. Before they could head to the gym for practice, Joe moved aside the living room furniture, pulled out the boxing gloves, and sparred a few rounds with each of them.

"I didn't have a dad growing up, so I always wanted a bunch of sons," Joe said. "I got a chance to raise them, be good to them, but also be tough and mean and strict."

What Joe never wanted to be accused of was favoritism toward his boys. When it came to his role as the Rockford Five-0 coach, that meant they had to be, in his words, "ten times better than everybody else" to make sure no one would ever second-guess how much playing time they got. The team practiced in the evenings, but Joe also put his four boys through a before-school workout at the local YMCA.

"I was getting them up at the crack of dawn every damn morning," Joe said. "Rooms had to be cleaned and beds had to be made. We'd get to the Y, and I had these thirty- or forty-pound vests and they would have to play in 'em. They were little guys, so I had to duct-tape the shoulder parts on them so they wouldn't slip off. The guys playing pickup on the other courts were like, 'This dude is crazy.' But that's what they had me doing when I was boxing in the Army. I wanted to teach the boys toughness, because I wasn't always going to be around to hold their hands. I felt that if you knew how to protect yourself and you were tough, you could survive. And all these boys, man, they were all tough-minded. They didn't take no shit."

No one more so than Fred. He played primarily for two AAU teams, both based in Rockford: Pryme Tyme, run by Anthony "Doc" Cornell, and Rockford Five-0, modestly funded by the Rockford Police Department (hence the name, a reference to the TV show *Hawaii Five-0*).

Fred rarely played for Five-0, but that didn't affect his attitude in the least. When Five-0 showed up at LeBron James's now defunct Shooting Stars tournament in Akron, Ohio, Joe was stunned to see a six-foot-ten kid in their seventh-grade bracket.

"I was like, 'What the hell did I get my damn self into?'" Joe said.

Fred, still a fourth grader, was undaunted. "The six-ten kid said something to J.D. or Darnell," Joe recalled. "Fred walked right up to that dude with his head at his waist and pushed him. I just started laughing and said get your ass back over here."

Pryme Tyme Elite allowed Fred to play against his age group, where he was still undersized but there was no reason to hold him back.

"I told people, 'Fred VanVleet is the best guard in the country and that is why we're winning,'" Doc said. "There was no rhyme or reason to why we were beating the teams that we did, but I can tell you one of the main key factors was that Fred was arguably the number one point guard in the country."

Scouting services and recruiters were less inclined to believe that because Pryme Tyme Elite was not a shoe-sponsored team. The shoe-sponsored teams, on the other hand, were well aware of what Doc had in Fred after facing him. Former NBA power forward Antonio Davis, who coached Illinois Central Elite, went so far as to have dinner with Joe and Susan and offered to cover any costs if Fred would play for him. Fred, as a sixth grader, reluctantly tried it for a year. The experience was valuable in that he got a glimpse of the life, via Davis, that making it to the NBA could provide. It also introduced Fred to flying on a plane for the first time. But leaving behind the friends, teammates, and coaches who had helped make him into a player that nationally recognized, shoe-sponsored programs wanted felt selfish and like a form of betrayal.

"All these teams would say, 'He needs to be playing with us,'" Doc said. "But Fred has always been loyal. He was like, 'If they're going to see me, they're going to see me. Plus, I'm not leaving my guys. These are guys I can go spend the night with. I can hang out with them. I'm going to see these other [shoe-sponsored] guys every blue moon. I'm just going to show up at a tournament and play? That's not what I do.'"

Fred's ambition was to be more than a player: he wanted to be a leader, and he couldn't very well do that parachuting in on weekends to play with a group of boys he didn't know. That kind of bond took time and familiarity.

"I was taught point guards were judged by wins and losses and it's a bottom-line business," Fred said. "And I was taught that at an early age. Those were the things instilled in me: Don't turn the ball over, make the right plays and reads. It ain't about all that other stuff. That was just the way I was raised up."

Fred had also cultivated Doc's trust to the point that Doc told people he felt like former NFL coach Tony Dungy coaching a young, future Hall of Fame quarterback, Peyton Manning. "I took care of the defense and I let Fred run the offense," Doc said.

Fred's offensive wizardry began with watching what did and didn't work for Rockford Five-0.

He accepted that a certain degree of size, strength, and speed were needed to compete, but he observed that those weren't prerequisites for winning. What were: Execution. Poise under pressure. Trust. Effort. And efficiency. The differentiators were less about physical superiority than mental and intellectual strength. Understanding what needed to be done and how to get a group to do it could overcome any physical disadvantage. And that *was* a gift that Fred had.

"I feel as though I'm a leader of men in real life," VanVleet said. "So by the time you get to basketball, it's easy. There are leadership positions in every sport, and I just naturally had that as a God-given. My whole game is based off of who I am as a person. The rest of that stuff is just me figuring it out, being an athlete and a hooper. But pretty much all of my advancement and success and accolades come from who I am as a person. It ain't nothing on the exterior, you know what I mean? I didn't get those gifts. I didn't get the height or the hops or some supreme blessing like that. It's more so just about what's inside my chest."

Don't cue the dramatic orchestral string music quite just yet. Fred may have been born with a desire to lead, but he didn't always know how.

"He was a jerk," said Susan VanVleet. "He would tell his teammates they sucked."

The turning point came when Fred entered high school and chose to follow Darnell and J.D. to Auburn rather than the local high-powered private school, Boylan Catholic. Auburn had three boys' basketball teams–one for freshmen, one for sophomores, and the varsity–and played them in an informal summer league program. Joe volunteered to coach the sophomore team, and although Fred was an incoming freshman, the varsity coach moved him up to Joe's team. Fred quickly established himself as its best player and they routed most of their opponents. One game, Joe subbed Fred out in the third quarter with a particularly lopsided score. Fred was incensed. Here he was again, playing for Joe, sitting on the bench.

"Why are you taking *me* out?" Fred said angrily.

"We are up by damn near a hundred," Joe said. "Let these other guys get in and get some run because they're not going to get a lot of time during the season."

Fred stomped over to the bench, threw himself into a chair, and, when Danforth walked past, stuck his leg out in an attempt to trip him. Danforth wheeled around, picked Fred up, his legs literally kicking in the air, hauled him out into the hallway, and lined him up against the side of a concession stand. "Who do you think you are?" Danforth snarled, towering over him. "You're going to sit your ass on that bench and cheer for your team and you're going to enjoy it. You understand?"

"Yes sir," Fred said quietly.

Susan VanVleet witnessed the entire episode. "He came back in a changed man," she said of Fred, who dutifully sat down on the bench and cheered for his teammates.

"He wasn't the best teammate at first because he didn't understand at a young age why people didn't play hard like him," Cornell said. "But after he started maturing, instead of getting on them, he started helping, and then people wanted to play for him. Some of his teammates told me years later, 'Doc, we didn't want to let Fred down. We saw him dive on the floor, setting picks, rebounding, and going against the so-called best player from the other team. If he was doing it, we felt we had to do it.'"

The switch flipped for Fred when he realized that a leader can't demand teammates follow him; he has to inspire them.

"We all have the same twenty-four hours and I knew they weren't working on their game as much as I was," he said. "But I had to learn that people are more likely to follow someone they love than someone they fear."

It was also acknowledging that he, too, had room for improvement.

"Being coachable starts with accountability," he said. "If

you don't have an issue with accountability, then you're not going to have an issue with coaching. If I know I'm wrong before the coach gets to me, then I'm going to receive his message versus being surprised that somebody's yelling at me. You're not paying attention to how that message is delivered, you're thinking more about 'How do I get it right?' And once you're on that track, you start to understand what coaching is. The ultimate goal is to win the damn game. So if you keep that in mind, then everything else kind of falls underneath that."

Fred wasn't interested in playing for anyone who didn't value accountability. Hence, joining a high-profile team to play in the biggest national tournaments held no appeal. He knew the coaches would be less likely to challenge him or any of the other players for fear they'd skip to some other high-profile program that catered to them. He would be just another one of the thousands of young, promising players flying around the country concerned only about catching a college coach or recruiter's attention. Despite Fred's reluctance, Doc persuaded the director of Nike Elite 100, an annual camp and showcase for the top one hundred high school players in the country, to extend him an invitation.

"Fred hated that stuff because it was more about one-on-one basketball," Doc said. "Nobody played team basketball. And he was about team. He ended up breaking down and going, and then his competitive spirit kicked in. But he had a demeanor that was just different from the average kid. To him, it wasn't a tournament; it was a business trip. His gym bag was his suitcase."

In many ways, Fred personified his hometown: overlooked, underestimated, but with a blue-collar toughness, pride, and work ethic. There were no guarantees when it came to what playing basketball ultimately could do for him. But having seen the reaction to the success he brought to Auburn High and

Pryme Tyme Elite, he knew what playing basketball could do for Rockford. It could inspire a new identity and a ray of hope for every player that came after him.

"Relatedness is a top-three motivator in elite performance," Professor Kimberly Shaffer said. "Fred was motivated by his connectedness to other people. It takes us off our island and allows us to know 'it's bigger than just me.' Core values are at the heart of why we, as humans, make most decisions. They are our North Star. His sense of loyalty is absolutely a core value. Losing his father at such a young age, the connection with his brothers, that all plays into his 'why.' We feel a cognitive dissonance when our actions don't align with our core values."

No wonder Fred listed "perspective" as his greatest strength.

"It's being able to see things from different viewpoints and different angles, which allows you to react and adjust to different situations," he said. "There are way more undrafted guys trying to make it to the NBA now. When I talk to kids, they always ask me, 'What's the secret?' I'm like, 'It's really a thousand decisions you've got to make on a daily basis. Little decisions that you've got to get right and not only when it's beneficial. You've got to do that shit when it doesn't matter, and then, over time, it'll add up to something.'"

It is still jarring to see VanVleet in an NBA locker room, a Yoda among Darth Vaders. There's nothing that would suggest he's one of the best basketball players on the planet when he walks into a room. He hasn't grown an inch since his senior year in high school, when he topped out at six feet. The imaginations of most recruiters and scouts are sparked by height, long arms, big hands, quick feet, willowy agility, and leaping ability. VanVleet would not be described as elite in any of those categories, or "measurables," the word scouts and recruiters use for the quantification of an elite basketball player's physique. He has a cherubic face and a 195-pound build some might describe as chunky. There are no NBA draft combine measurements for vertical leap or agility because he wasn't among the nearly eighty prospects invited to the weeklong event to be tested, interviewed, and observed in various drills and scrimmages by team executives. This predraft assessment by one scout explains why: "At 6' with a 6'1.5" wingspan, VanVleet lacks great size, length, and explosiveness for a point guard."

Not exactly a rousing endorsement. So what did he have? An intangible that is hard to quantify: supreme toughness. Losing his biological father as a five-year-old, one-on-one basketball games on a gravel driveway with a brother three years his senior that often ended in fistfights, and a prizefighting stepdad who taught him how to box produced a six-foot-tall bulldog that was afraid of only one thing: not being given a chance.

Joe Danforth insists he merely honed a toughness that Fred already had. "He took everything I said to heart," Joe said. "Despite him not being my blood son, people would say, 'God damn, he acts like he's mean and tough. He acts just like you.'"

That toughness was augmented by an even greater attribute: the ability to instantly calculate space and angles and timing, a genius that could only be identified—and appreciated—by watching him play and seeing the results. Joe describes him as part obscure brainiac superhero—Charles Xavier, or Professor X—and part Will Hunting, the Matt Damon character in the Boston-based movie *Good Will Hunting*.

"He was a mutant," Danforth said, laughing. "If he was a superhero, he would be Charles Xavier because he had a mind for stuff, man. His brothers had the agility and the speed and the quickness and the hops and all that other kind of stuff. Fred was just a regular little dude, but he was just so smart. He just understood shit. His IQ has to be through the roof. I used to call him an egghead all the time because he just got it. He was in gifted classes and he begged me and his mom to take him out. He just wanted to be regular."

Much like Will Hunting, Fred didn't care about being "wicked smaht"—as Will's friend Chuckie Sullivan (Ben Affleck) described him in a Boston brogue—if it was only of value to him. He helped J.D. and Darnell with their homework. He could've got by without studying or attending class, but he did so to inspire his teammates to do the same. He also considered it his responsibility to identify their strengths and how to help make the most of them on the court. He couldn't do that if he were focused only on showcasing his skills.

Wichita State head coach Gregg Marshall didn't know anything about Fred when one of his assistant coaches first mentioned his name. All he knew was that a self-sponsored team out of Rockford, led by a point guard not listed in the ranking services, was crushing AAU teams loaded with D1 prospects. And underdogs capable of beating more celebrated opponents were exactly what Marshall needed to transform Wichita State into a powerhouse.

"My personal internal competitiveness is, unofficially, by my calculations, more than 99.5 percent of the people in the world," Marshall said wryly. "Fred is in that top 0.5 [percent]. His competitive nature is the greatest that I've ever seen."

VanVleet wasn't listed in the rankings, but he still impacted them. Yogi Ferrell, then the No. 1–ranked high school point guard in the country by some scouting services, got knocked down to No. 2 after facing and being beaten by Fred. Which elevated future North Carolina Tar Heel Marcus Paige to No. 1. Paige, playing for Martin Bros Select, sat out—ducked, says Doc—a subsequent game against Pryme Tyme with a sore ankle. When Pryme Tyme took on the Houston Defenders with two Kentucky-bound six-foot-six twin brothers Andrew and

Aaron Harrison, Doc sidled up to the Harrison twins' dad, Aaron Harrison Sr., and suggested he not have them guard Fred or they might have their Kentucky offers rescinded.

"I watched them beat teams with three and four guys going to the ACC or the Big Ten," Marshall said. "Not just beat them but throttle them by 20 or 30 points. Fred was out there with one other guy, a kid [Marcus Posley] that ended up going to St. Bonaventure, and then a bunch of DIII guys. They literally had nobody over six-two. They were tiny and Fred was out there just taking the ball from people and shooting layups and getting people wide-open shots with his penetration and playing unbelievable defense. They didn't go back to half court and pick you up man-to-man. They got in your ass as soon as the ball was inbounded, hounding you for ninety-four feet. It was just incredible to watch."

In his own playing career, Marshall, like many coaches, was longer on effort and basketball IQ than athleticism. VanVleet's search for a ticket out of a challenging environment also made them kindred spirits. For Marshall the environment was a shrinking Appalachian town–Roanoke, Virginia–and Randolph-Macon College, at the time a Division II school just up the road from the state capital, Richmond, provided the ticket.

"I was six-foot-two, 145 pounds, skinny, weak, couldn't really jump, had a questionable jump shot," Marshall said. "There's no reason that I, physically, from an athletic or basketball-skill standpoint, should have been a college basketball player. It was simply because I was unbelievably coachable."

Randolph-Macon head coach Hal Nunnally convinced Marshall that players willing to be students of the game and give supreme effort could punch well above their weight. During Marshall's four-year Yellow Jacket career, Randolph-Macon earned three Division II NCAA tournament bids. "He found guys like myself and just blended us together," Marshall said of Nunnally, now enshrined in the Virginia Sports Hall of Fame. Nunnally took note of Marshall's attention to detail and competitive spirit and upon graduation asked him to join his coaching staff.

Marshall landed his first head coaching job at Winthrop University in Rock Hill, South Carolina, less than one hundred miles northeast of his birthplace, Greenwood. He took over a program that had suffered eight consecutive losing seasons and immediately flipped it, winning a conference title and making the first of seven NCAA tournament appearances in his nine-year tenure. It took him a little longer to find success at Wichita State: five seasons to earn his first NCAA tournament bid. Then VanVleet showed up and Marshall had his defensive and offensive spearhead. Four more tournament bids followed.

"My forte was defense," Marshall said. "My coach had me guard the best player on the other team who wasn't the center and just basically be a pain in the ass. And that's what I always looked for in players."

A tip to any athlete looking to play for a particular coach or program: Identify what they appreciate and value most and make that a hallmark of your game.

"I always had a guy that played my role, and I glorified that defensive-stopper role to the point where that was the guy getting all the praise," Marshall said. "And Fred had that. Fred had that all the way."

Every spring, beginning with his sophomore year when he led the Missouri Valley Conference in assists and shot a team-leading 42 percent from 3-point range, rumors would arise that Fred was going to declare for the NBA draft. But after some exploratory calls, Fred would opt to stay and continue to work on his game and his college degree.

"He did his own research," Danforth said. "He asked a

bunch of people a bunch of different things and I just don't think he liked what he heard."

The feedback after his senior year was only slightly better. NBA scouts didn't know that he played with a hamstring injury and still managed to lead the MVC for a third consecutive season in assists and take Wichita State to a conference title and NCAA tournament appearance. Fred's no-excuse philosophy meant refusing to acknowledge to anyone outside the team that he was playing injured. Not being invited to the NBA Draft Combine meant arranging private workouts. He visited eighteen teams in thirty days. The Toronto Raptors were the eighteenth.

"It was literally our last workout of the predraft process," said Raptors assistant GM Dan Tolzman. "We had to reschedule with him several times. We just wanted to see him up close. The competition level is always a bit higher in the draft workout and it's against bigger, longer athletes than he would've seen at Wichita State. When we finally got him in, it was like, 'This was why we worked so hard to see him.' He was very much what you see today, just really calm and in charge."

Rather than diminish his accomplishments, Fred's lower-profile path worked in his favor. If he could make the most of limited means in Rockford and Wichita, the Raptors imagined what he'd do with a steady diet of tougher competition and unlimited resources.

"The moment a player gets to the NBA, it's 24/7 basketball if they want it," Tolzman said. "If a guy is wired that way and then you give him a weight program and nutrition and high-level competition on top of it, there's usually greater progress made by someone who is new to that level of resources, as opposed to the high-pedigree guys who have been given everything from the time they were ten and take it for granted."

The Raptors also valued intangibles more than measurables. Their starting point guard at the time, Kyle Lowry–listed as six feet and 196 pounds—was built very similar to VanVleet, with the same bulldog demeanor, earning him his second season as an All-Star. And while Fred may not have had the classic attributes of a high-level basketball player, he wasn't devoid of unique physical assets. Whether it was wrestling with his older brothers or boxing with his stepdad, he had developed strong hands and an unusually stout frame that allowed him to take a shot to the chest from a bigger player and stand his ground.

"During that exact time we had Kyle Lowry, who is an anti-measurable guy himself, and we were having a lot of success with him running the team," Tolzman said. "We had an example that, if a guy has the heart and knows how to play, size doesn't matter. The biggest thing is: Can they defend? As long as they're not going to get picked on defensively, that will help them push through and survive in the NBA. Freddy's been a guy from way back hanging his hat on defense as much as he has offense. You see his strong hands and his ability to chest up people and not get backed down in the post, you think, 'Okay, he's not the fastest, most athletic guy, but he plays the right way and he doesn't give up an inch on the defensive end.'"

There was just one problem: the Raptors didn't have a second-round draft pick at their disposal. Both the Atlanta Hawks and Orlando Magic, on the other hand, had two of them and indicated to Fred's agent that they planned to use one on Fred if he was still available. But they also made it clear that there wasn't a roster spot for him or even necessarily a contract. They would be drafting him to have his NBA rights as a future asset, hoping he might still grow a few inches or develop physically in some other way. Miller asked Fred how badly he wanted to hear his name called on draft night or if he'd be okay going to training camp with a team as an undrafted free agent. Second-round draft picks have a slightly higher chance of being offered a contract simply because an investment has been made in them; conversely, an undrafted player can survey all thirty NBA rosters, choose one that appears in the greatest need of his services, and procure a camp invitation. But it's invariably on a non-guaranteed contract for the NBA minimum wage.

"I didn't know that teams could call you and tell you that they're going to pick you or not," VanVleet said. "So when we had that conversation, I said, 'Yeah, I do want to hear my name called, but if the team is telling me I don't even have a chance to make it, I don't want to do that. I want a chance to make the roster before anything.' I knew I had one person in the Toronto front office who was a fan, Dan Tolzman. I'm like, 'All right, cool. I'm going to just work with that.'"

Miller put out the word to the rest of the league: Please don't draft Fred if there isn't a roster spot he could potentially win. The Raptors were offering no more than a potential path to the NBA but it was enough for Fred.

"We didn't even really need a point guard at the time," said Tolzman. "We had just drafted Delon Wright the year before. We had Kyle, of course, and Cory Joseph. So we had three very legitimate point guards and our G League program was very much in its infancy. We had struggled the year before and needed somebody to steer the ship. It was like, if we can find ourselves a really good young point guard, they're going to spend a lot of time with the [Raptors] 905 and could develop through that process. As we were preparing for the draft, we just kept coming back to Freddy as the guy who fit that profile."

With no guarantees about what would happen, Fred held a draft party for 150-some friends and family at a local bar and grill anyway.

"That was a weird night," he said. "I was sitting in a room full of people, knowing I might not get picked, and everybody's wondering what's going on. I had to get up there and explain to everybody why. They still didn't understand it."

As uncomfortable as the moment might have been, that Fred handled it the way he did spoke volumes about his vision.

"His entire approach to finding his way into the NBA reiterates his ability to see the bigger picture, especially with him being okay without the gratification of having his name called on NBA Draft Night," Shaffer said.

The Raptors called as soon as the draft was over and reiterated their interest, inviting him up for a minicamp the following week with a chance to play for their Summer League team, a training camp invitation, and, at the very least, a spot on their G League squad. Fred accepted the offer. It still didn't take the sting out of not getting drafted.

"Even though I knew I probably wasn't going to get drafted, it was the finality of it," he said. "That was the first time it was real and public and I was, like, 'Damn, I ain't getting drafted.' I had a couple drinks and by the next day my mind was already on going to Toronto and trying to figure out how to make it out of Summer League. I got back in the gym and went back to work."

Minicamp ended with the Raptors being even more impressed. The instant chemistry he demonstrated with their first-round pick, an Austrian center named Jakob Poeltl, had them adjusting their expectations for what VanVleet might be.

"He shows up and it's obvious there's a lot more to this guy than just being a solid player," Tolzman recalled. "We flew in Jakob and Freddy at the same time. We were treating the guy like, 'Dude, we targeted you. If we had a second-round pick it would've been you' sort of thing. They start workouts together—Jakob, the No. 9 pick in the draft, and Fred, this undrafted, undersized point guard—and there was no talent gap at all. We just got this big young Austrian center and this Midwestern brickhouse point guard. They both had something to 'em where those workouts were pretty incredible to watch, like, 'Whoa, summer league's going to be pretty fun if we've got these two guys.'"

What the Raptors didn't tell VanVleet is that he was one of six undrafted free agents invited to be part of their Summer League team. Not that it fazed VanVleet. By now he had become fairly adept at sizing up the competition and figuring out how to squash it. He also knew that Raptors coach Dwane Casey liked to carry three point guards on his roster, which meant with Lowry, Joseph, and Wright as the incumbents, he was one injury away from getting a shot. That injury occurred in Summer League when Wright dislocated his right shoulder and had to have surgery to repair a torn labrum, sidelining him until February.

"I ended up falling into that third point guard slot, and that's pretty much what got me over the hump," Fred said.

But consider all the decisions Fred made that led to that opportunity. Even though he had already been through seventeen workouts and had secured interest from a couple of teams, he flew to Canada to go through an eighteenth for a team that didn't even have a second-round pick. When it came to the draft, he sublimated the ego-feeding—and temporary—gratification of hearing his name called in front of family and friends to pursue the best avenue to his goal.

The rest of Fred's career has been essentially the application of the same principles: Take advantage of every opportunity given, prepare as if it's the last one, embrace whatever is asked, learn as much as possible, and keep aiming higher.

Being undersized made it harder to impress scouts and recruiters and GMs, but not Toronto's hockey-oriented fans, who were quickly enamored with the bearded, barrel-chested rookie who had the temperament, in hockey parlance, of a mucker and a grinder.

"Freddy was the point guard of a five-man unit off the bench, and they might've been more popular than our starting five, because when they got up to check into the game, the crowd would go crazy and the place would just ignite," Tolzman said. "And, then, incrementally, his role just got bigger and bigger and the culmination is we're in the championship series and he's making key shots, key defensive plays, and getting Finals MVP votes. You could see it coming, but you didn't realize the snowball effect would happen as fast as it did."

Tolzman, reflecting on VanVleet's journey, believes the catalyst was Fred's clear understanding of who he is and what he can do. All he needed was someone else to see it.

"So much of this game is players actually believing in the skills that they have and what they're capable of," Tolzman observed. "How many of the most talented players in the world come into the NBA and they struggle and never find a footing because they don't have that? Or they don't have a team or a coach backing them? Wichita State, at the time a very small school and no real high-level basketball history, believed in him and he believed in the message they were sending. That was our situation, too. He had no business picking us because of the depth chart of point guards ahead of him. But early in the process we were showing our interest and relaying to his people that this isn't just surface interest: we actually see something in this kid and think we know where we can take him. Knowing that we've done our research and we actually do see a fit, it helped him put trust in us and we put the trust in him and it was a mutual decision to do something together."

An athlete has to have a vision of where they want to go and who they want to be. But the first sign that they are where they're supposed to be is that who they are playing for, or with, has a vision of who and what the athlete can be as well. It may not be the vision the athlete had hoped for, but that's okay as long as there is one. Besides, plans and visions are mutable.

"A lot of problems that people have with their kids and why they fuck up when they get to college or to the league is because they've been told their whole goddamn life, 'Oh, you perfect, it ain't your fault. It's the coach's fault,'" Danforth pointed out. "I was never like that. If you played fucked-up or played like shit, I wasn't going to sugarcoat it. That's where people mess up with their kids, treating 'em like they're perfect and handling them with kid gloves instead of telling them the damn truth, like 'Man, you ain't as good as you think you are. You got to get your ass to the fucking gym.'"

That's where Fred's early years of observation from the bench proved particularly invaluable. He watched how some big-name players dodged responsibility for a mistake, how their parents harped on the coaches or referees, and how all that impacted the team as a whole. He saw those same parents and players being approached by, or showing up on, a different team. The takeaway: if an athlete shows any degree of ability, there is sure to be someone ready to tell them what they want to hear to lure them away. Fred eventually experienced it himself. Fred's advice to athletes and their parents or mentors: Don't succumb to promises. Being told you're not good enough is a gift, not an indictment.

"There are so many opportunities, you can just jump from situation to situation, depending on the outcome," he said. "But you're not even thinking about the long-term effects. You're just thinking about what's the best situation for us right now, and it sets a bad precedent for the kid. Then they never really learn how to make it through anything."

THE OPPORTUNITY TO GROW AND learn and develop a craft is not specific to conditions or circumstances. As VanVleet demonstrates over and over again, it is learning how to fully utilize our strengths and minimize our weaknesses. It is, as some would say, "an inside job." Psychologists refer to it as a "growth" mindset rather than a "fixed" mindset. A fixed-mindset person believes failure is finite and a reflection of their innate limitations; a growth-mindset person believes failure is merely an indication that they need to improve, which can be accomplished through practice and better preparation. Improvement doesn't require special circumstances. Embracing whatever tools are available to us—a stepfather willing to go to a gym to train every morning, a mid-major college coach offering the chance to lead a team, a scout extending an invitation to be part of a summer league team—is all that is necessary to advance or find out what's needed to do so. Having the mentality that certain prerequisites are needed to reach our full potential—a location, organization, or mentor—is placing a dependence on elements that are beyond our control. Which then creates a built-in excuse for not reaching our full potential. ("I'd be better if only I had X, Y, or Z.") There can't be qualifiers or prerequisites for giving our best. The challenge is not to find the ideal or most attractive building blocks but to fully utilize those readily available. And, as Fred demonstrates, when we exhaust our resources, there is inevitably someone offering new ones out of respect for anyone with a track record of making the most of their opportunities.

Seeking to accomplish a goal greater and more magnanimous than personal success also is a powerful motivator, particularly if it involves people and programs we know intimately. If the goal is a self-centered one, what happens to our drive when we reach it? On the other hand, to be of service to those around us is a never-ending well of inspiration. Fred has never lost his drive despite all that he has accomplished, because it's never been just about him. It's also about everyone around him. That's a perspective worthy of a superhero.

TRUTH 5

Humble or Humbled, It's Your Choice: Brandi Chastain

BRANDI CHASTAIN'S JOURNEY TO SCORING THE MOST ICONIC GOAL IN U.S. women's soccer history began long before she placed the ball on the front edge of the chalked twelve-yard spot, spun on her heel, and marched back toward the top of the eighteen-yard penalty box, resolutely keeping her eyes off Gao Hong, the Chinese goalkeeper. There was nothing she could do, though, about the 90,185 sets of eyes in the stands locked on her. The overheated crowd squirmed breathlessly as they waited for Chastain to answer their prayers.

However anxious the fans in the stands were, they truly would have been on edge if they had known Chastain wasn't supposed to be taking this kick, that her missing a penalty against Hong three months earlier had convinced the coaching staff not to have her among the team's first five penalty takers. And the fans might've done a group rendition of Munch's *The Scream* if they had been aware she was about to take the kick with her left foot, something she had never done in a game in her entire life.

What a moment to try it for the first time. This was the 1999 World Cup final between two global titans and heated rivals, the USA and China. And it was not just any ol' penalty kick. This was the fifth and final one in an overtime shoot-out, the one that could end this two-hour-plus marathon on a Rose Bowl field that felt like an oven and had the players' legs twitching and threatening to seize up from fatigue and dehydration.

If all that wasn't enough pressure, the formation of the world's first fully professional women's soccer league was also riding on Brandi's kick. She and the rest of the team knew going into the tournament that, if they won the cup, a group of investors was prepared to start the Women's United Soccer Association, an eight-team league that would provide them an opportunity to get paid for showcasing their skills right here at home. But only if they walked away champions. Which they would–if Chastain quieted all her many demons and converted this kick.

Brandi was letting it all ride on her untested, unproven left foot because that's what coach Tony DiCicco asked her to do. She trusted him because she was only here, on this team, in this game, in this moment, because he had asked her to do something completely unorthodox, totally out of her comfort zone, and she both accepted the challenge and answered it. So when assistant coach Lauren Gregg asked Brandi if she wanted to be the fifth kicker, she said, "Yeah, no problem. I got it," and when DiCicco walked up a minute later, put his hand on her shoulder, and said, "You're going to take it with your left foot," before quickly walking away, she had the same response.

"I didn't spend too much time thinking about it, honestly," she said. "That's what he wanted me to do and I said, 'Okay, no problem.' I trusted him. He brought me back to the program. And he never let me down. So I just felt that whatever he asked of me, he wouldn't be asking if he didn't think that I could do it. So that's how I felt."

But to get to this moment required a decade of Brandi reshaping who she thought she was, and what she was capable of, to fit what someone else saw in her. The fact is, without becoming coachable and her subsequent transformation, there is almost no chance she would have been in the Rose Bowl that day, much less providing an image that would forever change the perception of women's soccer in particular and women athletes in general. Brandi ripped off her jersey and dropped to her knees in her black sports bra, shaking her fists as she shouted in joy, a celebration that felt somehow intimate and personal despite taking place in front of an entire stadium and a national TV audience. Perhaps that's because it was so much more than the celebration of a goal. Brandi was also celebrating the personal transformation that made it possible for her as well. Once an arrogant challenger of authority ready to quit the sport rather than confront her shortcomings, it was her selflessness and resilience that put her on that field and prepared her for that moment.

Ironically, she had the chance to score that goal only because she had been willing to stop defining herself, first and foremost, as a goalscorer. It meant handing over the thing she'd had a talent for all her life—and the thing she loved more than anything—to others. Don't think for a minute it was easy. Scoring goals is the most exciting and prized part of the game, and those who are adept at it are placed on a pedestal—a pedestal she had enjoyed from the time her dad, a former marine, coached her and the rest of the eight-year-olds that were part of the

Blossom Valley Horizon in San Jose, California. *Soccer America* named her Freshman of the Year after she found the back of the net fifteen times at Cal Berkeley and added fourteen assists. She topped that in 1990 with 22 goals at Santa Clara University, good for the national scoring title. It was the skill that first earned her a place in the U.S. national team program, which she displayed by scoring 5 goals *in a row* in a 12–0 win over Mexico for Team USA on its way to the 1991 CONCACAF Women's Championship title.

But that's not who she was going to be for this U.S. national team. Not if she wanted to be on it. And after being dropped by the program for a full cycle, how badly did she want back in? Badly enough not just to accept without argument—which was not in her nature—but to embrace what DiCicco wanted her to do?

Chastain didn't know she was about to face that question when DiCicco called her into his office to tell her he wanted her on the team. "Of course, immediately you feel this warm, fuzzy excitement that is almost unexplainable," Brandi said. "And then he dropped the bomb of 'Well, but not as a forward. As a defender. We want to play different.' And I mean, at first I was like, 'What just happened? What is he saying? I want to score the goals.'"

Ten years earlier, Chastain's response would have been simple and swift: "No. Hell no. Don't you know who I am? What I can do? I don't need your national team roster spot." She might have stormed out of DiCicco's office, much the same way she stormed off the Santa Clara practice field when Broncos coach Jerry Smith, exasperated that Brandi was begging out of another conditioning drill, finally told her, "You know, we don't need you," to which Chastain shouted back, "Well, I don't need this!"

The Broncos were several games into the 1989 season when Chastain quit. It was neither the first time she butted heads with a coach nor that she bailed on a team. The headbutting began with the Horizon. "My dad was my coach for the majority of my life," she said. "I would get sent home from practice for acting up or for not doing the right thing. I was fighting his information. And I got sent home quite a few times."

Sent home, but not kicked off the team. Her goal-scoring talent, combined with an almost unshakable confidence, allowed her to get away with acting up, or out, and she knew it. "As far back as I can remember, I had this belief and this assertion and this confidence of invincibility," she said, "and I brought that to the playground, to the math class, to everywhere I went. Everything was a competition. Everything was like, 'I can do it.'"

After winning three city titles at Archbishop Mitty High in San Jose—delivering crucial goals in two of the three championship games—she had her choice of top programs and decided to join a powerhouse close to home, accepting a full ride at Cal Berkeley. A torn anterior cruciate ligament in her left knee, suffered playing for a club team in the spring of her freshman year, exposed how much camouflage her soccer success had been providing. Her identity was wrapped up in being a goal-scoring star; how she felt about herself as a person depended on how well she played. The injury forced her to redshirt her sophomore year, and without soccer as a compass and confidence booster, she felt lost. She wasn't the Cal Bears' vivacious goal-scorer now. She was just another one of the 30,000-some students dotting the campus. Neither of her parents had attended college, so she didn't think they would understand how she was feeling. Besides, this was about making them proud that their daughter was on a full ride at a prestigious university.

The last thing she felt she could do is admit to them that she wanted to give it up, that it was too much for her. But her failing grades gave her no choice.

"I was not prepared for the academic rigor, the being-on-my-own rigor," she said. "I excelled in the soccer piece only because I was good. I had a talent that I spent time on, but I was not a complete package. And so now I had to really see, okay, who am I and what do I have going?"

She enrolled at nearby Merritt College, a two-year community school, to get back on track academically, thinking smaller classes and the strict schedule of waking up every morning to catch a 6:00 a.m. bus to class would discipline her, ground her, make her whole. She still lived in the same apartment with the same Cal roommates, her plan being to reenroll in the fall to resume her soccer career. But her heart wasn't in it; returning to Cal felt like something she was supposed to do rather than something she wanted to do. Instead, she confessed to her parents about her academic struggles, enrolled at another community college–West Valley, closer to their home in San Jose–and moved back in with them.

"I had not been telling myself the truth," she said. "I had been lying about what I wanted to do. The idea of going back to Cal was only to make my parents proud."

Her move coincided with one by Jerry Smith, a longtime local boys' high school coach, who had agreed to coach a women's team for the first time. Along with coaching the Homestead High boys' varsity squad, Smith served as an assistant for the Foothill College men's program. When Foothill started a women's program, he agreed to serve as head coach.

"I was fascinated by how coachable our players were and how much they wanted to learn and how much better we were in game six than we were in game one," he said. "I was like, 'This is fricking awesome! I love this!'"

After that first six-game trial season ended, one of his players invited him to an NCAA Division I match between Cal Berkeley and UC Santa Barbara to get a taste of the women's game at the next level. That's where he first saw Chastain, who scored the game's lone goal. When the job of coaching the women's team at Santa Clara University opened up, he jumped at it. He was well aware of how competitive collegiate women's soccer was in the Bay Area with two perennial powerhouses in Cal and Stanford and knew it would take extra work to attract and cultivate the necessary talent. When he heard that Chastain had dropped out of Cal and was attending junior college, he tracked her down and invited her to join his team. Chastain might have been struggling with her identity as a student and a person, but it had done nothing to dent her confidence in who she was on the pitch with a ball at her feet—which was far too good for the fledgling Broncos.

"No, I'm not interested," Smith recalled her saying. "I'm going to a big-time program and Santa Clara's not big-time." Smith laughed. "She said that to me straight out. It was a real short conversation."

But no big-time programs came calling. The '88 collegiate soccer season came and went without her. The Santa Clara women had a second winning season and established themselves as an up-and-coming program. Smith reached out to Chastain again.

She had been following the Broncos' success. She had also been humbled. Being a godsend for a hometown team after a season of feeling forgotten appealed to her. Besides, there was no way her parents could afford to send her to SCU on their own dime. If she wanted to get a four-year degree and play D1 soccer again, this was her only option. This time she said yes.

This is going to be the turning point, she remembered telling herself.

It was. Just not in the direction she expected. A week later, playing in a club tournament in Las Vegas, she made a move she'd made a thousand times, pivoting on her right leg as the ball came across her body to hit a left-footed shot. Her entire body whipped around but her right foot remained planted. She immediately felt a familiar knifing pain, this time in her right knee. *Not again*, she thought.

Yes, again, it turned out. She'd torn her other ACL.

"The first question for a lot of people when that happens is 'Why me?' and that's where I was," she said. "I felt sorry for myself."

Lark Chastain, Brandi's mom, wouldn't allow it. A former flight attendant, she had left the friendly skies when she became a mom. Despite not having a college degree, she talked her way into a Silicon Valley company and then worked her way up to vice president. This was in the days when women in corporate executive suites, no matter how accomplished or educated, rarely did more than deliver coffee or answer the phone or take dictation.

"My parents were absolutely paramount to the person and the player that I turned into," Brandi said. "They were always supportive of me, wherever it was, whatever environment that I was in. But if I ever had a moment of doubt or if I wasn't feeling comfortable with a coach, they didn't jump on the bandwagon with me. They would listen. They never tried to put any pressure on a coach or tried to bypass any guardrails that might have been around. They didn't try to involve themselves unless I needed them."

Lark convinced her daughter that challenges were only given to those strong enough to face them. It was enough to get Brandi to do the necessary rehab to be on the field in the fall for training camp. Neither the injury nor the bulky hip-to-ankle brace she was required to wear diminished her prima donna attitude, though.

"I still was not coachable because I was still in the I-don't-have-to-do-what-the-other-people-have-to-do-because-I'm-already-good-at-this mindset," she said.

It presented a conundrum for Smith because he had built his program on the idea that the Broncos' edge was going to be outworking their opponents. Brandi provided him a vital injection of talent, but her attitude made him question whether the team was actually better for it.

"Brandi's baggage was the same baggage that a lot of talented people have," he said. "When you're super talented, you sometimes don't always have the work ethic, and Brandi didn't. When it came to anything with the ball, she pushed, and then if I took the ball away and it was just conditioning, her knee hurt. It finally came to a head. As a new coach, the whole team's looking at me like, 'Hey, Coach, what are you doing about this? She's bailing out when the rest of us are working.' Because I had told them, 'Look, we are not that talented yet, so we are going to win by being a blue-collar team.' Well, Brandi was the antithesis of a blue-collar player. I've got this blue-collar team with a blue-collar mantra and Brandi's sitting out when the going gets tough."

The gulf widened when the Broncos faced her old team, the Cal Bears, in an early nonconference match in Berkeley. While Santa Clara practiced and played on natural Bermuda grass, Cal's field was artificial turf, which is notorious for being less forgiving on an athlete's ankles and knees. Make a sharp cut or pivot and the turf didn't always let go the way a natural surface did. It was decided that the risk of Chastain getting a cleat stuck and wrenching her tender knee, or suffering another injury landing on her brace on what was essentially carpet, was not worth it. Brandi the godsend would be a mere spectator.

Chastain embraced being a cheerleader, encouraging her teammates from the sidelines, and the Broncos pulled off an upset, breaking Cal's twenty-seven-game home winning streak. But it also raised an unspoken question with the entire team, Smith included: Do we really need Chastain?

After another practice in which Brandi begged out of conditioning, Smith pulled her aside and said she'd have to participate in everything if she wanted to stay on the team. An argument ensued.

"That's it, then," Smith said. "You're done."

"Well, that's fine," Chastain responded. "I quit."

"Good. We don't need you."

"And I don't need this!"

She didn't tell her parents or anyone else that she had quit. She spent several days in a daze far deeper than when she had left Cal. This felt like her last chance and she was throwing it away. She had to accept a hard truth: she wasn't who she thought she was.

"I was regretful right away," she said. "I had to ask myself, 'What kind of point are you trying to make? What do you think you're going to get out of this?' I was giving up the one thing that I knew, deep down inside of me, I loved. Every day I'd wake up thinking about it. Every night I'd go to bed thinking about it. I am constantly emotional over how much I love this thing, and now I'm going to give it up because someone's challenging me?"

It is human nature to treat anyone with immense natural talent in anything–coding, writing, science, sports–as special and therefore worthy of special treatment. The danger is when that treatment consists of allowances or concessions, particularly from parents and coaches. The gifted performer can easily acquire a sense of entitlement and believe they have a license to pick and choose when and how they want to perform. Every extraordinary leader I've ever met or studied, from Gregg Popovich to the late Steve Jobs, shared the same philosophy: Be the hardest on and demand the most from their best talent. To do otherwise not only does a disservice to that talent but sends the unspoken message to everyone else involved that fulfilling one's potential is not a priority. And what is the point of being coachable if that isn't the objective?

Looking back, Chastain now admits that fear of failure drove her reluctance to give everything she had. She resisted doing anything that she might not do well or easily rather than risk looking less superior than how she wanted to be perceived.

In Santa Clara's timed conditioning exercises, everyone had to make the allotted time before the team could move on to the next challenge or get back to working with a ball. Brandi was the one routinely holding the team back and she sensed her teammates were losing respect for her. Her value as a goalscorer had allowed her to circumvent anything she didn't like to do for so long that now she questioned whether she was capable of doing those more mundane or arduous tasks. Those inner doubts were only compounded by her two knee surgeries. Treatment and recovery from ACL tears was not at all as routine as it is now. If she went all out, she–along with Smith and her teammates–might find out she was no longer the player she thought she was. Better not to give 100 percent than really try and possibly fail. "I would use 'Oh, my knee is bothering me' as an excuse when things were really hard," she said. "Maybe it was trying to overcome being scared and not really knowing how to handle it. I'd never been challenged in the way I was being challenged. I was not as mentally strong as I thought I was. I thought I was tough, and physically I was, but I really was weak mentally. I just didn't know it."

It became clear that Smith and the team didn't need her–at least, not the version they had seen so far. She was not the godsend to the Broncos' program; actually, the program was a godsend for her. She needed Smith, her teammates, and the program—or, more specifically, she needed the challenge they were presenting to her: the challenge to find out exactly how good she still could be. To find out exactly how much she was willing to do to find out how good she could be. To find out, as a player and a person, exactly who she was when faced with the prospect of failure.

"If you choose a team sport, there is this camaraderie that I believe is an accelerant to a flame of enthusiasm and belief," Chastain said. "But at the end of the day—or maybe, even better said, at the beginning of the day—the only person who can get you going is you. So I believe part of the coachability equation is there has to be a vessel that is willing to be filled. And if that vessel is porous and the water or the energy or the information seeps through it, it will never stick."

Chastain's point is that there are two essential parts to a performer realizing their absolute best: they need someone willing to pull it out of them, and they need to have the hunger and courage to have it pulled.

That desire drove her to Smith's office after class to ask for a second chance. Smith granted it. He then ripped up his practice plan for the day and filled it with every conditioning exercise and drill that Chastain had sat out or failed to finish in time, along with a few particularly grueling ones he hadn't used in years.

"I don't know if we saw a ball for most of the day," Chastain said. "We did all the things that I hated, all the things that I didn't feel I was good at."

Smith wasn't simply trying to punish Chastain or test her limits. He wanted to give her a chance to prove something to her teammates.

"I'm a big fan of eleven-on-eleven training," Smith said. "I like to get into 'This is what our opponent is going to do, and this is what we're going to do.' And that was the right thing for the team, in terms of what we had in front of us getting ready for the next game. But this became the bigger issue. Is this person going to be on our team or not? Showing me that you want to be on the team is a small part. She had to show her teammates. After those couple of practices without Brandi, the team was like, 'Okay, that's fine. We actually might be better.' And maybe they were right. But if you could get that talented goal-scoring machine to also be invested, now you get the best of both worlds. We all had to find out where she was. I basically chucked my practice plan and we did real hard running. We did three-hundred-yard shuttles, this thing called downers, goal line to half field and back, full field and back. A lot of coaches will do one-to-two ratio: one minute of work, two minutes of rest. We did everything one-to-one work-to-rest ratio. We did ten downers in a row. People were dropping like flies. Then we did what we call doggies, five yards out and back, ten and back, fifteen and back, twenty and back, twenty-five and back. That's a lot of turning and cutting, which is hard on the knees. The downers are not as bad: you're just running. Then we did the soccer version of the Cooper test, which is running a set number of laps around the field in twelve minutes. This is stuff that I hadn't done in a long, long time, but it was about creating a big challenge for Brandi and her having a chance to prove herself and earn her way back into the team."

Chastain finished first in every challenge, leading from start to finish. "Never saw the back of anyone's jersey," she said.

It would take more than one practice, though, to win back Smith and her teammates.

"She killed it, but it wasn't like, 'Welcome back,' and we're wrapping our arms around each other," he said. "It was like, 'Okay, good first step.'"

She was on the team again, but she wasn't *in* the team.

That came one practice and one game at a time. Brandi was now not only the Broncos' most skilled player, she became one of their hardest workers, and that transformation galvanized the team. They not only received their first NCAA tournament invitation but received a first-round bye, pitting them in the second round against a familiar team for Chastain: UC Santa Barbara. The Broncos won, 2–1, Chastain scoring one of her team-leading 11 goals. The run ended in the semifinals with a 2–0 loss to Colorado College, but the Broncos were now firmly on the national map and looking to make an even bigger splash the next season.

"As soon as you think you're good enough, that's when you're not, so a large part of success is being in an environment that keeps you humble," said Michael Lardon, a sports psychiatrist and clinical professor at the UC San Diego School of Medicine. "Most super-elite athletes have been able to maintain a core group that keeps them grounded. Because if you have sycophants everywhere, you go from swagger to arrogance. You develop an 'I don't need to learn anything; I don't need anybody' attitude. And then you get in trouble."

Perhaps nothing illustrated how much Brandi had changed more than her selection as a team captain. Freed of that cumbersome knee brace, she led the nation in scoring with 22 goals as the Broncos roared to a 17-0-1 season and earned another first-round bye and another second-round rendezvous with the UC Santa Barbara Gauchos. This time the win was even more convincing, 2–0, setting them up for a semifinal match against the University of Connecticut Huskies in Chapel Hill, North Carolina, where they suffered their only loss of the season, in double overtime.

Goalscorers always being in demand, Brandi's exploits caught the attention of the U.S. national program. She earned her first international cap, or appearance, in 1988 and was part of the national team that won the inaugural Women's World Cup in '91.

But the requisite baseline in skill, focus, and conditioning increases at every level. After the five-goal burst in Team USA's CONCACAF opener against Mexico, Chastain scored once in another 12–0 win, this time over Trinidad and Tobago, and again in a 10–0 win over Martinique. She went scoreless in her two World Cup appearances. Brandi had learned the value of being in tip-top shape to be her best as a goalscorer, but there was another lesson to be learned: how to be of value and work just as hard at contributing in more mundane ways than putting the ball in the back of the net. When it came time to select the roster for the '95 squad, Chastain didn't receive a call.

"In the initial cycle, she was more of an attacking player and she was a star," said Lauren Gregg, a former U.S. national team player and national-team assistant coach from 1989 to 2000. "She had scored a lot of goals for Santa Clara. She was a very skillful player, but her training habits weren't quite where they needed to be. She got caught and challenged by some of the younger players. We knew what she had to offer, but there were a lot of players knocking on the door with a little bit better training standards. And as an attacker, she wasn't quite making the contribution that I think we knew she could on both sides of the ball."

The game of soccer was evolving into what we see today: attackers aren't just expected to score goals, defenders aren't just expected to stop them, and midfielders aren't just the connective tissue between the two. Defenders with ball skills who can make a timely pass or make an overlapping run or be a threat on set pieces in the attacking third of the field add a new wrinkle. Chastain wasn't scoring goals at the same rate as the other available strikers, but if she was willing to do the dirty work of a left back, DiCicco envisioned her as an occasional surprise threat. The U.S. program directors, Gregg said, hoped that being left out would motivate her to take her preparation and "professionalism" to the next level.

A disappointing bronze medal finish in the 1995 World Cup and a brief strike by nine national team players over bonus clauses for the 1996 Olympics resulted in Chastain getting an invitation to a pre-Olympic training camp to see if she'd gotten the message. After checking with the nine striking players—many of whom had been her teammates in 1991—if they'd be okay with her accepting the invitation, Chastain, now approaching her twenty-eighth birthday, came to camp once again looking to not see the back of a single jersey. She knew she was capable, thanks to answering Smith's challenge at Santa Clara eight years earlier. When the strike ended, Chastain was the only replacement player asked to stay.

Wrapping her head around DiCicco making her inclusion in the squad incumbent upon her accepting a role at left back took some reflection.

"Brandi, all you wanted to do was be on this team," she told herself. "You never said, 'I want to score as many goals as Mia Hamm.' That made it really easy. And then I got into the nuts and bolts of, like, holy shit, can I really do this? Because I've never played that position before, and it's not in my wheelhouse. But I quickly also realized that I was going to be between Kristine Lilly and Carla Overbeck. I was pretty sure they were going to take care of me. Those are two really good people to be between. Carla is a great leader and Kristine is probably the most hardworking, diligent person that's ever played for the U.S. national team and has played more international games than any human on the planet. So I was fairly certain that was a good spot for me to be in and it gave me some confidence."

There were still growing pains. Five minutes into the World Cup quarterfinals match against Germany, Chastain, under pressure by a German player, played the ball back to goalkeeper Briana Scurry only to see it slide past her and into the net, giving the Germans an early 1–0 lead.

There's no more crushing mistake for a defender than an own goal. Brandi couldn't hide how distraught she was. Germany took a 2–1 lead into halftime, which is when Overbeck pulled Chastain aside and said, "We need you."

Four minutes into the second half, Chastain delivered. She made a decoy run to the near post on a USA corner kick as the ball was swung high to the back post. Her goal-scoring instincts kicked in and she reversed her run as a German defender headed the ball back into the middle of the box. Brandi pounced, hammering a side volley off the inside of the right post for a 2–2 tie. Redemption. She celebrated by screaming with joy as she slid onto her back and spread her arms wide on the grass as if to say "Thank you" to the soccer gods before cupping her forehead in disbelief. For the first time she realized that she shouldn't define herself as an attacker or a defender but as a performer looking to do whatever is necessary to win.

"What I learned–and this is a part of being coachable–is that we all have these tools that we rely on and we use them the same way all the time," she said. "And sometimes we fail to examine how those tools are interchangeable in different scenarios. You can take a screwdriver and drive a screw into the wall, but what if you have a nail and you don't have a hammer? Just turn the screwdriver around and use the butt of the handle to drive that nail. And that's what I had to do."

CHASTAIN HAD HAD A DIFFERENT fall from grace months earlier, playing in the championship final of the Algarve Cup against–and hosted by–the same Chinese team they would meet in the World Cup final.

When Team USA played in the first-ever Women's World Cup in 1991, not much thought was given to preparing for a penalty kick shoot-out. That nearly proved disastrous in the final, where the U.S. women faced Norway and were two and a half minutes away from going to a shoot-out when Michelle Akers-Stahl scored the winning goal.

"We literally had nobody that wanted to take a penalty kick," Gregg said. "It was a real lesson. It became a part of our daily process and preparation from that point on. By '99, penalty kicks were as much of a daily routine as stretching."

The players not only practiced kicks, but Gregg kept detailed notes and statistics on individual results. Chastain's accuracy earned her designation as the in-game penalty kick taker, which is how she came to taking one in the Algarve Cup final against Gao Hong with China leading, 2–1.

Hong had a reputation for staring down opponents to intimidate them, but this time, perhaps emboldened by being on her home turf, she went a step further. As Chastain bent over to place the ball on the penalty spot, Hong left the goal and walked right up to Chastain. When Chastain straightened up, she found Hong in her face. That didn't bother her.

"I used to watch boxing with my dad and it was like two boxers in the middle of the ring, and it was kind of cool," Chastain said. "It was a stare down."

What Hong did next, though, did rattle Chastain. Hong smiled and winked before returning to take her stance on the goal line.

"I was like, 'Whoa, what the hell? What's going on here?'" Chastain recalled. "It did have an impact on me. There's an interesting relationship between what you think and how your body acts. Your mental side can really impact or inhibit your physical side. My thought process was 'What was she doing?' instead of 'I'm going to slam this past her' or 'This is going in the back of the net.' It was just enough to throw off my concentration. I didn't mis-hit the ball in terms of the velocity or speed I wanted, or even how I struck the ball. My technique was just off a tiny bit. I missed where I wanted the ball to go by two inches."

It was enough. Taking it right-footed, she aimed for the upper left corner. The ball clipped the crossbar and ricocheted back down and away from the goal, preserving a 2–1 lead and eventual win for China without Hong even having to touch the ball.

A player without the experience of being in a dark place and pulling themselves out of it might have been haunted by that result, particularly when faced with a nearly identical situation. But Chastain by now had fallen short or been disappointed a multitude of times and had to find a way to work her way back to earning another crack at being successful. She had come to understand that the only part of the equation she could control was how prepared she was when another opportunity came along. And dwelling on the previous opportunity that she failed to capitalize on—beyond identifying why she didn't and making a correction—had no value; in fact, it was detrimental, stealing focus and energy from finding and honing a solution.

When she was physically or mentally drained, when gremlins of doubt appeared, she would return to the memory of coming back to the Santa Clara team, unsure if her knee would hold up, unsure if she had the stamina to complete Smith's relentless conditioning tests, but deciding to give whatever she had and live with the result. She went from suspecting she wasn't quite as good as she thought she was to discovering she was better than she imagined simply because she gave herself permission to go all out and still fall short, if it came to that.

"That was a moment for me that changed everything," she said. "The feeling was like a weight had been lifted off my shoulders. I let go of the fear of failure, the fear of disappointment, I'd been holding for years. I realized at that moment the thing that my mom always used to say, which was 'Find your yes.' This was the thing I wanted to do more than anything in my life. My biggest hurdle was getting over myself. I felt like I was so good, but then I was so weak at the same time, and that was really a scary place to be. I realized it's okay to be vulnerable, to wonder if you're good enough or how good you can be, because it has turned into a great strength for me."

Being left out of the national team and then successfully reinventing herself was one more lesson—and more proof—that she was capable of adapting to whatever she was asked to do. That Tony inspired and then rewarded her for that reinvention gave her complete faith in anything he might ask her to do—a faith that would prove indispensable not only for them but the entire team.

"Tony was such a good player's coach because he was willing to listen," she said. "He wanted to know how you were feeling, and he wanted you to be able to articulate the things you needed. And he was a good judge of like, 'Okay, I've listened to what you're saying, and whether I agree or I don't, I'm going to make the decision, and you're going to be okay with that because you know that I've listened to you.'"

Leading up to the World Cup final, DiCicco had Chastain practice penalty kicks with both her right and left feet, telling her that the Chinese might be surreptitiously scouting their practice sessions, and if they were, he wanted to leave them guessing should she have to face Hong again. The old Brandi might have questioned the strategy, maybe even balked at it. The new Brandi took it as a compliment.

Privately, the coaches were wrestling with what the psychological impact might be on Brandi if she had to take another high-pressure penalty kick against Hong, especially right-footed. They decided to punt on the issue going into the game by not including her in the first five kickers. But then Michelle Akers-Stahl, who was designated as the fifth kicker, had to leave the game due to a concussion. DiCicco and Gregg still wondered if they were being fair to Chastain by putting her up against Hong. Would she try too hard to fool Hong about where she planned to go with her shot and mis-hit it? They debated whether to go with Chastain or Lilly. They finally decided that Chastain taking it left-footed would turn the psychological tables on Hong.

"Tony didn't want Brandi to go against this goalkeeper who saved it a few months earlier," Smith said. "But now the goalkeeper's getting ready for Brandi and she's like, 'Wait a minute. She's on the other side of the ball!'"

A player who is concerned about making sure their shot is accurate will take a penalty with the side of their foot. It means losing a bit of power but gives them more foot-to-ball contact. Despite all that was riding on her shot, despite the fact that she'd never done this before with her left foot, Chastain had no such worry. She hammered the shot with the laces on her left foot. Hong guessed correctly that Chastain would take the same approach with her left foot as her right foot and shoot for the opposite post. Despite diving all out to her left, it didn't matter. Chastain put the ball in the upper right corner and the celebration began.

"That moment right there, it's such an incredible thing this many years later," said Smith, now married to Chastain. "It's hard for me to fathom the courage it took to do that. Brandi laced it left-footed. She rifled that thing. The only left-footed penalty kick in her life in competition, in the World Cup final, and she chooses to lace it and tucks it right inside the post. That is something that very few people in the world could do."

The journey to taking that left-footed shot, more so than

the goal itself, is what Brandi said has informed her life ever since.

"Now I'm more comfortable than I ever have been with challenges," she said. "I might not get it right. I'm okay with that. But what if I go for it and I get it? That would be amazing! I say to people all the time now, 'Coach me; I've been coached my whole life. Tell me how to do it.' I'm taking a business class online. I am learning the piano. I mean, I'm fifty-five. Why am I doing these things? Because I just love that uncomfortable, learning, coach-me kind of environment. Now it's become my lifeline."

NATURAL TALENT, PARTICULARLY WHEN IT appears at an early age, can be a blessing and curse: a blessing because it assures myriad opportunities and the means to build confidence; a curse because it can lead an athlete to rely on those natural gifts and not develop others. It also tends to inspire a level of special treatment from parents and coaches alike, both within the sport and outside of it. That special treatment, particularly if it starts early, is not in the best interest of the athlete. It ingrains the idea that the rules are different for someone with God-given gifts and that less should be expected of them when, in fact, it should be more. This may sound counterintuitive, but the greatest way to instill gratitude and humility in someone for being born with an unusual ability is to hold them to a higher standard. If the special treatment begins at an early age, a performer is apt to become accustomed to that treatment and expect it. That leaves them vulnerable, for at some point that treatment is sure to end. Their talent will no longer be special, either because they are surrounded by greater talent or the years of special treatment discouraged them from cultivating that talent as much as they could have. Being treated like everyone else at that point, with no special dispensation, can have all sorts of consequences: loss of confidence, rebellion, or depression. Having never had to learn how to stand out by means beyond their natural talent then leaves the performer ill-equipped when the playing field has been leveled.

Having the most valued talent a soccer player can have—scoring goals—put Brandi on a pedestal at a very early age and resulted in special treatment that eventually boomeranged on her. It allowed her to skirt some of the other, more demanding aspects of the game and left her wholly unprepared to tackle challenges off the field. She discovered how fragile that pedestal truly was and how essential those other aspects were.

It took several tough lessons in humility for Brandi to grasp that talent alone could take her only so far. Perhaps the harshest (and most valuable) lesson was that she was replaceable, that the opportunity to compete was a privilege earned, not granted or assumed. Brandi is the exception, not the rule, when it comes to performers who are able to reinvent themselves quickly enough to resume their upward trajectory. That her mother was a groundbreaking executive and her father was a former marine certainly provided her living examples of what facing obstacles head-on could produce. She accepted a role on the national team that required her to mold herself to what the team needed, even if it meant developing completely different skills and sublimating her ego. For as much fame and glory as her goal provided her, the real benefit has been what she took from the experience of being rejected and humbled and reinventing herself. Where once she avoided anything that might test her limits, she now finds joy in being a novice and a student. The prospect of doing something she's never done before is no longer seen as a threat to her ego but an invitation to become someone—and something—more.

TRUTH 6

Tunnel Vision Is a Black Hole: Dirk Nowitzki

HOLGER GESCHWINDNER FOLDED HIMSELF INTO HIS VELVET-covered seat at the Naismith Basketball Hall of Fame ceremonies and smiled puckishly as protégé and fellow German Dirk Nowitzki identified the people responsible for him standing onstage. One by one, he gave their names and a word that described their contribution.

It might go down as one of the most organized and exact Hall of Fame acceptance speeches ever.

"Very German of him," Geschwindner said, chuckling.

Very Geschwindner of him as well. Holger, of course, was one of those mentioned in the speech, being the first to recognize Dirk's potential and subsequently having spent the next twenty-plus years cultivating it. The word Dirk assigned him was "innovation." The *New Oxford American Dictionary* definition: "a new method, idea, product, etc." And what, exactly, did Holger innovate?

Not what–who: Dirk Nowitzki. Or, to be more precise, the Dirk Nowitzki standing at the podium that night in Springfield, Massachusetts, invited to join the exclusive club that is the Naismith Basketball Hall of Fame. While there had been seven-foot-tall players capable of taking and making jump shots before Nowitzki, the array of ways in which he launched shots from distance–off one foot (either one), fading, spinning, spinning *and* fading, and beyond the 3-point arc–and the frequency with which he launched them was unprecedented. Before he came along, anyone who was seven feet tall was expected, first and foremost, to play center and employ that extraordinary height by operating within a few feet of the basket. Shooting jump shots on occasion was tolerated, but not as a staple. Why waste all that height? It didn't matter if they were seven feet tall but slender and without the core girth to back down an opponent; a big man who didn't try to get as close to the basket as possible was labeled as soft or taking the easy way out. And you didn't have to be seven feet tall to be a center, but if you were that height or bigger, you almost certainly were expected to play the position. (The stigma was so prevalent that eventually some ultra-thin seven-footers, such as Kevin Garnett and Kevin Durant, refused to be categorized as centers and insisted on being listed as six-eleven or shorter so they'd have the freedom to play away from the basket.)

If Stephen Curry deserves credit for revolutionizing the role of point guards, Nowitzki deserves credit for doing the same for seven-footers. During the course of a twenty-year career, well over 50 percent of his shots were taken sixteen feet from the basket and beyond. (For comparison, the top three seven-footers in the league in Dirk's first season–Shaquille

O'Neal, David Robinson, and Dikembe Mutombo—took 90 percent of their shots *inside* sixteen feet; for O'Neal and Mutombo, 90 percent were inside ten feet.) Dirk also played a significant role in erasing the demarcation between power forward and center and popularized the concept of a "stretch four," basketball jargon for a power forward who can play away from the basket and thereby stretch the previously standard space in which a power forward operated.

Had Dirk never met Holger, he still almost assuredly would have enjoyed a career as a professional basketball player. Already six-foot-nine as a fifteen-year-old and mobile enough to play handball and tennis, the top German clubs already had him on their radars after seeing him play for his local lower-division team, Würzburg. In fact, Holger made it clear to Dirk that he didn't necessarily need Holger's help or insight.

"I told Dirk at the beginning, 'If you want to be the best player in Germany, we can stop practicing right now,'" Holger recalled. "'Nobody can stop you from becoming that. But if you want to play with the best guys in the world, we have to invent something. We have to show those guys something they have never seen before.'"

What he didn't tell Dirk was how they would accomplish that—largely because Holger did not know. All he really knew, or at least wholeheartedly believed, was that to be a great basketball player required a whole lot more than simply being great at basketball. And the most important word he used was "we," in that developing Dirk's full potential would be a collaborative effort. And one of discovery.

"Nowadays, if you go to an NBA basketball clinic, the NBA players tell you exactly what you have to do," Geschwindner said. "And if you do what they tell you to do, every day, day and night, you will be better. Bullshit." He laughed. "All the creativity of individual players is gone. They are like chess figures. We saved a lot of time by not looking at how other guys shoot. We just tried to get as close as possible to the theoretical optimum for Dirk. Everybody made jokes about his rainbow shot at first. It ended up in the Hall of Fame, so it could not have been too wrong."

Holger's theory was relatively simple: the idea that the arc and method of shooting a basket is the same for all players makes no sense because the relationship between every player and the basket is not the same. A player's height, arm length, and where and how they release the shot are all naturally unique. If Dirk's high-arcing shot looked unusual, it was in part because no one was used to seeing a seven-footer shoot from a long distance, especially one releasing the ball from above his head.

He defied the same logic when it came to a player's height determining where and how they played. Nowitzki might have been only an inch shorter than the seven-foot-one Shaquille O'Neal, but he was eighty pounds lighter. There was little chance he was going to win a wrestling match under the rim.

"The principle was always the same: how to shoot with the minimum amount of effort and have the greatest margin of error," Holger said. "Dirk was not a guy who could post up with guys like Shaquille O'Neal under the basket in those days. So I said, 'If Shaq pushes you out, okay, go out. If he pushes you out again, go out one step further and now he has to make a decision. If he goes further out, he can't get the rebound anymore. So take one more step and then shoot it.'"

It is no easy task for a coach to tailor skill work and tactics to squeeze the most out of a group of uniquely talented athletes, but that challenge is not exclusive to someone in charge of a sports team. Holger tried to convince NBA coaches to seek insight from other leaders charged with team building. Nowitzki served as captain of Team World in the 2017 NBA Africa Game, a charitable fundraiser between NBA players from around the world versus a group of the league's African-born players in Johannesburg, South Africa. During the festivities, Geschwindner met former U.S. Army general Martin Dempsey, who had been asked to serve as the chairman of USA Basketball. Seeing as Dempsey's job in the military involved utilizing a group of men to coordinate both defensive and offensive strategies, Holger asked him if he'd be willing to share his perspective and experience with NBA coaches. When Dempsey said yes, Holger went straight to San Antonio Spurs and U.S. national team coach Gregg Popovich and relayed Dempsey's interest. Popovich, a U.S. Air Force Academy graduate, welcomed the idea and Dempsey spoke at the NBA coaches' annual fall get-together.

With military terms and references being commonplace in sports—"The game is won in the trenches" . . . "Take the fight to them" . . . "It was a war out there" . . . "It's a next-man-up mentality"—the appeal of hearing from a distinguished military figure was understandably not a hard sell. Holger's attempt to have the coaches sit down with a symphony conductor didn't fare as well.

"I tried so many times," he said. "A symphony orchestra, like a basketball team, has all these players and the conductor has to be able to get those guys to play one piece of music. But it never really happened simply because the sports guys don't understand enough about music, and the music guys felt the sports guys were dummies."

Holger has the presence of a more buttoned-up and neatly coiffed Doc Brown, the irrepressibly passionate and quirky scientist responsible for creating a time-traveling machine out of a gull-wing DeLorean in the *Back to the Future* movie franchise. Some consider his methods controversial, and after one critic called his approach "nonsense," he named his summer camp near Germany's Lake Starnberg the "Institute of Applied Nonsense." He is adept enough at physics and calculus to identify the ideal arc for Dirk's shot based on his height, arm length, jumping ability, and release point–60 degrees–and yet has enough of an artist's soul to insist that basketball and jazz, performed at their best, share a common level of inimitable creativity. Nor does he consider it an accident that basketball and jazz came into existence right around the same time, at the end of the nineteenth century. Credit his awareness to Ernie Butler, the first Black man to play in Germany's Bundesliga and one of Holger's early mentors who later became an accomplished jazz saxophonist. Butler introduced Holger to the basketball-is-jazz concept and, in turn, Holger introduced Dirk to Butler. After Holger insisted that Dirk learn to play the saxophone in order to refine the touch in his fingers and his overall manual dexterity, he arranged for Dirk and Ernie to have a couple of jam sessions together.

Dirk proved to be a seven-foot Marty McFly to Holger's Doc Brown. In his acceptance speech, Nowitzki recounted how Geschwindner's training methods for him included learning to play the saxophone, doing handstands, "and sometimes doing handstands while playing the saxophone." He could have added "and with a vacuum cleaner running," because Geschwindner didn't want Nowitzki's sense of accomplishment clouded by how the saxophone sounded when the purpose wasn't to develop a musician's ear but his touch and dexterity. Geschwindner believed that practicing a discipline outside of sports that relied on a particular skill that was an underlying element *in* a sport could provide a physical edge–developing the finger control needed to play a sax enhancing a basketball player's shooting touch, for example. Holger also had a custom-built fencing suit made for Dirk so he could work on his reflexes and hand-eye coordination to improve, well, everything. It also served to keep Dirk's ego in check, making him aware that being gifted at basketball did not make him universally gifted.

"Dirk was nineteen and fighting against a sixteen-year-old kid, one of the younger guys," Holger recalled. "The kid killed Dirk six times before he could react."

Holger's general philosophy: Make every exercise applicable but also fun and different.

"I wish every kid and parent could hear Dirk's story, because it is the antithesis of what we're seeing in youth sports right now and it has resulted in a lot of burnout," Kimberly Shaffer, the Barry University Professor, said. "My brain went instantly to Rocky Balboa training in the woods, carrying logs, and all the other unique ways he trained–only in Dirk's case it was real life, which is awesome. Developing skills in nontraditional athletic settings shifts an athlete's perspective from 'I am an athlete and only an athlete'–the dumb-jock identity–to 'I am a person who can do many things because I am an athlete.' I know Holger's training methods were all based on athletic development, but from a psychological perspective they also got Dirk's brain thinking about different avenues of success."

If any of Holger's young charges had an idea, he welcomed it as well. One summer his basketball campers proposed that the conditioning workout consist of swimming across Lake Starnberg and back, roughly three miles. Holger had his doubts about their aquatic abilities but let them try, following one hundred yards or so behind in a boat. When he saw them start to flail and struggle on the way back, he pulled them into the boat and rowed them home.

"If somebody came up with a crazy idea and it was not close to suicide, we tried it," Holger said. "You have to let boys at that age test their limits."

That included mixing a social life with their sporting one. One night Holger asked the older teenage campers if they wanted to go to the P1 Club, the biggest disco in Munich, roughly thirty minutes away. They were shocked but immediately said yes. The legal drinking age in Germany is sixteen and the boys took full advantage as they danced the night away. As Holger drove them back to their camp quarters, they tried to persuade him to cancel the next day's first workout. He refused and the next morning they dutifully reported, discovering that carousing and conditioning don't mix.

"We called it an alcohol evaporation workout," Holger said. But the point was made: preparation for peak performance is a twenty-four-hour commitment.

While Holger is granular about the finer points of basketball, he also believes it is vital to the success of an athlete to see the world as a whole lot bigger than a basketball court.

"When he came to my parents' house and talked about his vision, it was always about growing as a person, not only as a basketball player," Dirk said. "Obviously my parents were thrilled with that approach. In Germany, we have all sorts of different high school diplomas we can get. I was in the highest level, but I was struggling a bit and was thinking maybe I'd go overseas and do tenth grade in the States. Holger was like, 'No, you're staying. You're focusing on your education here. If basketball doesn't work out, if you blow out your knee, you have to fall back on something.' I had to take tons and tons of tutoring in certain subjects. He pushed me not only on the court but off it to finish school, to get that high school diploma, to learn an instrument and learn another language or get better in English. He was always giving me books to read every year to keep going. It was definitely about full character development and not only just developing moves on the court."

That relationship, built on more than basketball, proved to be invaluable years later when Dirk earned league MVP honors by leading the Mavericks to their first sixty-seven-win season, only to be upset in the first round of the playoffs by the Golden State Warriors, led by Nowitzki's first NBA coach, Don Nelson. (The upset meant so much to the Warriors franchise at the time that a hole in the wall outside the visiting locker room, created by Nowitzki when he heaved a trash can after being eliminated, was preserved behind plexiglass as a historical monument.) Rather than sit at home or prepare for the upcoming European championships, Dirk and Holger spent six weeks in Australia, exploring the outback in a Jeep.

"I took '07 as hard as anyone can take anything ever in life," Dirk said.

"I didn't even want to take the MVP trophy. I was so embarrassed. A few weeks went by and I told Holger, 'Hey, I just want to get away.' We backpacked; sometimes we slept in the car. We just went completely off the grid. It was so cleansing. I didn't touch a ball. I'm almost thirty years old, traveling with this sixty-two-year-old coach. Guys were looking at me crazy. But we talked all the time, driving, sitting by the campfire at night. Holger has traveled the world; he's studied math and physics. I could pick his brain about anything."

Eventually, the pain of not living up to his MVP accolades dissipated. They began to talk about what happened and what Dirk needed to do to prevent it from happening again.

"We talked about life, hoops, what do we need to do, how do I need to get better?" Nowitzki said. "I was definitely hurting deep in my soul and questioned everything that I'd ever done. When I came home, I was excited again. I wanted to work out, to have a good European championship. That trip really gave me a new perspective. I was looking forward again to another new season and new challenges."

Dirk and Holger were just as adventurous in how they approached training. Walking around the gym on his hands was part of Holger's theory that learning atypical physical acts enhanced an athlete's brain to execute more traditional ones. He applied the same philosophy to shooting and dribbling: he'd have Dirk warm up using his weaker hand to sharpen his mental capacity to shoot and dribble with his dominant hand. The most important exercise for a shooter, according to Holger? Push-ups done on their fingertips to strengthen the last–and most overlooked–appendage that directed the ball toward the hoop.

Weight training became an essential element in basketball in the '90s; before that, it was considered a detriment, inhibiting a player's flexibility and reach and ruining his touch on the ball. Holger, contrary to popular belief, isn't averse to weight training; he simply believes it should be tailored to each individual athlete and that there are a variety of ways to build muscle. Much like a jump shot, the weight training should be calibrated to an athlete's size. Seven-footers shouldn't necessarily be lifting the same weight or doing the same exercises as six-footers because, by virtue of the length of their limbs, their joints bear a different level of torque.

Holger rejected any type of training or advancement that lost sight of, or undermined, the game's essence: the ability to shoot, dribble, and pass a basketball.

"You know those fifteen-kilo plates for weight lifting?" Holger asked. "Let a guy carry one of those around, one hand or both hands, it doesn't matter. Then add six hundred grams to it without him knowing it and hand the plate back to him. He cannot tell the difference. Well, the basketball is six hundred grams."

Weight lifting, in Holger's mind, also isn't the most efficient use of time or energy. Activities such as rowing develop coordination and rhythm along with strength without impacting an athlete's touch. Exercising in ways that leave a player unable to differentiate the weight of a basketball is naturally questionable, if not outright counterproductive.

"Even though he had kind of weird methods, I was having fun and what we did was never really the same," Dirk said. "We were doing some stuff that was totally trial and error. We would try an exercise and I'd give him feedback. We would work through stuff. Or when I got tight during games, he'd be like, 'Hey, try this.' I would try it the next day, and if it didn't work, we'd go find another method that did work. It wasn't him giving me answers for the test; it was trying out possible solutions. Through my feedback, we'd find something that worked for me. Obviously he was way different than me. And so whatever worked for him might not work for me. It's important that a mentor or coach show the student or player ways to do stuff. But there is not one way. You have to keep evolving. You have to keep trying stuff, and eventually you find something that works for that particular player. So that's what we did. We tried a lot of stuff. We threw out what didn't work and kept plugging along. I was improving and that's how he earned my trust. That's big in being coachable. As a player, if I think, 'This is not going to work' or 'This coach is nonsense,' then of course there is some reluctance to listen. But I stuck with it because I really did trust him 100 percent."

Holger's presence at Dirk's induction completed a circle that began some seventy years earlier with Holger's boarding school instructor, Theo Clausen. Basketball became part of the Olympic Games hosted by Germany in the summer of 1936, with twenty-one nations taking part, making it the largest field for any team sport. Basketball was not at all popular in Hitler's Germany, and it showed: the athletes who failed to make the Olympic handball team were invited to participate in the games as the nation's first basketball squad. They were summarily spanked in all three of their games, losing 25–18 to Switzerland, 58–16 to Italy, and 20–9 to Czechoslovakia. Clausen's teacher, Jim Naismith, was on hand to award the gold medal to Team USA after its 19–8 victory over Naismith's native Canada, the low score attributed to the fact that the game was played outside on grass in a driving rain, making it a challenge to simply hold on to the ball and eliminating almost any thought of trying to dribble it.

It's unlikely that any German knew more about the sport than Clausen, but while he attended the games, he was not involved with the German Olympic basketball program. Being proficient in English, he had returned to Germany to work as a translator in the Olympic Village after spending the previous two years attending, on scholarship, Springfield College in Springfield, Massachusetts, where in 1891 Naismith first nailed a pair of peach baskets ten feet high at opposite ends of an indoor gymnasium and instructed his PE students to try and huck soccer balls into them. Government officials, made aware of Clausen's passion for basketball and embarrassed by Germany's underwhelming performance, commissioned Clausen to travel the country preaching the gospel of hoops in hopes of raising the nation's global basketball profile. World War II derailed that mission as Clausen was drafted into service, but immediately at the war's end he went back to it. He is credited with creating the first official national basketball department, the first basketball magazine, and national championship competitions for both men and women, and he even served as the German men's national team coach from 1947 to 1951.

It was during his years promoting the wonders of chest passes and set shots that Clausen worked as a boarding school teacher in the little town of Laubach and helped convert a movie theater into a makeshift basketball court. The lid from a baby grand piano served as a backboard and the court was dissected by a *Kegelbahn*, or German bowling alley. One of Clausen's students, named Holger, would grow into a six-foot-four, lean and athletic basketball devotee, embracing the game as passionately as Clausen did. Holger would eventually serve as captain of the country's Olympic squad in 1972, averaging nearly 14 points a game, and play pro until he was forty-seven years old, winning several German league championships.

Along the way, he played for a countless number of coaches. "I survived twelve national team coaches alone," he said. He dutifully did whatever they asked, but he kept a mental list of the drills and philosophies that were inefficient or downright unproductive. He considers line sprints, a staple for most teams at every level, to be mindless. One coach would have him run a sprint every time he missed a free throw. "Does your free-throw shooting get better if you sprint?" he asked. "No. I experienced all those ugly practices and the mentality of the coaches and wanted to get rid of all the bullshit. If you're starting with young kids, especially, it has to be fun." The players in his summer camp work out four times a day: gymnastics at 7:30 a.m., rowing on the lake from 9:00 to 11:00 a.m., individual skill work from 2:00 to 4:00 p.m., and scrimmages in the evenings where the players have to implement the moves or mechanics they learned in the afternoon session.

The Institute of Applied Nonsense grew out of Holger's work with Dirk, which was sparked when Holger, nearly fifty years old, showed up at a small gym to play for his amateur men's team and caught the end of a youth game that featured a six-foot-nine kid with shaggy blond hair and unremarkable skills, but a unique instinct for spacing and positioning.

Their two teams were assigned the same locker room, and as Dirk walked in and Holger was walking out, he asked, "Who is working with you?"

"No one," Dirk said gruffly, annoyed by the fact that his team had just lost.

"You do a lot of things with great instinct," Holger said. "You move well with your long body, but you really don't have a lot of skills."

Dirk softened. "Thank you," he said. "I only practice once or twice a week. I haven't really concentrated on basketball. I still like playing handball and tennis."

Nothing more was said, and Dirk didn't think any more about the exchange. "I had no idea who he was," he said. "He was some older balding guy. I forgot all about it."

Holger did not. He had been taciturn in talking to Dirk, but Holger was enthralled with Dirk's potential. He reached out to Dirk's Würzburg club and informed them they had a special talent on their hands. Dirk may not have known who Holger was, but the Würzburg directors did, and his endorsement carried a lot of weight. He then offered his services as an assistant coach even though he ran a business-systems company an hour away, due east, in Bamberg.

When word reached Dirk's mom that the great Geschwindner had recognized potential in her son, she showed up at his next men's league game in Würzburg and approached him. Helga was very aware of Holger's pedigree, having played for the West German women's national team around the same time Holger was part of the men's squad.

Helga and Jörg-Werner, Dirk's parents, took a relatively hands-off approach as soon as their son showed promise, even though both were extremely accomplished athletes themselves. Jörg-Werner played for the German national handball team and coached a handball team with Dirk on it, but that was it. They showed him, by example, what a good work ethic was and left it up to him to decide what to do with it.

"Obviously they were both competitors, so I always saw them competing the hardest as I was growing up," he said. "My dad had to run a company at the same time, and so he'd get up at six o'clock and work all day and then still go to practice in the evenings. They were there for support, but they never sat me down and said, 'You have to keep going.' There was something in my DNA from them, I guess. I was tall, I had a lot of talent, and I didn't want to be that guy that wastes his talent. I wanted to get the maximum out of my abilities."

Dr. Jean-Charles LeBeau, an assistant professor of sport and exercise psychology in the School of Kinesiology at Ball State University, said every truly great performer has Dirk's mentality.

"Studies show that the best of the best get their drive from two places," LeBeau said. "Not just from winning games and championships and trophies, but also finding ways to improve, to be able to say to themselves, 'I was better today than I was yesterday.' Those are the athletes always looking for little things to try to get better, challenging themselves, utilizing the latest technology or training technique, the latest diet or whatever thing they can find to improve themselves. Both types of motivation, what you would call the ego orientation–focusing on being the best–and then the task orientation–focusing on just continually getting better–[form] the ideal combination."

Some of Dirk's motivation to maximize his athletic potential came from the knowledge that his parents had forfeited theirs to provide for him and his sister, Silke.

"My dad was a good handball player," Nowitzki said. "He was six-foot-four and played left wing. He was a goal-scorer. He's super proud of the fact that one year he was the Würzburg Athlete of the Year. He still has the trophy at home. He played in the German second division, because he didn't really have the time to do more. He could have easily played in the first division, but he had to help run his dad's business starting at age sixteen. My mom started working super early in her life as well. She was five-foot-eleven and played center. I think she had one national team appearance. She could've played first division at a bigger club but because of work couldn't leave Würzburg. So they were great local pro athletes, but they weren't able to pursue their dreams or find out how high they could really go."

They also didn't have the time or inclination to be consumed with Dirk's development as an athlete.

"They just trusted Holger," Dirk said. "My mom knew who he was, having watched him play in the '72 Olympics for Germany. They trusted his knowledge and then, after meeting him a couple times, they agreed on his vision and kind of let Holger completely take over and teach me everything about the game of basketball. I know that kind of handoff is not normal, especially today. A lot of parents are way too hands-on and think they can do better than most coaches. So that was a big move by them trusting Holger, trusting that he would do the right thing for me and my career."

Helga and Jörg-Werner did not make a point of impressing all that on their kids, as if they were owed something for their sacrifice. Their priority, first and foremost, was always on the principles they were teaching them, not the progress Dirk and Silke were making toward some preconceived objective.

Holger did his best not to be consumed by Dirk, either; had Holger been obsessed with making Dirk, and only Dirk, a world-class player, Dirk surely would've sensed that, felt that pressure, and eventually been overwhelmed by it. While Dirk's talent clearly stood out, Holger gave the same attention to every player on the team in practice, teaching the art of shooting as comprehensively as possible.

"He would take one guy over to the side hoop and start from scratch–where you put the ball in your hands, how you followed through–and work for ten to fifteen minutes," Dirk said. "Then that guy would go back into the team practice and he'd work with the next guy. That's how we did it for a couple of years. I've been around the sport now for thirty years. I've never met anybody who teaches the details of shooting down to the fingers, down to the breathing, down to the eyes, down to the legs, down to balance. I mean, there's so many details in his method of teaching."

It didn't take long for everyone else to see Dirk's potential. At sixteen he started playing with the Würzburg men's team and the top European clubs at the time–Alba Berlin, Bayer 04 Leverküsen, Barcelona, Bologna, Real Madrid–tried to lure him away. There were also agencies willing to arrange for him to attend school in the United States; several of Dirk's teammates on the German national team took that route. Most NBA teams at the time were fairly skeptical about international players being physically, mentally, and athletically capable of competing in their league and dealing with the necessary cultural adjustment. Holger met with Dirk's parents and suggested none of that was necessary and might even be detrimental. Playing for a club in a bigger city would require transferring schools and living elsewhere on his own. Playing overseas would be an even bigger adjustment. Sacrificing his educational and social growth as well as, potentially, his emotional and psychological well-being all for his development as an athlete was neither worth it nor, in Holger's mind, necessary.

"I leaned heavily on Holger's guidance; that's why he was my mentor," Dirk said. "He told me and my parents, 'I don't want to rip you out of your school to go somewhere else. That's really only if we have to. You're going to leave home soon enough.'"

While the competition, facilities, and resources might have been a little more robust at a bigger club, Holger also warned the Nowitzkis that Dirk might not get the same playing time or attention in Berlin or Leverküsen. In Würzburg, he could practice and get some playing time with the first team in the second division, play a bigger role with its "B" team in the third division, and be the undisputed leader of his youth team.

"Getting experience playing against older men who were

better than me was important," Dirk said, "but Holger was worried that if we went to a really good club, the pros there would be way better than me and I'd sit on the bench. I would not get the playing time I needed to improve. Staying in Würzburg, I could play for three teams at the same time. Looking back, it was a great decision. Now guys in Germany ask me sometimes, 'What should I do? Should I go to this big club?' And I advise them to go to a smaller club, get more touches, be 'the man,' and get more playing time over sitting on the bench at eighteen, nineteen years old."

For Holger, staying in Würzburg was not about sentiment but science, particularly with Dirk picking up the sport in his mid-teens. He rejected the notion that playing time only against the most elite talent available was useful.

"My calculation was you need about one thousand playing hours before you really can deal with the best guys," Holger said. "So if you played forty minutes every game in one division, you will be twenty-seven before you have a thousand hours. That means your career is almost over. So Dirk played with the youth team, the third-division team, and the second-division team. We had to shortcut that stuff."

For a teenage kid in a town as far off the basketball map as Würzburg, it took a leap of faith by Dirk to devote himself to Holger's atypical perspective. Rather than look at what other players in Europe had done to make it to the NBA, Dirk took a results-based approach to everything Holger asked him to do. As novel and eccentric as Holger's methodology may have been, his explanation for everything made sense and he was consistent in always explaining the purpose behind every idea.

There is nothing more psychologically empowering than having a personal Yoda. "What Dirk found is ideal—unwavering trust and faith in a leader or captain," said Shaffer. "It allowed him to let go and say, 'We'll see where this goes,' as opposed to being obsessed with reaching a particular destination. Finding that right coaching match is huge. Holding on to the right coaching match; no matter what, is even bigger."

Equally important is the fact that Dirk didn't stick with Holger because of his parents; he developed his own faith, one day, one practice, one conversation at a time.

"If I wouldn't have gotten better in a year and my shot would've gotten worse, I would've probably said, 'Okay, this old man is silly,'" Dirk said. "He said my shot was completely wrong and we started from scratch, from where to put the ball in my hands. I saw steady improvement and that's what helped me buy in even more. I just believed and trusted his vision and basically put my whole career in his hands. That's what a mentor was to me: a guy who has been there before, knows his stuff, and passes on his knowledge to the next generation."

Or, as Holger noted, smiling, "Clausen learned it from Naismith, I learned it from Clausen, I gave it to Dirk, and then he came back to Naismith. Hey, we got it in four steps!"

With one important distinction: every exchange was a collaboration between a coach and a player or a teacher and a student. It wasn't a static perspective on the game that was passed along. Every new generation listened to the previous one and every old generation was open to adapting to accommodate the new one. Dirk's induction into the Naismith Hall of Fame was a testament to the value of being both a disciple of the old ways and an innovator of new ones.

PERHAPS THE MOST VALUABLE ASPECT of Dirk's story is that his success wasn't driven by some standard, preconceived concept of success—reaching the Hall of Fame or becoming the greatest German basketball player ever or even making it to the NBA; it was unearthing what Dirk, and only Dirk, could become and contribute to the game. It is an oft-used saying but it is no less true: "Comparison is the thief of joy." Maintaining an open mind, having a willingness to experiment, and judging methodology strictly by what led to his improvement allowed Dirk to fully realize what he could be in a relatively humble basketball environment without ever stepping inside a sports lab or cutting-edge training center or playing against or with top-tier talent. He introduced a way of playing that transformed the sport of basketball, but that was never his goal; it merely proved to be his destiny.

As a seven-footer with spatial awareness and a fair amount of coordination, Dirk was already elite at a young age in Germany and would have made a living as a pro basketball player—and perhaps even reached the NBA—had he and Holger never crossed paths. But because he held no contempt for Holger's suggestions prior to applying them, it not only expanded his perspective on how to play the game but made him conscious of what a small part of the world basketball occupied. His parents modeled that same idea by not only building a healthy work-family-sports dynamic but by not being preoccupied with Dirk becoming a great basketball player. They made it very clear to Dirk from the start that their faith in Holger had as much to do with his desire to see Dirk evolve as a person as a performer.

It would have been infinitely harder for Dirk to trust Holger's unorthodox methods if the latter (a) hadn't been able to explain the logic behind them, and (b) didn't have the adaptability to discard or pivot away from anything that Dirk didn't find helpful. The seeds of Dirk's faith that he could overcome any setback—even one as devastating to him as being a league MVP bounced in the first round—were planted by their joint years of trial and error, of interpreting a setback, no matter how painful, as simply information to be applied going forward.

Like every performer in this book, underpinning it all was

Dirk's sense of being part of something much bigger than himself and an obligation to realize his potential as much for those around him as for himself. Being cognizant of his parents' sacrifice, Holger's devotion, and his lineage to Clausen, the founding father of German basketball, Dirk never shrank from a challenge or a setback because he recognized, and sought to honor, all those who made his basketball journey possible.

TRUTH 7

Anyone Can Be the Answer to a Need: John Staton IV

JOHN STATON IV GREW UP A FAN OF FOOTBALL IN GENERAL AND THE University of Georgia Bulldogs in particular. His mother, Maggie, was raised in Athens—home of the Bulldogs—and although she and John III raised John IV and his two sisters in Atlanta, they'd regularly make the hour-and-change drive east for family get-togethers with more than two dozen cousins, aunts, and uncles.

"I loved Atlanta, but Athens just always had a special place in my heart," he said.

He's not sure exactly when he first latched on to the idea of not just visiting but playing on a UGA championship team, but latch on he did. Even when he graduated from high school as a six-foot, two-hundred-pound linebacker with limited prospects—nothing more than a couple of Division I preferred walk-on offers and not a sniff from UGA—he did not let go of one day running onto the field at Sanford Stadium as a Bulldog.

It wasn't exactly the way he had imagined it, but four months later he was doing exactly that.

It is a tried-and-true axiom that it only takes one person—albeit the right person—to believe in you. That person, for Staton, was Ross Newton, the linebacker coach and director of recruiting at Samford University in Homewood, Alabama. Atlanta was the home base of Newton's personal recruiting region and he was very familiar with Staton's high school, the Lovett School, and its football coach, Mike Muschamp. Lovett was the No. 2 Christian private school in all of Georgia, with a tradition of strong academics and football success. Mike was the older brother of Will Muschamp, a former walk-on Georgia safety who has coached at both the pro and college level.

The Staton name contributed to the success at Lovett even before John Staton IV. John Staton III was a standout three-sport athlete—football, wrestling, and track—and went on to play a year of football at North Carolina.

The expectation that John Staton IV would follow in his dad's footsteps, or possibly exceed them, was forged early. He had the body control and fearlessness as a kid to do flips and gainers off a diving board. He was ambidextrous, capable of playing golf and swinging a baseball bat right- or left-handed. And he routinely blazed by the other tots as a running back in Pop Warner football.

"He was just always one of those gifted kids," John III said. "Fast, strong, and not afraid. Liked contact."

By high school, though, John IV's edge in pure athleticism had diminished.

"I was a really good athlete growing up," he said. "I wouldn't say everyone caught up with me, but I didn't shine as a physical specimen or a recruit in high school the way I thought I would. I soon realized that I needed to find a way to separate myself from others. And the best way to do that was to be coachable."

That did not come naturally. Like a lot of ambitious, aggressive athletes, Staton could get wrapped up in his own performance and react petulantly if he didn't play well. He collected technical fouls as a point guard in basketball, a few penalties for late hits in football or running over the catcher looking to score a run in baseball. It was more overzealous than malicious behavior, but the result was the same: his competitive fire throwing him, and his team, off track. As much as John III appreciated his son's uber-competitiveness, he knew it would ultimately get in his way if he didn't learn how to channel it.

"I always tried to make sure that he was levelheaded," said John III. "Sportsmanship was extremely important to me and sometimes I had to force that because he was so passionate. If things didn't go his way or the result wasn't what he wanted, he would struggle with that. Aside from working on the physical side, you've got to work on the mental side as well. I spent a lot of time working on that with him."

The most memorable incident for father and son occurred when John IV was twelve years old and playing for the Buckhead Red Sox in Little League. As the starting pitcher, he was warming up in the bullpen when the pitching coach pulled him aside and offered some pointers on how he should throw his curveball. Staton threw predominantly fastballs, wasn't particularly fond of the pitching coach, and didn't appreciate the advice. He lobbed a lazy curveball as a way of expressing all that. The pitching coach took note, told him he was no longer the starting pitcher, and sent him to the dugout.

When Staton was finally put into the game to take an at-bat, he hit a line drive to left field. The first base coach signaled for him to stop after rounding first base but, still angry about not pitching, he kept running in defiance and was thrown out at second base.

The game was on a Saturday. Sunday morning the Red Sox

coach stopped by the Staton home after church. "That was a real eye-opening conversation," John IV said.

The three of them sat down together—coach, father, and son.

"We just had a heart-to-heart talk," John III said. "We told him there are different things that you need to be thinking about. You've got to be able to harness that competitive juice to your advantage, to be super efficient, whether it's in your emotions or your movement or your mind. All that will make you a better player. And there are things other than wins and losses. This is how you factor everything together to become a better person, because sports is only going to last so long and you've got to have perspective about it."

The situation could not have been handled in a more ideal way. The Red Sox coach waited twenty-four hours, allowing emotions to cool on all sides. It also put distance between the game and its outcome and the topic, which was John IV's behavior toward, and relationship with, the coaching staff and his teammates. The Red Sox coach didn't ask John IV to come to his house, either, which could've felt as if he were being called to the principal's office. The coach cared enough about John IV to take time out of his Sunday to drive to the Statons' house. That John III said, "We told him"—meaning he and the coach—indicates they spoke beforehand about the purpose of the conversation and were on the same page. This wasn't the coach coming to convince the father and son that John IV's attitude and behavior had to change; it was the adults giving guidance to a young man.

Not that it was the last father-son conversation about the subject. John III laughed and said, "Oh, man, I couldn't even count 'em," when asked how many subsequent talks there were. But the bottom line is those subsequent conversations were had. His answer could have been "As many as were needed to get the message across." Because that's what happened.

There is a line of thinking among some parents that competitive fire is so valuable and vital—the fiercest-warrior-wins mentality—that nothing should ever be done to tame or tamp it. There's a quiet—or sometimes not-so-quiet—admiration for young athletes so obsessed with winning that they act out when they lose, their parents making light of the histrionics with a smirk or shrug.

John III, having been one of those athletes when he was younger, knew better.

"I was always a sore loser in sports," he said. "I hated to lose and I did everything in my power to not lose or to not have my team lose. As I got a little bit older and a little wiser, I realized there were other parts of the game that were more important than the score or a statistic. It's not about getting twelve tackles or rushing for sixty-eight yards. There was a skill set to learn—resilience, situational awareness, sportsmanship—that you could take into life to face real-world challenges with that same competitive nature. If you could come out with that competitive edge a little smoother, your chances of success and having an impact on society were probably greater because you would have a more enhanced skill set than someone else."

While John III coached John IV briefly, he took his role as a dad in shaping his son as a person to be more important than molding him as an athlete. So he left the coaching to the coaches. "In youth sports there's too much parental involvement," he said. "I never liked that 'daddy ball.' When I was coaching, I was a little bit harder on him because I expected more from him. That wasn't necessarily fair to him. I was so glad when he graduated into professional coaches, if you will—high school coaches. That's when your mental support, your moral support, your perspective as a parent, can be applied at a greater level or more intensity because you are seeing the whole field as a dad now."

Before every game, beginning in high school, John III would send his son a text—*Have fun, be a good sport*—to remind him to see the big picture in some way. John IV would read his dad's text before he left the locker room.

"He made sure to send me one every single game of my career," John IV said. "It helped me get into the zone of being competitive but also respecting the game and my opponents."

John IV also adopted a couple of routines on the field to keep his composure. In football, it was helping up an opponent, whether they tackled him or he tackled them. In baseball, if he had a frustrating at-bat, he'd stop on his way to his defensive position to draw a smiley face in the infield dirt. Not every coach understood, but his dad did and that was enough.

"There were numerous times in high school and college that coaches would get pissed when I helped up an opponent," he said, "but for me it was to stay fully present. The smiley face in baseball was a reminder to be happy, that it's not that serious. But helping people up off the ground is when it started. That was my cue to remain in the game and in the moment."

The refined version of John Staton IV is what Newton saw on the gridiron and baseball diamond. Some of that competitive spirit had been channeled into knowing the game plan and being a good teammate, with plenty left over. He didn't have the classic size for a linebacker in a program like UGA, but watching him perform as an all-state outfielder convinced Newton that John had enough intangibles to potentially play at the next level—especially for a lower Division I program like Samford. Knowing that Staton had a walk-on offer from his dad's alma mater, North Carolina, Newton pitched him on the idea that he had a better chance of actually playing at Samford.

"At places like North Carolina it's a one-in-twenty chance for a walk-on to play," Newton said. "At a place like Samford, it's a one-in-five chance. It's still hard to do, but the odds are more in your favor. So I put on the full-court press, went after him like a full recruit, brought him in for an official visit, kept him overnight and everything. You never really know, but I was convinced he would play for us one day."

Unbeknownst to Newton, he had a notable recruiting tool the Tar Heels couldn't match: a game against the thirteenth-ranked Georgia Bulldogs that very next season—in Athens. Staton accepted Newton's preferred walk-on offer.

"My motivation was to make the bus to Georgia and to play in front of all my family in my mom's hometown," John said. "That drove me a lot."

The chance of his being on that bus when preseason workouts began could not have been more remote. College football travel squads are smaller than the full roster and John was at the bottom of that. Newton's belief that Staton would play for Samford "one day" was a lot further away than John anticipated, in part because the defensive coordinator apparently did not share Newton's enthusiasm. While Staton was officially on the roster, there were no plans to actually have him play that year—not as a linebacker, nor even as a blocker on special teams. Which meant he certainly wouldn't be on the trimmed-down travel squad for away games, i.e., going to Athens. "In college football, the first thing that they do after your first team meeting, before your first day of practice, is have a special teams meeting," John said. "And if you're not in the special teams meeting, then they don't expect anything of you. And I was one of the six or seven dudes who weren't in the special teams meeting that first day."

As discouraging—and unexpected—as that might have been, he already knew what it was like to be both patient and resourceful. More than anything, he wanted to be on the field, contributing in any way possible, and special teams offered that. He didn't view a smaller role as a downgrade but rather a stepping stone, a means of demonstrating to the coaches his grasp of a game plan and attention to detail.

"I realized that there's a lot more opportunity on special teams," he said. "There can only be two or three linebackers out there, but there can be eleven people on special teams across four different units. I didn't care what the role was. I even practiced being a long snapper."

He wasn't afraid to ask for a chance to do more. As a high school junior, he was a backup linebacker. When one of the starters was injured, he didn't wait for the coaches to decide; he asked for a shot at the starting spot. They granted him one and he never relinquished it.

"I realized the worst thing that somebody can say to you is 'No,' and then what are you going to do?" Staton said. "That's it. And then you just go, 'Okay, well, that might not be a person that I want to do business with or be involved with or play for,' but if it is, you can always circle back and ask again and try to prove your worth."

Being so far down the depth chart, John knew before he could ask for a shot that he had to demonstrate why he deserved one. That began with making himself as visible as possible, which meant not only putting in extra work but doing it at times and in ways that would catch the coaches' attention.

"I would try to be in the football facility all day long if I could," he said.

The next step was having a clear idea of what he was attempting to accomplish.

"I had to set a goal and then create the right mindset and headspace to accomplish that goal," he said. "Once I set the goal, I had to figure out, 'How long is this going to take? What do I need to do to separate myself from other people? How do I, in theory, play the game inside the game?' That was a big part of my success: figuring out how to play the game inside the game. Do I need to be in the film room at this time for this long to learn this much and does it look good to the coaches if they see me up there? Or: How do I take extra reps and bring people along with me to take extra reps on the field or in the weight room so they can see that I'm working on more than just what's beneficial to my success. Things like that."

In the case of making the bus to Athens, he created a specific plan in the notes app on his phone, working back from the day the team bus was scheduled to depart. "The game was week three of the season," he said, "so I back-channeled to where I was starting. Preseason camp is here and I'm in this position: How do I make it out of the end of camp on the two-deep depth chart on special teams? And then, how do I perform and find a starting role? And then, obviously, I couldn't mess up too bad in the first two games."

With a lot of successful people, there is some inherent gift that gives them an advantage and is critical to their success. With high-level athletes, it is often some physical trait. John Staton IV is proof that there is another way. Newton pointed to Staton's ability to create ambitious goals and the efficient game plans to reach them as his superpower.

"John had tremendous ability to set accurate goals that he could achieve, but they were still high enough," Newton said. "Some people set goals that are too high and you're like, 'Come on, be realistic.' Then some people set goals that are too low. He could set lofty goals, but then he could tell you his plan to achieve them. And a lot of eighteen- and nineteen-year-olds can't do that. They can set lofty goals, but they can't come up with a plan to achieve 'em. He was great at that. And he was a tireless worker. He took great notes in meetings from day one. You have to teach a lot of guys in college to do that. He understood the value of taking great notes, learning from the older guys and from his coaches."

John's innate skill is one that psychologists routinely teach to athletes and performers.

"We teach people how to make achievable goals," assistant professor Rachel Hoogasian said. "Because if you make them too big, then you don't have the motivation to persist through them and you get down on yourself. It's counterproductive. The natural ability to be able to do that probably comes from someone's personality traits: openness, conscientiousness and extroversion, a willingness to engage. It's someone who can see things in a balanced way."

Staton was so far down the depth chart when he arrived at Samford, though, that his first goal was to be invited to the meetings that required taking notes and included the coaches and older players that could counsel him. He came in early to do extra weight training and stayed late to watch extra film. When everyone hit the showers, he helped the strength coach put everything back in order in the weight room and wipe down the equipment. He wasn't doing it merely for show. He had lost fifteen pounds from a bout with mononucleosis in the spring of his senior year at Lovett and was working to get his strength back. He couldn't be sure how or where an opening on special teams might occur, so he studied every scheme they ran and every position's role in it until he could perform all of them. If an opening appeared, he was prepared to fill it.

"It didn't guarantee me anything," he said of the extra work, "but it guaranteed people were going to respect me. And once you have that respect, it goes a long way into translating into opportunities."

Despite all of that, camp rolled along and he wasn't moving up the depth chart. When special teams lined up, he was standing on the sidelines. When he felt ready to show what he could do, he went by the special teams coordinator's office.

"He's not afraid to ask for an opportunity," John Staton III said. "I've told him he should be in sales, because he's not afraid to ask for the order. And when they say, 'Yes,' you better be ready because you usually only get one shot. He's always been able to pull it together and deliver."

The extra time in the weight room paid off in a way he couldn't have anticipated. When he walked through the door, the coordinator just happened to be in a meeting with the strength coach.

"I'll do anything to be on the scout team or special teams; just give me one opportunity, one chance," John Staton IV told the coordinator.

The strength coach vouched for him. The next day he was on the scout team's kickoff return unit and flattened the player he was assigned to block.

"The rest," he said, "was history."

It's a phrase Staton uses fairly often, and reflects his mindset: *Just give me an opportunity and I'll do the rest.* But the truly historic part was still a few years, challenges, and accomplishments away, and no one would have predicted it had they seen his very first play in the season opener against Kennesaw State.

Staton was one of two upbacks, the two-man blocking line directly in front of the kick returners. He had a simple goal in mind: Just don't do something that gives away you are a true freshman walk-on. Well . . .

"I got my ass planted on the ground on the opening kickoff," he said. "I got hit so hard, I had a quad contusion."

Luckily, because the ball sailed into the end zone and was ruled a touchback, it was inconsequential as far as the game was concerned. But Staton was worried that when the team reviewed film on Monday it would be on full display and he'd lose his spot.

"My saving grace was because it was a touchback, there was no film of me getting laid out, so it basically didn't happen," he said.

What was caught on film was his partial block of a Kennesaw State punt and a near recovery of the subsequent loose ball despite that bruised thigh. It was enough to keep his spot. In the next game, against West Alabama, his assignment was a former defensive end who had transferred from the highly competitive Southeastern Conference, where Georgia plays. This time Staton turned the tables, delivering the big hit.

"I was like, 'All right, maybe I am supposed to be here,'" he said.

All of which put him on the bus to Athens with a mix of excitement and be-careful-what-you-ask-for apprehension. He had attended enough Georgia games as a fan to know how raucous 92,000-seat Sanford Stadium could get, packed with tailgate-fueled UGA fans. But first and foremost in his mind was that there were thirty-some friends and family among them.

"It was like, 'Oh my God, don't embarrass yourself in front of your grandmother,'" he said.

For John Staton III, seeing his son realize the goal that seemed so fanciful a mere month earlier was "completely surreal," he said. "There's 90,000 screaming rednecks there and you see your kid on the field, eye black on, playing and sweating. An emotional full circle. We knew lots of people there were pulling for the Georgia 'Dawgs and for John. It was pretty magical."

John, meanwhile, was hoping he had a trick up his sleeve. His assignment: block UGA's Lorenzo Carter, a six-foot-six, 243-pound senior linebacker who would be drafted that spring by the NFL's New York Giants.

"As a Georgia fan growing up, it was crazy watching film and knowing the guys that I was going to block," John said. "When you see Lorenzo Carter as your responsibility, you're like, 'Oh, boy, this might not be a good collision here.' So I knew that going into it. You just try to stay on your feet and don't miss."

He did not miss. In fact, he got tangled up with Carter, resulting in a mini-skirmish to start the game. Staton wasn't just on the field; he was making his presence felt.

"It was just a normal block, but in my mind I was like, 'I'm not letting go until I hear the whistle,'" he recalled, smiling at the recollection.

For his dad, who had enough firsthand knowledge playing collegiate football that he had a healthy apprehension about his eighteen-year-old son's safety going up against young men several years older and forty to fifty pounds heavier—perhaps with that first Kennesaw State kickoff in mind—it was confirmation that John IV hadn't set his sights too high.

"It was a moment where I thought, 'Okay, he has recognized part of his dream, but there's another chapter or two because he didn't get smoked,'" said John III. "He was competitive, he was prepared, he was big enough. I realized from that moment on that there were other chapters to be written."

John Staton IV credits his fearlessness taking the field that day to having, step by step, earned his right to be there.

"I really did feel like I was supposed to be there, just knowing that I had earned that opportunity and no one had given me anything," he said. "I'm a big believer in manifestation and knowing that if you believe in your values and work hard, it will pay off. Whether it's playing at Georgia or against Georgia, it's really the same kind of principle."

Going nose-to-nose with Carter and not backing down also erased any concern about him being a private school product by his teammates. As much as he might have been thoughtful and considerate off the field, once he was on it, he demonstrated a toughness and nastiness that defied his privileged upbringing.

"John wasn't a saint," Newton said. "He'd get into it with people. Sometimes these guys get portrayed as goody-two-shoes guys, and they don't make it. He is a great young man, but on the field he knew how to turn it on and flip that switch."

That presence and confidence led to his role being expanded over the course of the game, the special teams coach adding him to the kickoff coverage squad as well. Samford held its own until halftime, scoring a late first-half touchdown to trail 21–7 before Georgia's superior depth took over and doubled the difference for a 42–14 win. But at the end of the season Staton had played in all twelve games and recorded six tackles—more games and tackles than the two full-ride freshman recruits combined. He even won special teams player of the week after their final regular-season game, a 26–20 win over Furman.

While he didn't get a chance to play linebacker, he prepared as if he might. That earned the respect and assistance of the two upperclassmen ahead of him on the depth chart: Shaheed Salmon and Deion Pierre, both future pros. He also took note of how their respect for him was contagious.

"If the best players on the team trust you, then the coaches are going to trust you," he said.

Playing alongside Staton on special teams and seeing how he approached that role inspired not just their mentorship but a bond that transcended their disparate backgrounds.

Staton euphemistically called the three of them the Triplets.

"They loved that because I told them, 'I'm trying to be like y'all.' They knew I wanted to work for it and be where they were, and they were nice enough to give back to me in a way that really impacted me. Sharing the field with them on special teams gave them the confidence that I had potential. It really comes down to the little things. They'd say, 'Hey, this technique needs to be a little bit better.' Or 'This is the way that you do these drills.' Or 'Hey, this is how you take the angle on the running back.' And I obviously was not afraid to ask questions. They realized that and instead of me even asking, they would just tell me, which was very helpful."

Newton took note of Staton's ability to forge relationships

with Salmon and Pierre. Staton wasn't just preparing to play; he was preparing to lead.

"You have 105 different people on a team, and I don't know how many different groups," Newton said. "It's probably ten to fifteen. And some guys can only relate to guys that are like them. Some guys can relate to a lot of different people. He learned how to relate to everybody. It probably took me eighteen months to recognize it. You see bits and pieces of it and then it's 'Oh, wait a minute, we've got something really special here.'"

Staton was adept not only at goal setting but also at role recognition. The upbacks are primarily responsible for blocking the fastest and most adept tacklers on the kick coverage team to give the returners a chance to find a running lane and accelerate. But they occasionally wind up catching the ball if a kick is short, and some players might be inspired to show what they can do by running with it rather than securing the ball and voluntarily taking a knee. Staton wouldn't have hesitated to take off running with a short kick in high school, and later in his Stamford career he did. But running with the ball opens up the possibility of fumbling it, especially in the mayhem of a kickoff, and the opponent then recovering it with outstanding field position. Staton understood the meaning behind the saying, "There's a time and place for everything." The risk, for a freshman newly added to the special teams squad, was in no way worth the reward.

"I prayed to God they didn't kick it short or kick a short, high one and I'd have to make a play," he said. "I definitely wanted it and I wasn't scared of it. The kick did come to me a couple times in my career and I did not fair-catch them; I was trying to take it to the house. But at that time in my football career, I was just trying not to stand out for the wrong reasons."

Newton awarded Staton an athletic scholarship his sophomore year. With Salmon and Pierre graduating, Staton's role expanded beyond special teams and he didn't waste any time making an impression, forcing a fumble and recording three tackles in the first game of the season. At the year-end awards ceremony, he was named the program's special teams player of the year.

The expanded role didn't lessen his drive and willingness to put in extra hours; it heightened it. By his junior year he was named a captain.

"Going into his third year, he knew the defense backwards and forwards. He took notes and asked questions as if it was his first year," Newton said. "I thought, 'This is going to be my coach on the field.'"

Along with the text message from his dad before every game, Newton left a handwritten note in his locker. The note outlined the task at hand and how Newton had complete faith he could perform it.

"It's one of the things that I'll carry with me forever," Staton said. "Whether you were the last guy on the totem pole or at the top, he did it for everybody for every game. That little touch of love made you feel like you were a part of a family."

Staton had also figured out how to be at his optimal best, physically. Being undersized initially prompted him to add nearly thirty-five pounds as a sophomore, but it wasn't all good weight. He trimmed down and found that with the proper technique he could be more effective ten pounds lighter. The former walk-on led the Southern Conference and finished nineteenth in the nation in tackles, earning him first-team All-Conference honors at season's end.

Samford had just begun its spring practice for the 2020 season when the Covid pandemic hit. Staton was named a preseason All-American and had every intention of completing his career with the Bulldogs when the season was pushed to the spring. It gave him time to complete his degree and think about how to best utilize his final year of eligibility. The defensive coaching staff, including Newton, had been let go. Staton's great-grandfather had been All-Southern Conference at Georgia Tech and the thought of putting on the same Yellow Jacket uniform, even for a year, was appealing. There was also the option of following in his dad's footsteps at North Carolina. And then there was Georgia. He was still keeping close tabs on the program and was confident that they would be contenders for the 2022 NCAA title. How sweet would it be, he thought, to finish his career helping his mom's favorite team bring home a championship?

"I thought he was crazy," John Staton III said. "I mean, flat batshit crazy. I was like, 'How's this going to work again?' I knew the why but not the how. But the same way he lasered in on Samford and made that happen, he lasered in on Georgia and made that happen. He did that on his own."

It's important to understand why he made the move. John Staton IV uses the "IV" wherever and whenever he provides his name out of an immense family pride. He points to his late grandfather, John Staton II, a well-known Atlanta lawyer who dedicated time and energy to a variety of programs at his alma mater, Georgia Tech, as one of his biggest fans and inspirations. Being part of the Georgia program, regardless of the role, was sure to bring his family more enjoyment and satisfaction than anything he could do at Samford.

"I would be nothing without my support system and the people that helped me get there," he said. "That's such a critical part of my story. Something I will always carry with me, no matter what I do for the rest of my life, is that you're never bigger than the team. And the best thing I've learned to do through those experiences with football, and where I feel the most fulfilled, is in bringing people together."

It's also why choosing to give up being a star linebacker for the less celebrated role of a special teams blocker wasn't difficult: because he wanted to be part of something bigger than himself.

"It wasn't about leaving Samford; it was just about me being able to accomplish my dreams, which was to play college football under the brightest lights," he said. "I never had any desire to play in the NFL. My dreams, my top of the mountain, was winning a national championship at the University of Georgia. That was my mindset the whole time."

Staton knew that Georgia's director of football operations, Jay Chapman, had deep ties to Samford. He'd earned an undergraduate degree there, he had worked as the football program's director of operations before going to Athens, and Chapman's son had played football at Samford. Even before Staton officially entered the transfer portal, he reached out to Chapman to see if the 'Dawgs might be interested in an All-American linebacker looking to join them as a special teams walk-on. Chapman talked to Samford head coach Chris Hatcher, watched tape of Staton, and decided he was worth a shot. Staton enrolled as a preferred walk-on graduate student with no guarantees of seeing the field but confident that he could replicate what he had done as a Samford freshman.

The challenge, he discovered, was once again more daunting than he expected. Every week of the season was essentially a tryout to be on the field. And because he had sat out the delayed 2020 season, he had not played football for an entire year.

"When I showed up, it was like riding a bike, only they're asking you to ride the bike at a hundred miles per hour against the best cyclists in the world," Staton said. "It's not as easy as you'd want it to be. There's no real way to replicate football training or football speed. You can do all the sprints you want and work with a coach or whatever, but there's just no way to replicate the pressure or the environment. But I would say the biggest hurdle was being a twenty-one-year-old senior. You're in meetings with all the freshmen and now I had six months, not four years, to get it done. The playbook was a lot more sophisticated than it was at Samford. We had five or six dudes that would end up playing linebacker in the NFL, and they wanted all the starters and five-star recruits to play on special teams, and I was not a five-star linebacker. Figuring out all of those pieces of the pie and trying to put 'em all together in such a short period of time was definitely the biggest hurdle. So, at the start, just trying to fit in wasn't easy. It wasn't a straight line. I had a lot of mountains to climb. But I knew that I had in my back pocket the blueprint that nobody else had."

He also was going back to a very familiar environment, having grown up in Georgia and spent plenty of days and nights in Athens.

"Going to Samford was me making the decision to write my own story," he said. "It really forced me to put myself out there. Most of the people I grew up with took the SEC route right out of high school. Going to Georgia was almost like coming back into the bubble I'd grown up in because I knew so many people there. By then I knew what was important to me: visiting my grandma every week or going to my aunt and uncle's house or getting tickets for my family. It made it, in some ways, easier than Samford."

The need to prove himself every day and every practice to climb the ladder at Samford, combined with his intense film study and attention to detail, prepared him well for playing under Georgia coach Kirby Smart. In the week leading up to their first game against Clemson, Staton was put on the scout team to play the role of the Tigers' star middle linebacker, Jeremiah Trotter Jr. He impersonated Trotter so well that Smart acknowledged him in a press conference. "That gave me all the confidence in the world," he said. And it earned him a spot on the travel squad that week. But Staton knew that there was no carryover–that he'd have to prove his worth all over again, week by week.

"It worked out that I traveled every week, but it was never a given," he said. "I was the most nervous person in the building on Thursdays when they put up the travel roster."

Before the season was over, he would get the chance to play linebacker in several blowout wins and even started on Senior Day in a 56–7 win over Charleston Southern. Smart didn't care about a player's accolades coming into the program. It was about his capacity to do what needed to be done in a particular role.

"If you do it his way and commit at the level that he wants you to commit for all the different aspects of being in the program and representing that brand, that will result in success," John Staton III said. "Now, he'll tell you that success might be that you're on the practice squad all year. It may not necessarily be playing, but you are part of something that is greater than you are."

John Staton IV already had developed that mindset before he arrived.

"The most fulfilling thing that's ever happened to me was having a big-ass family reunion on the sideline on Senior Day at Georgia," he said. "A lot of what I did, in the back of my mind, was to make them proud."

The most memorable moment for all the men who carried the John Staton name, though, occurred the following week in Atlanta against Georgia Tech. Before kickoff, John II shared with his son the significance of John IV running onto the Bobby Dodd Stadium turf.

"I didn't want to tell you this because I didn't want you to tell John [IV]," John Staton II said. "But do you realize it has been one hundred years since a John Staton stepped on the field at Georgia Tech?"

John III had not, until that moment. "That one made my hair stand up a little," John III said.

John IV heard about that piece of family history before he boarded the team bus back to Athens after the 45–0 win. All those Georgia touchdowns meant a healthy amount of playing time for Staton and the rest of the special teams squad. His hair stood up a little, too.

"It couldn't have meant more," he said of the historic moment for his namesakes. "It was one of the most proud moments of my life, knowing how much deep-rooted love, passion, and respect that my grandfather had for Georgia Tech. It just felt like I was supposed to be there that day."

Staton's willingness to do whatever was asked of him was put to the test a week later in the SEC Championship Game against Alabama.

"They put me on the front line of kickoff return, which is, in my opinion, the worst position that the Lord created in football," he said. "They needed somebody to block one of their bigger linebackers. And I did it."

That earned him a starting spot on special teams in both Georgia's 34–11 win in the national semifinals, and again, ten days later, in its 33–18 rematch win over the Crimson Tide for the 2022 title.

John Staton III sent this text message the night before the national championship game:

> *Night Bud! Love u! Not sure how we are all here but The Dawgs have a chance to win a "Natty" as you said when you decided to enroll at Georgia. Enjoy the day and seize the moment! Lock in and do what you are trained to do. Pretty simple at this point . . . Get er done!*

He then sent a second one the day of the game, his standard reminder since John IV's freshman year in high school that attitude and conduct were more important than the outcome:

Have fun today! Enjoy! Play Hard! Heads Up! Good sportsmanship! Go Dawgs!

An athlete creating a pyramid of achievable goals is only one part of the equation, assistant professor Rachel Hoogasian said. Having people the athlete knows and respects is just as vital.

"The other side is the nurture or caregiving environment," she said. "The important people in this person's life have modeled how to set a goal and achieve it, so that when they say, 'We believe you can do this thing you want to do,' the athlete has reason to believe that he or she can. If they set a goal that is too big, let 'em fail. It's still a learning experience. They know next time around to reel it in a little bit. A developmental theorist named Lev Vygotsky created the zone of proximal development. It's about how to teach people and encourage them along the way, getting them from where they are to where they want to be by scaffolding each move. As John Staton IV demonstrates, that is a skill worth developing in and of itself."

IN THE END, JOHN STATON IV said the ultimate value in winning a championship ring was participating in such a monumental collective achievement. He told his dad at one point that he learned more about running a business by playing for Smart than he did in any of his sports management classes.

"I didn't accomplish anything," he said. "We, as a team, accomplished everything. It's crazy how many people play a small part in such a big goal. And being there from day one when it was the stated goal that we were going to go win a national championship and seeing how locked in everybody was, from the janitor all the way to the head coach—that was my favorite part of the experience. It was being a small part of a very large goal and doing it with people that had the same mentality and mindset from the top of the organization to the bottom."

In the end, John Staton IV credited his willingness to be coached as the key to everything.

"I wasn't really that coachable until I got to college," he said. "I was always really good at football, and so I kind of did things my own way at Lovett. In college I became a listener and a problem-solver and the person that wanted to do things that others didn't want to do. That was instilled in my dad, who instilled it in me."

His definition of being coachable:

"Understanding your situation and your circumstance as it relates to your position on a team and your position individually—and then being flexible and thorough in figuring out the best way to maximize that position, whether it's through coaching, or having conversations with coaches, or doing the little things that coaches or people in leadership roles will notice—[is what] separates you from your counterparts."

Asked if he has found a use for that blueprint since, Staton said, "Every single day, 100 percent. The No. 1 thing I learned that translates is you need to understand what important people value and how you can help fulfill that value. Once you do that, you can do things each and every day that mold you around the most valuable thing to them, and it proves that you're an asset that they need to trust and believe in and give responsibility to. That's the same with relationships and social life and school and charity work. It's just the way that you do the little things in life."

There may not be a better example of how doing the little things can translate into a major accomplishment with patience and persistence. John Staton IV has set the bar incredibly high for John Staton V, if one should come along, but as John Staton IV can tell him, there is a way to clear it. Draw a picture of the right-sized ladder. And then, rung by rung, build it.

IT TAKES A COMBINATION OF patience and persistence to reach almost any goal—persistence in looking for ways to improve and get a step closer to that goal, patience in understanding that there are an untold number of steps to reaching that goal. That's why there has to be joy and gratitude taken from the incremental gains: earning a teammate or coach's trust, mastering a skill that we didn't have a week or a month or a year earlier, or experiencing enlightenment courtesy of a conversation we wouldn't have had if not for the pursuit of our goal.

Balancing confidence and humility is also particularly important for anyone looking to get their foot in the door or reach the next rung on the ladder. It requires the confidence to self-advocate or accept a wholly unfamiliar role, and the humility to ably fill it without, at least initially, trying to expand it. John Staton IV learned to see what was needed and dedicated himself to being a solution. He climbed the proverbial ladder at Samford and again at Georgia by aiming for the next rung—and designing a plan to reach it—rather than worrying if, or how soon, he'd reach the top.

Although Staton didn't reach the pinnacle of his sport the way a number of athletes in this book did, he shares many of the same traits, which ultimately allowed him to reach his personal pinnacle. Success can't, and shouldn't, be measured by how high we climb but whether or not we climbed as high as we were capable of climbing. What John Staton IV took away from his college football career is a clear understanding of exactly how that is done, both by an individual and a team.

TRUTH 8

The Greatest Goals Are the Ones You Can't Reach by Yourself: Paolo Banchero

RIGHT AROUND THE TIME THAT PAOLO BANCHERO BEGAN TO SHOW he might have a future as an elite athlete, his father, Mario, decided that making that a reality should not, and could not, be the family's focus.

"I actually had sort of an epiphany when Paolo was probably twelve or thirteen years old," Mario said. "Whenever I went to a game, I always watched kids and their parents and how they interacted. I watched who the top guys were in high school. And I realized that if I made Paolo the best athlete who ever lived and he was a bad kid, I wouldn't be proud of him. But on the flip side of that, if I made him the greatest guy who ever lived and he was a terrible athlete, I'd be extraordinarily proud of him. From that point on, it was like, 'Hey, your mom and I understand sports, but our focus is on you as a young man.'"

That Mario and Rhonda, parents of Orlando Magic forward Paolo Banchero—along with his sister, Mia, and brother, Giulio, also accomplished athletes—"understand sports" is a modest statement. They met at the University of Washington, Rhonda starring for the women's basketball team and Mario serving as a backup tight end on the Huskies' top-twenty–ranked football team. Rhonda graduated as UW's all-time leading scorer and went on to spend a season in the WNBA with the Sacramento Monarchs before becoming the basketball coach at the all-girls Holy Names Academy in Seattle. Mario took over the family butcher business, Mondo & Sons, and coached Pop Warner football.

As former high-level athletes, they believed playing sports, if approached the right way, could help make Paolo a great person, whether or not he became a great player. But it was a learning process for them, especially once he showed some uniquely elite promise, to figure out where to set the boundaries of behavior, what to encourage, what not to accept, and what to refine. As both of them well knew, playing a sport not only asks an athlete to test their physical, emotional, and psychological limits, it also demands being both creative and disciplined, to adhere to a game plan but adjust if the situation demands it. Finding the ideal line for an athlete between the latitude to test limits and adherence to certain principles is not easy. The siren call of success, and all the perks and material rewards that come with it, certainly was tempting for the Bancheros. But Paolo's development as a human being first, and athlete second, served as their guiding principle.

"Habits that lead to being coachable and accepting challenges are ingrained early," said Barry University professor Kimberly

Shaffer. "How a kid views work ethic and success and their ability to give up when things get hard is both how it is modeled and the feedback they get from their parents. Those habits can be reshaped even if they're not instilled early on, but it takes a conscious effort because there isn't necessarily immediate gratification."

That development as a human being for Paolo meant acquiring a trait that is in short supply today: being able to take criticism without taking it personally.

"With the success that I had as a player, I was able to say, 'Listen, I don't care if times have changed: when you get to college or you get away from here, it's going to be how I'm telling you, which is, it's going to be hard,'" Rhonda said. "'Your coach is going to get on you and yell at you.' And I think Paolo was able to see, 'Okay, I can get yelled at and get some feedback that might not feel great, but I've still got to go. They're still expecting me to go out and perform.'"

Having discussed how they hoped to raise Paolo and his siblings before any of them came along, Rhonda and Mario were able to work as a team. Paolo remembers very clearly the first time he went against a coach's instruction and how his parents responded.

The coach: Mario. The team: a Pop Warner youth football team, the Rainier (Washington) Ravens, Paolo's first taste of organized sports.

"My dad coached me playing football for probably two or three years growing up, and I was the quarterback," Paolo recalled. "The quarterback and the head coach have got to have a good relationship. Being the quarterback and having the ball every play, that comes with a lot of responsibility. My dad would try to stress that to me. And we went at it a couple times when I was younger. Fifth, sixth grade. I was a pretty good quarterback, so there might be times where he called a play and I'd look at my wristband with the plays on it, and I wouldn't like the play he called. So I'd look at him on the sidelines, thinking, like, 'Man, why are we calling this play?' And then one time I called a different play from the one he called and it actually didn't work."

As the two remember it, Mario called for a quarterback sweep and Paolo, believing the defense was ready for that, changed the play to a handoff for the running back. It lost yardage.

"I got a good earful after that," Paolo said.

The Ravens were a powerhouse team and the outcome of this particular game was well in hand, but that didn't matter: Mario was focused on the big picture, not the scoreboard. He couldn't let Paolo think defying a coach's instruction was acceptable. He also knew from firsthand experience that a single possession could decide games against the best competition. He didn't want to open up the possibility that a game would be lost because he and his quarterback were not in sync.

When they got home, Mario and Rhonda sat down with Paolo. Mario asked Rhonda what he should do if he told a player to do something and they did something else. Rhonda turned to eleven-year-old Paolo and did not mince words.

"We don't do that," she told him. "Your dad calls a play, run the play. If it doesn't work, so what? You guys can figure it out later. But don't go off the script. Don't be *that* guy. Don't be uncoachable."

There was genius in the way Mario and Rhonda addressed the incident. By inviting Rhonda to illustrate how Paolo's decision appeared to someone not directly involved, it shifted the conversation from a difference of opinion between Mario and Paolo about a particular football play to the violation of a principle. It kept Mario and Paolo's relationship as coach and quarterback clean, which allowed them to move on to discuss a solution.

As Mario also knew firsthand, the best coach-player relationships are collaborative. A player on the field, if he or she is paying attention, can see and feel elements of the game that a coach from the sideline can't. Mario liked that Paolo was thinking unselfishly and didn't want to discourage Paolo from reading the defense to anticipate what its plan might be. Had the focus been simply on Paolo changing a play and making sure he never did it again, the potential to develop some positive elements would have been lost. And the only reason Mario—or any coach—would have a hard-and-fast rule not to change a play would be out of distrust of the player or the egotistical notion that he, the coach, had all the answers and shouldn't be second-guessed.

"He saw something and he thought that in this scenario, because of these factors, his idea would work better," Mario recalled. "And so I was like, 'This is not something to frown upon. This is something to develop. Let's talk about what you see.' I still think I know what I'm doing here and you can't just go changing every play you don't like, but let's look at this as an opportunity to say, 'Hey, how can we develop this skill set where you're out there in the middle of it and seeing things?' If you see something at the last minute, now we can introduce audibles. I figured we were a few years away from that, but we got to the point pretty quickly where he could start doing some of that."

It wouldn't be the last conversation the family collectively had about the coach-player relationship, because they saw it as the blueprint for future relationships that their son would hope to build.

"My wife and I were both athletes," Mario said. "We both recognized how much our lessons in sports helped us as people, as friends, as businesspeople, as professionals, as parents. We realized how valuable all of the life lessons of sports are. So when we first had kids, that was the motivation: for them to learn these life lessons through sports. It was all very pure at that point. 'Hey, be a great teammate: when you get knocked down, get back up.' All of those stereotypical sports analogies, that's where our focus was."

Almost every parent has dreams of their kid being special and the first indication that they might actually be inspires an instinctive rush to support it, nurture it, maybe even obsess over it. The Bancheros were no different. After Paolo played in a couple of national basketball tournaments and showed he was as good as any twelve-year-old in the country, they began to think about what sort of training they needed to get him to make the most of his talent. Weight trainer? Shot doctor? Sports psychologist?

With all their personal experience in the world of competitive sports, the Bancheros could have easily barreled ahead, confident they knew best. But they were humble enough to seek a second opinion and an outside perspective. A tempering influence, if you will. A childhood friend, Daryll Hennings, provided it. They trusted him not only because they had grown up with him—Rhonda and Daryll went to the same elementary school and Mario and Daryll played pickup hoops on the weekends throughout high school—but they knew what motivated him when it came to his involvement in sports.

Hennings is now the Seattle Rotary Boys & Girls Club athletic director. He was working as a paralegal when he started coaching basketball in his free time in Seattle's Central Area Youth Association (CAYA) program. Having participated in the city's vibrant high school basketball scene, he was convinced that the local talent could compete on the national level if it only had exposure. Dan Finkley, a fellow coach in CAYA, agreed. But they needed proof. A trip to Reno, Nevada, where they took several CAYA teams to play in a tournament, provided it in the form of Jason Terry. Daryll and Dan sat next to Jason's mom as her son, a middle schooler, torched a squad from Slam-N-Jam.

"We knew Jason was very, very good, but he wasn't the best player in our area," Hennings said. "We figured if we can get our best players together and give 'em an opportunity, we might be able to help get 'em on a path where they can be successful or at least go to college. We weren't even thinking about the NBA; it was more so, just, let's help them get to college."

That was the inspiration for an AAU program first named Seattle Style, and later changed to Seattle Rotary when it moved its headquarters to the Seattle Rotary Boys & Girls Club. Before Seattle Style, the Seattle hotbed for basketball talent, as far as college recruiters were concerned, was literally an island–Mercer Island, which sits between Seattle and Bellevue and is one of the more affluent neighborhoods in the country. The late legendary coach of Mercer Island High School, Ed Pepple, would put together a team for national AAU tournaments, but players on the other side of the western bridge were not in the mix. The predominantly Black high schools–Garfield, Franklin, and Rainier Beach–were vying for state titles, but the title of "playground legend" was the pinnacle for most of their players. Enter Hennings and Finkley.

"We weren't trying to use kids for anything more than to help 'em win basketball games, get good at the game, love the game, and be a good person all around–meaning academically, socially, and athletically," Hennings said. "And some of them took it to the max. Some of them used it to build discipline. Some of them used it to stay out of trouble. Seeing what it was doing for our community, that's driven us to keep it going. And we've been lucky to run into some very talented kids."

THOSE KIDS WILL TELL YOU they were lucky to run into Seattle Style/Rotary. The program has produced more than a dozen NBA players, at least half of them leaving their mark as team leaders and community ambassadors. There's Terry, an NCAA champion at the University of Arizona and an NBA champion with the Dallas Mavericks; three-time Sixth Man of the Year Jamal Crawford; and Brandon Roy, a three-time All-Star for the Portland Trail Blazers, beloved despite having played only five full seasons, his career cut short by knee issues.

Seattle Rotary is now sponsored by Nike, but Hennings said the funds are not extravagant and only defray their operating costs. Where AAU programs and coaches can get rich is accepting financial gifts from college boosters or agents in exchange for steering players to their schools or agencies. Hennings and Finkley have resisted that temptation.

"I still live in the same house I started out with," Hennings said. "I still do the same things. I have the same friend base. All of the coaches that have been with Seattle Rotary, we haven't really gained a whole lot out of it, other than the riches of our community loving us."

That example was important to the Bancheros. Seattle Rotary was exactly the athletic incubator they sought for their son.

"Seeing the world of youth sports and the money that was involved, the influence that's involved, and seeing the decisions that adults make around that is so disappointing on so many levels," Mario said. "Especially when you get out on the circuit and start doing the travel tournaments and the big ones in Vegas. And then you have a guy like Daryll, who runs a program that is still 175 bucks and has all volunteer coaches. He's never taken the hundred thousand or the 5 percent to get his top-five

NBA player guys into a room with an agent or a financial advisor. He's never done any of that stuff.

"I know that he subscribes to our principles and our values. I know, at the end of the day, if my son's spending time around this guy, he's going to come out with the same type of messages that I would give him."

Hennings was valuable in keeping the Bancheros from expecting too much of Paolo as well.

"I remember one time Paolo was crying about something and he slammed the wall," Mario said. "I told Daryll, 'He shouldn't be crying out here. He's being a poor sport.' And Daryll said, 'I don't worry about the ones who cry. I worry about the ones who don't. The fact that he's mad that he missed a layup in the third grade is a great thing. The passion is there, the competitiveness is there; we'll shape it.' That was interesting."

Daryll also reassured them that Paolo had all the exposure he needed; sending him across the country to one of the elite post-grad prep schools or the IMG Academy was not necessary. The combination of advanced technology and money to be made off of elite athletic talent meant that however good Paolo became, the entire world would know it.

"Hey, listen, most guys get what they're supposed to get," he told Mario. "I haven't seen a kid missed on in a long time. In this day and age, people don't get missed. There's too many eyeballs, too many cameras."

Paolo, at the time, didn't grasp that he was being developed in a unique and thoughtful way and the advantage it would give him down the line. He only understood, because it had been drilled into him, that his first objective had to be showing he could and would do what was asked by a coach.

"They stressed it to me a lot when I was young, and at the

time you might not understand it or even get frustrated over it," Paolo said, "but I look back on it now and there were a lot of good lessons. Whatever sport I played–football, basketball, track–they would always just tell me to listen to my coaches. They obviously would do their due diligence in putting me with the coaches that they felt they trusted. But once they did that, they would send me off to practice. It was simple: No excuses, be coachable. Listen to whatever your coach has to tell you. They made it pretty simple for me."

One of Paolo's early memories was tagging along to the Holy Names practices as an adolescent and seeing and hearing his mom bark at her players.

"My mom was a coach from the time I was born into my teenage years," he said. "Every day I was with her, watching her coach her girls, and I would see just how hard she was on them. I saw every day how she treated them, which was with love and care, but she expected a lot out of them, too. So when she would do the same to me, I knew that it wasn't just me or just because she's my mom. That's how she coached, that's how she treated her players."

Mario, after his epiphany, took a different approach. Almost every family has experienced the heated ride home after a young athlete has played poorly or underperformed, the parents conveying their disappointment with chastisement and a half dozen derisive questions that start with, "Why didn't you . . . ?" or hindsight directives that start with, "The least you could have done was . . ." The Bancheros, early on, were no different. But Mario believed there had to be a healthier way. So one day, after making the three-hour-plus drive from Seattle to Portland for a Rotary game only to watch the team lose and Paolo play poorly, Mario resisted the urge to question Paolo about his performance and instead struck up a conversation with his younger son, Lio.

"Pablo gets in the car afterwards and it's quiet, and he's probably expecting me to ask him about the game," Mario recalled. "And I just start asking Lio, 'Hey, did you see a friend? Were you guys shooting baskets over there?' We have this whole conversation unrelated to Paolo. We get thirty minutes down the road and there's a lull in the conversation and Paolo says, 'What did you think . . ." and he starts asking me about the game. I was like, 'This is amazing. And so I tried it again and it worked. I've tried it with my other kids and it's an incredible technique.'"

He even coined a term for it: artificial ambivalence.

"All I wanted to do was talk about the game, get down to the bones of the matter, but I bit my tongue," Mario said. Allowing Paolo to start the conversation changed its tone completely. Instead of Mario telling him what he should have done differently, Paolo was asking what he could have done differently.

For any parent looking to set up their young athlete for success, Mario suggests two tactics: artificial ambivalence about their performance and finding coaches that share their principles.

"Find a like-minded coach, a coach that subscribes to your principles, your values," Mario said. "Man or woman, someone who's a good example to the kids and somebody who's going to hold them accountable the same way you would. We found that at a fairly early age at Rotary. I didn't have to yell from the stands because when I'm thinking, 'Get your butt down there and get some rebounds; you're the biggest guy on the court,' the head coach yells it right before I'm almost at my limit. So then you get in the car, and, again, you don't have to have those conversations. They'll say to you, 'Coach was telling me I should play defense.' And you're like, 'Oh, well, I see what he's saying.' You can just kind of support the coach. It takes you off the hook. That's a role that is probably not best suited all the time for parents anyway."

The Bancheros had a fairly good idea that Paolo had a future as an athlete when he grew to six-foot-five in seventh grade. The rest of the world did, too; ranking services had him among the top fifty eighth graders in both basketball and football.

"Paolo was a better quarterback than basketball player from second to seventh grade," Mario said. In the Football University All-America Game in San Antonio, Texas, a national all-star event gathering the top eighth graders in the country, Paolo threw for three touchdowns and 250 yards, outshining several quarterbacks who would go on to play for major college programs, including Kyle McCord at Syracuse and Preston Stone at Southern Methodist.

But the previous summer Paolo had had a glimpse of just how good he could be playing basketball for the Seattle Rotary's U17 team as a fourteen-year-old. It convinced him it was time to give up football to concentrate on basketball. That would have been disappointing news to all the O'Dea High School alums, who were already salivating at the prospect of Paolo leading the school not only to four basketball state titles but four in football as well. In part because his size made him appear much older than his age, in part because he was so mature in the way he carried himself and interacted with people, it was easy to forget that the expectation to win eight state titles was being thrust upon a newly minted teenager before he'd stepped on campus.

It was the one time, though, that Mario insisted that Paolo play a certain sport for a certain team. It wasn't about upholding the family tradition—Paolo is the third generation of Banchero men to attend O'Dea, with Mario having started at tight end on a state-title winning team before making the Washington squad as a walk-on—but about making an informed decision.

"Listen, you have to play," Mario told Paolo. "I don't care if you're on the freshman team, the JV team, the varsity team, I'm not going to go talk to the coach or anything, but you're going to play."

Paolo did it begrudgingly at first, but as the season progressed he appreciated the experience. It didn't hurt that O'Dea won the state championship. Despite splitting snaps at quarterback and drawing attention from several Power 5 conference football schools, it would be the last time Paolo played organized football. Starting that winter, he focused strictly on basketball. By Paolo's choice and Mario's approval.

When friends asked how he could let his son quit after such an auspicious freshman year, Mario laughed and told them, "That was the easiest decision ever. If you can have that experience and have fun and win a ring and still know you don't want to do it, then it was clear."

One of the many lessons to be drawn from the Bancheros is that establishing very clear principles and a collective, cooperative way to adhere to them can preempt a lot of potential problems down the line. Every parent has to ask themselves, *Is it my kid that wants to play on the super team or is it* me *that wants to say my kid plays on the super team?* As tempting and understandable as it may be to make the goal all about being part of the most prestigious team or program possible, play the long game. That elite team or program may not be the right fit for a kid at that time in their development. Case in point: my daughter was invited to be part of a shoe-sponsored AAU basketball travel team after her freshman year in high school. I went to the first practice. Several of her older high school teammates and a number of talented players from the area were there. The bleachers were full of proud, attentive parents. Every kid, mine included, clearly felt special and elite. But there wasn't much coaching, individually or collectively, and I knew that's what my daughter needed at that stage. Neither her game nor her physicality were as developed as the other girls'. We would've been doing it for the prestige of saying she played for a shoe-sponsored travel team. We declined the invitation–and I say "we" because I explained my concerns to my daughter and we came up with an alternate plan with the help of her high school coach. A former collegiate Division I All-American, she offered to work with my daughter one-on-one at no charge; she asked us to take what we would've paid her as a trainer to hire a sports psychologist to work on her confidence. Every Sunday I'd drop my daughter off for a two-hour pickup run the coach knew about that was all former women high school and college players to let her experiment in an unstructured setting. There is never any certainty about how any plan is going to work out, but she went from being a very good high school player to a Division I walk-on to a collegiate Division II All-American to a Division I scholarship athlete. Not being on a shoe-sponsored AAU team might've cost her some free swag, but that's about it.

The greatest value of her entire experience is having an unshakable confidence that, with the proper guidance and work ethic, she can get to the next level in whatever she does.

"Many times we can see the direct connection between what we do and growth: I go to the weight room, I lift the weight, my squat goes from 225 pounds to 250," Shaffer said. "We see it happening. But developing a growth mindset or helping someone's mental toughness improve is such an abstract thing. You may not see the fruits of it until ten years down the road. And because there's delayed gratification, most people don't want to invest in it. But the people who have figured out what they don't have and are willing to work for it until they do, no matter how long it takes, are the ones who are ultimately successful."

The Bancheros didn't have to deal with other AAU basketball programs trying to lure Paolo away because they made it clear from the start that they weren't looking to market him to the highest bidder. Some local high schools tried to go to Paolo directly and convince him to transfer, suggesting their system would allow him to play more freely. Paolo might've been tempted by both had his parents not hammered home that developing wasn't about what he was allowed to do but what he learned to do. Understanding how to earn a coach's trust would serve him far more in the long run, on and off the court, than the instant gratification of being given carte blanche and a monetary enticement.

"I jokingly say this, but it's true: we never got offered the bag of money," Mario said, "and I think it's because it was pretty clear where we stood to the people who might. They'd be like, 'Listen, I'm not going to risk that conversation. I don't think it's going to go anywhere and it could get me in trouble.' And so I think that held off a lot of the shadier agents and recruiters."

Switching schools or programs in itself is not necessarily detrimental to an athlete's growth; it's a matter of why that switch was made. If it's for a specific inducement—a six-figure contract for NIL (name, image, likeness) rights or a starring role on the floor or simply greater exposure in a bigger program—and doesn't take into account who is offering those inducements and what their investment is in the person, not just the player, it's essentially a business transaction rather than a path to development. The focus is strictly on a short-term reward rather than a lifelong gain. It practically guarantees that an athlete will not realize their full potential, as a player or a person.

"I used to preach to Paolo, 'Stats don't matter,'" Mario said.

"'If you come out and play hard and have a great attitude and you're a great teammate, everything will fall into place. It translates to other things that you do.' We're not lost on how his journey has been unbelievably incredible. But he's going to do something when he's done with basketball for longer than he ever played basketball. Our emphasis now is on having those other things translate. I know people where the kid was successful–and I'm talking about No. 1 Player successful–and the parents kind of fell into this fan mode where the kid got extra leeway and they could miss school and they didn't have to do things because they were having so much success and the parents didn't want to interrupt it. And I've seen kids get all the way to the NBA, be successful for a year or two, and then it's all gone. They're not playing, the money's gone, the whole thing. And what invariably happens is the kid looks at Mom and Dad and says, 'Why didn't you discipline me? Why did you let me do all of these things?' So you can never lose sight of your role or responsibility as a parent."

Up until our conversation for this book, Mario shared his perspective only with those who asked. "I don't give unsolicited advice," he said. Those that did ask were often in search of different answers.

"A lot of these parents nowadays are trying to figure out how to make their kid a better basketball player," he said. "And what I tell 'em is: the way you move the needle as a parent is teaching them coachability, work ethic, character, and integrity. But they get left by the wayside because they're too busy worrying about his jump shot and his crossover. My son played in the Final Four, made collegiate All-American, NBA No. 1 pick, rookie of the year, and was an All-Star, all right? He checks all the boxes to a degree that people just don't check. But nobody wants to hear us talk about artificial ambivalence and not to coach them. They want to know, 'What magic dust did you put in his Cheerios to make him an elite athlete?' And the biggest kicker to the whole thing is if you go talk to any of his coaches—Jamahl Mosley at Orlando, Coach K [Mike Krzyzewski], Jason Kerr, or Daryll Hennings—they're going to say the reason he's great is the work ethic, the coachability, the fact that he cares about people and he loves his team and all that kind of stuff."

Mario pauses to gather himself.

"I get a little emotional talking about it," he said. "I can't tell you if it's going to make your son or daughter great at basketball, but what I can absolutely guarantee you is it'll make them great in whatever they choose to do."

Former Duke coach Mike Krzyzewski didn't know anything about the Bancheros or the way they chose to raise their oldest son. But he instantly recognized the result the first time he saw Paolo on a basketball court. Remember how the Bancheros worked out with Paolo how to stick with a game plan as a quarterback but earn the trust of a coach to adjust on the fly when necessary? That's what caught Krzyzewski's attention when he saw Paolo play basketball in person for the first time at the AAU Peach Jam tournament in Atlanta. Paolo was barking alerts and commands for the Seattle Rotary the same way he had on a football field for the Rainier Ravens.

"Peach Jam, Court Three," Krzyzewski says, smiling as he recalled the moment. "I am sitting there and I'm saying, 'Okay, this is a six-foot-ten kid who is talking the game. He is really smart. I've got to get this kid. He has things that normally I would have to teach. He already has them. I can take 'em, hopefully, to another level.' One of the biggest things for success as a team is you have to have at least one player on the court who's talking the game, because they're in the moment. I'm not in the moment as the coach. I can call a time-out or talk to my players during a free throw. But if you have a player who is understanding the game while the game is going on, how good is that? And especially if he's a big guy because he can see everything."

It's not as if Paolo didn't have moments when he questioned, or outright disagreed with, what a coach might have asked him to do or said to him when he didn't execute the game plan. Teenagers, after all, will be teenagers. But he learned very early on how to turn negative feelings into productive energy. Consistency and continuity were vital in teaching him that skill.

"I played for the same AAU program my whole life," Paolo said. "All my coaches had seen me since I was in first grade, all the way until my junior year of high school. So when I'd be a fourth grader and they would yell at me and tell me I wasn't playing well or whatever it was, I never took it personal. I never would cry or pout. I'd get angry, but I'd use it to my advantage. I'd use it to play harder, to do what they were asking me to do. And so I always looked at it that way."

All of that served him well in high school, particularly as a freshman. O'Dea is a private all-boys Catholic school with a high-powered basketball program led by coach Jason Kerr. The school has won four Washington State titles and made eight state championship appearances during Kerr's tenure. Paolo's arrival was certainly welcome but it wasn't going to change how Kerr coached the team. Or his commitment to a pecking order built on earned trust. No one, no matter how talented, waltzed into Kerr's program and received preferential treatment. So, despite being the team's leading rebounder, leading shot blocker, and second leading scorer, there were times that Paolo found himself on the bench after a missed assignment or simply to make way for a fresh, albeit less talented, upperclassman.

"I had to wait my turn being a freshman," Paolo said. "So, at the start of the year, I wasn't playing that much, even though I felt I was the best player on the team. Inside I was like, 'Man, this is bullshit. The coach doesn't know what he's talking about.' But obviously me being who I was, I would never lash out or anything because I'm coachable. But at that age I'm thinking maybe I shouldn't be coachable because this dude is sitting me on the bench. I struggled with that all the way through high school."

Most AAU programs see themselves as showcases for their most talented players, and their success is defined less by wins and losses than by how many of their players make it to the next level and receive athletic scholarships. The players are well aware of it and play accordingly, looking to showcase their individual skills. The priority of the best high school programs, the consistently winning ones, is team success: the wins and losses. Because of that, high school as well as college coaches are also more inclined to trust experience and consistency over pure talent. But it can be difficult for a player to go from the freedom of an AAU program to the shorter high school leash; a lot of it depends on how the AAU program is run. Paolo's O'Dea experience might've been a lot more difficult if his time in the Rotary program hadn't taught him not to take being critiqued or reprimanded as something personal—that it was simply part of the process of improving and the coach's priority was to do what was best for the team, not a particular individual. He knew to put his focus on how he could improve, not how he thought he was being treated.

He credits everything that he has accomplished—rookie of the year, All-Star, franchise cornerstone—to developing that ability.

"Honestly, looking back and then where I am now, regardless of how I felt in high school, there's something to be said for not being catered to the whole time," Paolo said. "I feel like, with AAU, high school, and even college nowadays, really, kids just ask, 'What can you do for me? What can I get? Is this set up for me to succeed? Am I going to have everything that I want?' And for me in high school, it was the opposite. I had to fit in to what the coach wanted, what my parents wanted, what the team and the school wanted. And at the time, like I said, it was frustrating that I couldn't kind of do what I wanted in terms of my own thing, but it teaches you how to fit in."

It required a disciplined approach by Mario and Rhonda as much as it did Paolo. Nothing changed when they began looking at college programs. As a family, they looked for a coach and a program that shared their principles.

When the Bancheros dropped off Paolo to begin summer conditioning, they stopped by Coach K's office and let him know what they were expecting.

"Coach," Rhonda said, "I wish I was there at the first practice where you just kick his butt and hold him accountable. I can't wait."

Krzyzewski was stunned. And grateful. And determined to bring the best out of Paolo because of the Bancheros' faith in him.

"Thank you for believing in me, but also thank you for believing in your son that he will accept that," Krzyzewski told them.

He also made sure Paolo knew what a tremendous gift his parents had given him by not catering to him, not allowing him to take the easy road, not making his elite athleticism a license to skimp on his development as a teammate and a person.

"When I got to college and got around Coach K, he told me how impressive and how rare it was to be that coachable and to come from that background," Paolo said. "That's when I realized the advantage I had. When you're a guy like me, who feels like they're one of one but then is forced to fit in, it helps you when you have to go to a school like Duke. Because Coach K was not going to change no matter who he was coaching. When he says, 'Oh, you're very coachable, you were raised right,' and he sees that in you, then it makes it easier for you to buy into his system, buy into what he's telling you."

For Krzyzewski, Paolo and his parents were a throwback to his days building the Blue Devil program, days when his promise to be honest and transparent and bring the best out of a player who chose to play for him was all he had as a selling point.

"As I was getting older, the guys I coached stayed the same age, but their environment continued to change," Krzyzewski said. "So a lot of the really good players, the talented players, already thought that they were at the level they're supposed to be at. Paolo didn't, and so much of that has to do with Rhonda and Mario. The key thing is that they wanted him to be coached, and they knew they couldn't do it. I know this is a bad expression, but they're 'old-school.' They wanted the coach to coach their kid. And I do believe they found a confidence in me to be able to coach him. A lot of people don't coach talent; they use talent. I got on Paolo really hard a number of times and he would always come back to me and say, 'Coach, you're right, I got it.' And I'd say, 'I know you got it.' He was as good as anyone I coached because he was in an era that didn't want to be coached like that."

Krzyzewski's commitment to Paolo did not end with his move to the NBA. He is proof that a coach, given a player willing to accept their coaching, will remain dedicated to helping that player no matter where he might be playing. He made sure Orlando Magic head coach Jamahl Mosley knew what he was getting in Paolo.

"I'm really close with Jamahl," Krzyzewski said. "I've met with him a number of times and I told him, 'Coach Paolo hard. He wants to be coached hard. He wants to know that you believe in him enough to coach him hard.' And that's a key thing. You're willing to do that because you believe he can be better."

Paolo is well aware that his current success in the NBA is due to the integral principles with which he was raised. A tattoo takes up the entire inside of his upper right arm that reads, "19th and Spruce," the address of the Rotary Boys & Girls Club. His faith in Hennings prepared him to put his faith in Coach K and accept the demands that he made, to strive for the bar that he set.

"Listening to Coach K, being coachable for Coach K, was one of the best decisions I ever made," Paolo said. "Because everything he told me, everything that he said would happen, happened. He told me that if I listened to him and if I came and played for him, I'd be the No. 1 pick. That I'd go on to be All-American. Everything that happened, happened because I was able to be coachable and listen to what he was telling me. All those experiences, from Little League through high school–it all helped build me all the way up to where I'm at now."

IT IS THE RARE PERFORMER who has the maturity to fully grasp the long-term value in the lessons and principles they are asked to adopt or practice at an early age. The performer has to trust not only that there will be a payoff but that it is one truly of value. It helps to have parents and coaches explain the "why" behind it all, but it still requires a leap of faith.

Paolo trusted how his parents were asking him to behave, not only because he knew they were successful athletes, but because they themselves modeled a willingness to accept counsel on how to conduct themselves, both from each other and from trusted outside sources. Parents and coaches can't realistically hold an athlete to standards and principles they don't adhere to themselves. "Do what I say, not what I do" is a losing proposition.

Today, more than ever, the concept of winning by any means necessary, in sports or business, the ol' ends-justify-the-means philosophy, appears to be in vogue. The idea of doing the right thing because it is the right thing to do seems almost quaint. But in the same way that Shaffer points out that it can be years before the dividends of taking a principled approach are realized and appreciated, there is a price to be paid for cheating the process as well. A runner or a business can take a shortcut to finish first, but it in no way prepares them to go the distance.

The Bancheros took the approach that unless Paolo worked as hard at being a great person as he did to become a great athlete, he not only wouldn't realize his potential as a leader or a teammate but would be less likely to fully utilize whatever influence his success afforded him off the court. There are legions of athletes—and doctors, musicians, and executives—who were materially successful but couldn't build on it because of the way they achieved it. There was no guarantee that Paolo would reach the heights that he has; the Bancheros just wanted to make sure that whatever opportunity or success came his way, he would be equipped to make the most of it. And himself.

What could be viewed as constraints on Paolo's growth as a basketball player—sticking with Seattle Rotary, making him play football as a freshman, having to wait his turn to have a bigger role at O'Dea—accelerated his development by teaching him the value of loyalty and respect and patience. Resulting in a level of maturity uncommon for a college freshman. Or an NBA rookie. Preparing him to take a leadership role for the Blue Devils and a year later with the Orlando Magic. Proving that the Bancheros' approach didn't hold him back. It spring-loaded him to take full advantage of bigger opportunities ahead.

TRUTH 9

Why Is More Important Than How: Landon Donovan and Caroline Marks

LANDON DONOVAN CRUSHED QUITE A FEW PRECONCEIVED NOTIONS on his way to becoming the most accomplished male player in American soccer history. For all his success, it was not an easy journey—and he might have never reached that hallowed summit had he not abandoned the preconceived notion of how to do it, delivering him to a coach who knew, better than anyone else, how to extract his best.

One of the crushed preconceived notions: to be the best—for an American soccer player—required, first and foremost, to play somewhere other than in America. Somewhere the game was played, and prized, as the absolute premier sport: the English Premier League, Germany's Bundesliga, Spain's La Liga, or Italy's Serie A.

Most of the top U.S. players over the years have subscribed to that idea. It is the iron-sharpens-iron theory: that the only way to realize your potential is to play against the best available competition on a day-in and day-out basis. Major League Soccer, the U.S. top league, has improved its competitive level and overall popularity since it was formed in 1993, but it still is not ranked among the top ten leagues in the world. Yet that's where Donovan played 340 of his 406 outdoor club matches. What Donovan proved is that if you know what it takes to compete against the best and you're willing to work until you meet that standard, you can.

Of course, even Donovan didn't realize that at first. As a self-admitted people pleaser, he sought to win approval by following protocol. Being coachable–i.e., incorporating someone else's perspective into his approach–was not his problem; it was identifying the right someone. If there was such a thing as being too coachable, Donovan embodied it.

"I got to a point where I'd been around enough good coaches and enough bad coaches that I knew some of them had no idea what they were talking about and some were really smart," Donovan said. "The challenge then was I wanted to please but there were a few different times with a few different coaches where I knew what they were doing was completely wrong but I also wanted to make it work. That's the challenging part about being coachable: you just listen because you're trying to be coachable, but maybe that's not always the right thing."

Anything that pushes us out of our comfort zone has value. But there shouldn't be any confusion about what a coach is asking a performer to do or how it contributes to the collective goal; if there is, that's leaving that performer without a North Star for motivation and improvement. No one ever gets to play their desired role in every situation. But the purpose of every role has to be clear to the person filling it; if it's not, the question "Is there a purpose?" will surface. Followed by the person in that role questioning if they have a purpose. When a relationship with a coach or an organization doesn't work or isn't fruitful, it's inevitably because of one primary reason: the athlete and coach didn't have a common goal.

When an athlete is as talented as Donovan, a certain degree of success is inevitable. Elite athletes can perform with their heart rates as high as 190 beats per minute; in fitness tests leading up to the 2002 World Cup, Donovan pushed his to 210. "Unheard-of," said Bruce Arena, the national team coach at the time. Donovan not only had more endurance than anyone else on the team, he was also the fastest, with the most technical skill—a truly Michael Jordan–esque combination.

But unlike Jordan, there was not an elite college program (North Carolina) with one of the greatest coaches (Dean Smith) just up the road to inspire him as a teenager and later hone that unique combination firsthand. A defined path for an American soccer player of Donovan's ability didn't exist. (Some would argue it still doesn't.) He would have to forge his own and, as with any trailblazer, it was not without wrong turns and backtracking and dead ends.

By the end, he realized that success on the pitch is far too transitory to let it determine how he felt about himself. Personal happiness couldn't be placed ahead of professional satisfaction. His quest proved to be as much about finding out what made him happy and whole as it was about becoming the best soccer player he could possibly be. Playing in the United States, where friends and family could share in his success, ultimately resonated with him in a way nothing else did.

Being true to himself also resonated with his teammates.

"When he embraced all of who he was, with all the warts and everything else, he became comfortable speaking up," said Pablo Mastroeni, one of Donovan's USMNT teammates from

2001 to 2009. "And then once he started speaking up, he put words behind his actions. And that's what makes you a leader, right?"

Going overseas, struggling, pivoting to achieve unrivaled success in the MLS and subsequently with the U.S. national team, allowed him to accept the biggest gut punch of his career far more gracefully than he would have otherwise.

National team coach Jürgen Klinsmann, an avowed anti-MLS zealot, left Donovan off the 2014 U.S. World Cup squad, effectively ending his international career. In hindsight, it's clear that Donovan's exclusion wasn't based on how he performed or his willingness to be coached but because he took a four-month sabbatical to deal with mental exhaustion after winning the 2012 MLS Cup, his fifth, while the national team went through qualifying. That Klinsmann, as coach of Bayern Munich three years earlier, lobbied for the club to take Donovan on loan from the Galaxy probably didn't help, either. Donovan came off the bench in six league matches for Bayern and didn't register a goal or an assist before the club sent him back to the United States; six weeks later Klinsmann was fired.

For Donovan, the four-month break was akin to Michael Jordan temporarily retiring from basketball to pursue a baseball career after winning his first three-peat of NBA titles; his physical and emotional tanks were empty.

In retrospect, he understands why the clash with Klinsmann happened: his need for a sabbatical didn't serve what Klinsmann needed as the USMNT coach. It taught him an invaluable lesson: there's no opportunity so valuable that it's worth partnering with someone who didn't have his best interests at heart. For a people pleaser, it was an enormous step.

"When a coach genuinely cares about a player and the player knows it, that's probably the most important thing to making them coachable," he said. "The coach might not get everything right, but if a player knows that the coach is trying to help him get better, they'll do anything for that guy. With Jürgen, you are dispensable at any moment . . . But I grew a lot more by being left out than if I had gone to the World Cup. To me, life is about growing as a person. It all happened the way it was supposed to."

He put aside his resentment, accepted a friendly farewell match against Ecuador, and even shook Klinsmann's hand after walking off the pitch for the last time. The most valuable part of the send-off came afterward, as he trembled and tears fell and the finality of it all hit home, when he shared a group hug with his mother, his twin sister, and his girlfriend (now wife), a moment that symbolized giving his personal circle priority over his professional one.

"It was a moment I'll never forget," he said. "That was real life."

Donovan, as with every other performer in this book, is proof that it's essential to grow as a person to reach full potential as an athlete. Rejecting a situation that is not conducive to overall growth is not quitting or abdicating responsibility. I've both experienced and witnessed toxic cultures at every level; no matter the resources or the talent involved, they invariably fail. Can they be fixed? Sure. But everyone involved has to recognize the toxicity and commit to removing it.

The subjects of this book are all proof of how our earliest years shape our approach to life, sports included. For Donovan it's where trying to be everything for everyone began, starting with his divorced parents, who had very different views of the role soccer should play in his life. Rich Motzkin was the first to suggest Donovan's view was what mattered most.

Motzkin, technically, is Donovan's agent, but he saw himself as more than a negotiator of contracts and endorsements.

He saw himself as Landon's life coach and surrogate father.

"Rich would always just be honest with me, and that helps you be coachable, because sport is dominated by male egos," Donovan said. "It's so valuable to have somebody, whether it's an agent or friend or family member, who can be really honest with you. A majority of people don't have that. They just have people telling them how great they are and how the coach was an idiot for not playing them, and that they're better than the other guy. If he said, 'I know you think you played well but I don't think you had a good game,' I listened. When you know someone like that, you can take your ego out of it and you're like, 'Okay, maybe I'm not that good.' He was consistent and full of integrity, and so I trusted him."

Donovan was fifteen years old and just beginning to draw attention for his soccer prowess when he met Motzkin, a pioneer as the first American pro soccer agent. Donovan's mother, Donna, asked him to meet with her, Landon, and her ex-husband, Tim, a former semipro ice hockey player. Motzkin hadn't seen Landon play but he'd heard of this young goal-scoring phenom from the Redlands and figured it was worth making the sixty-mile drive due east from Los Angeles to where the Donovans lived. Donna was raising three kids on a special education teacher's salary, which made making the most of Landon's talent kicking a ball particularly important. How to do that was the issue. Motzkin watched Landon play a high school game and then had dinner with the family afterward, quickly discovering that Landon's parents had very disparate views on what their son should do.

"His mom was a teacher and they didn't have a lot of money," Motzkin said. "The notion of Landon being able to get a college scholarship and have his education paid for was her goal, whereas the father's goal for him was to become a professional right away."

After watching Landon squirm as Donna and Tim pled

their respective cases, Motzkin asked Landon to step outside for a minute. They climbed into Motzkin's car and spent the next forty-five minutes getting to know each other. Discovering they both had a twin sister, putting them in a subset of 1.5 percent of the people on earth, gave them an immediate connection.

Motzkin finally said, "Listen, I know you're only fifteen and trying to appease everybody, but what is it that you really want to do with your life?"

It took years for Donovan to find the answer, but it planted the idea that happiness and success not only require knowing who and what you want to be but how you hope to get there.

The Donovans hired Motzkin as Landon's lawyer/agent/business manager. Offers poured in from Major League Soccer teams—a then-fledgling U.S.-based pro league—as well as several from overseas. Rather than make the long drive back and forth from home to Motzkin's LA office, Donovan began staying with the Motzkins.

"My wife and I jokingly—and not so jokingly—say he was our first child," Motzkin said.

It was no joke to Landon. That he met Motzkin before he achieved any noteworthy success and that Motzkin, from that very first meeting, made it clear to Donovan that his happiness held priority over his accomplishments forged something more than an agent-client relationship.

"He was basically a father figure," Donovan said. "Not basically—he was the father figure. It would've taken way more time to build trust if we'd met when I was twenty-five because you're just more skeptical of people in general. When you respect someone, and the starting point is at fifteen, it's different. At fifteen, he was in my life and always there."

Motzkin held Donovan accountable as he did his own kids, a girl and twin boys.

"He was seventeen, borrowed my car, and left it with literally no gas," Motzkin recalled. "As a result, I was late for a meeting. I chewed him out and told him if he ever did that again, I'd never let him borrow my car again. I believe you have to handle a young client no different than you would your own kid."

It's far easier to say than do; agents are often fearful they will lose a client if they are brutally honest with them. That Motzkin held Donovan to equal standards on and off the pitch from the very start was crucial.

"Landon would call me up after scoring a great goal," Motzkin said, "and he might say something like, 'Oh, I had a great game.' And I'd say, 'No, Landon, you scored a great goal. But, honestly, the rest of the game? You should have worked harder. The other team's goal was scored by your guy.' I could be brutal. But you've got to be real with people, especially athletes. Having somebody who provides a safe space for them but isn't just going to placate them or tell them what they want to hear is valued and appreciated."

Donovan, as an American world-class teenage soccer player, was as much a pioneer as Motzkin. At sixteen, he led the United States to a fourth-place finish at the 1999 FIFA U-17 World Cup and won the Golden Ball, the prize given to the tournament's best player. The German club Bayer 04 Leverküsen was so enthralled by his combination of speed, stamina, and touch that it signed him to a six-year deal for $400,000, an unprecedented contract at the time for any player still in his teens, much less an American.

It was a dream come true—and a nightmare about to unfold.

Going from club soccer in California to training and playing with the U.S. national youth team forced Donovan to mature more quickly than the average teenager, but it did not compare to hopping across the Atlantic to become a pro in a foreign and unfamiliar soccer hotbed.

"Landon blew up pretty quickly," Motzkin said. "Having things placed in front of him, he wanted to say yes to everything. For a long period of time, he had a hard time saying no. A lot of that was just that he didn't want to disappoint anybody."

Donovan was still a month shy of his seventeenth birthday when he arrived, all by himself, in Leverküsen to be introduced to the German press. When first introduced to one of the club's scouts, Donovan reportedly said, "What's a Bayer Leverküsen?"

Something else he didn't know: Leverküsen was already loaded with talent and considered him a prospect. The club stood near the top of the Bundesliga table with twenty-four players who were starters for their respective national teams. No one cared that Donovan was a full year younger than anyone else, didn't speak the language, and hadn't lived on his own before. His poise and technical skill on the pitch made it easy to overlook the possibility that he might not be emotionally and psychologically prepared to live in a foreign country unable to speak the language.

"They don't care about the mind of the player over there," said Frankie Hejduk, a U.S. national team defensive midfielder and wingback who was also on the Bayer 04 Leverküsen roster. "They show you what they want done and you're supposed to know how to do it. They only talk to you if you fuck up."

This was Hejduk's first time playing for a club outside the United States as well, but he was eight years older than Donovan, having played four years at UCLA and two years as a pro for the Tampa Bay Mutiny in the MLS. He caught Leverküsen's attention in the 1998 World Cup with a strong showing in a 1–0 loss to Team Germany. A few days later he was signing a contract put in front of him by Leverküsen's general manager,

Reiner Calmund. Hejduk didn't know much more about the club than Donovan did, but it was an irresistible invitation inside soccer's velvet ropes.

"I was so naïve," Hejduk said. "I was already on Leverküsen's radar and then I had a good half against Germany in the World Cup. Three days later I was signing a contract late one night at the hotel in France, not having any idea about the exchange rate. My agent wasn't much better. In my mind, it was like, 'Oh, they're going to pay you 50,000 deutsche marks a month.' I thought that was $50,000."

The conversion rate made it closer to $27,000 at the time—still a decent wage for a free-spirited California surfer—but nearly half of what he expected. Before taxes. He also was mistaken about the language barrier.

"They might know English, but they spoke German," said Hejduk. "I'd ask a teammate in practice, 'Hey, is it one touch or two touch?' They'd be like, 'No, it's free. You can play.' And I'd start dribbling the ball and the coach would be like, 'Frankie, what the hell are you doing? It's one touch.' They would mess with you and laugh. Imagine a training session and you have zero idea what the coach said."

What makes Americans attractive to European clubs is similar to the reason foreign players have become increasingly valuable to the NBA: it is such an honor to make the sport's top rung that they are willing to do whatever the coach asks. But as with foreign players in the NBA, there is a need to prove to their peers they actually deserve that honor.

"The players didn't respect you at all over there as an American," Hejduk said. "You had to prove yourself times ten."

Calmund had a reputation for plucking talent from unlikely sources. When East and West Germany were unified in 1990, he was quick to sign several East German players, most notably Ulf Kirsten, who would become the all-time leading scorer in club history with 240 goals. When Donovan showed up, Leverküsen already had the second-most prolific offense in the league, led by Kirsten, and were on their way to second-place finishes in the Bundesliga, the national tournament DFB-Pokal, and the UEFA Champions League. Donovan winning the U-17 Golden Ball, in Leverküsen's eyes, merely made him a prospect. He was so far removed from coach Christoph Daum's plans that he spent his first two years shuttling between the United States to train with the national youth programs and Germany to make appearances with the Bayer 04 Leverküsen reserve squad, scoring 9 goals in twenty-eight games. Leverküsen eventually loaned him full-time to a Major League Soccer team to get more playing time. The MLS, which assigned newly available national team players to upgrade its worst teams, allocated him to the struggling San Jose Earthquakes.

The addition of Donovan, along with several other changes, resulted in two MLS championships for the Quakes over the next three years. But the nagging question remained: Could he cut it overseas against the best of the best, not in a tournament setting, but week-to-week in diverse stadiums and conditions?

Maybe now, several years older, with several seasons of pro experience and a few championships on Donovan's résumé, both he and Leverküsen would see each other in a different light. Assured that he would be given a fair shot at playing for the first team, he returned for the final year of his contract.

His optimism was short-lived. They used him primarily as a wingback, providing limited opportunity to show his creativity and brilliance in the attacking third of the field. He made seven appearances, two of them in the starting lineup, before Motzkin and MLS negotiated a full release from his contract.

"Going to Germany helped him become a better soccer player, for sure," Motzkin said. "It helped toughen him up. And then he came to the realization that what motivated him and what he really wanted to pursue was his happiness. When Landon left Europe to come play in the MLS full-time, he caught a lot of grief for that. It's not the choice I would've made—it's not the choice a lot of people would've made—but that doesn't matter. Figure out who you are and do what you want to do. Over time, you started seeing him make these decisions that were the ones for him, not for others. That's an incredibly healthy way to live your life. And one I completely support.

"While you're caught up in the grind, you also have to find balance. Prioritizing relationships and being humble and empathetic are things that will actually allow you to perform at the highest level and make life and business more fulfilling when you succeed."

As it did when Donovan returned to the United States on loan, MLS assigned his rights after his full release from Leverküsen to the Dallas Burn—soon to change their name to FC Dallas—by virtue of their league-worst 6-19 2003 record. The LA Galaxy, seeing a chance of snaring a hometown hero, traded their top striker and the 2002 league MVP, Carlos Ruiz, to Dallas in exchange for the right to sign Donovan to what was then the largest MLS contract at the time.

Coming home wasn't all sunshine and rainbows. Earthquakes fans felt betrayed that he hadn't returned to the Quakes. Galaxy fans weren't exactly thrilled over losing Ruiz, either. And then there were those who saw Donovan's unremarkable time with Leverküsen as proof he wasn't all that great.

Donovan hoped to dispel all of that in the 2006 World Cup, which was hosted by . . . Germany. Was PTSD a factor? Who knows. But he and Team USA failed to collect a point in group play and went home after losses to Ghana, Italy, and the Czech Republic. Donovan did not register a single goal or assist.

"It was classic ego, being young and having so much success and just assuming I was gonna step on the field and be successful," Donovan said. "The depression came after that bad World Cup performance, just feeling that for the first time."

Resuming play in the MLS for the Galaxy wasn't the cocoon that it had always been, either, thanks to the arrival of English superstar David Beckham.

Sharing the spotlight—and giving up the captain's armband—first to Beckham, then Robbie Keane, coincided with Donovan seeking therapy. He wanted to be recognized as a great player while still being true to himself. He believed in being coachable but he also wanted to utilize his expertise and experience. "A reluctant superstar," his therapist labeled him.

"Landon was really humble in the way he approached his work," Mastroeni said. "From my perspective he should be cocky and arrogant, but it was actually the opposite. He was the most talented guy on the team, the hardest-working guy on the team, the guy that ran more than anyone else on the team, and yet he was the gentlest soul, the nicest guy to be around on the field. He would hold his hand up and say, 'My bad.' It was unusual for someone that talented."

Unusual, and not 100 percent beneficial. Acknowledging when you've failed at your part of a game plan only has value if you believe in the plan. Successful coaches—or leaders—aren't resistant to questions about their strategy; they invite them so they can be erased. They know that uncertainty leads to hesitation, which leads to disruption, which leads to failure. Ignoring a question to blindly follow a game plan is dishonest. Donovan's humility led to acquiescence, and his teammates could tell.

"He would speak, but it was almost like you knew he didn't believe what he was saying," Mastroeni said.

Donovan's leadership when he felt connected to the coach and believed in the game plan, on the other hand, was profound. If he believed, he could make others believe.

"His words would pierce your soul," Mastroeni said. "You

didn't know why you were making eye contact, you didn't know why you were buzzing inside. He had an ability to get players to work so hard around him because of the human being he was. It was his humility."

For Donovan, it was a matter of getting the confidence/humility ratio right. Most goalscorers are glory hunters. They have a supreme confidence bordering on arrogance that if their team can get them the ball, they can put it in the back of the net. Donovan had the rare combination of a finisher's bravado and an orchestrator's unselfishness, reflected in the fact that he finished his national team career tied with Dempsey in goals (57) and as the unrivaled leader in assists (58, 35 more than second-place Michael Bradley).

Donovan also adapted the way he played for the good of the team in ways that didn't show up on a stat sheet.

"He wasn't necessarily a guy that wanted confrontation," Mastroeni said.

"We were telling him all the time, 'Listen, just get into the next guy. Set the tone for us and we'll come up and clean it up after you.' What he didn't realize, for the longest time, was the impact he had on us when he was physical and not scared of contact. He went from a guy that would jump out of tackles to a guy that then started tackling himself. When the guy that's supposed to be your piano player is behaving like a piano mover, when he's making plays defensively, sliding and putting his body in harm's way, that is one of the greatest motivators for a team. It's like, 'Oh, if he's willing to do that, I'm going to go through a wall for him, man. I don't care who's coming with the ball.' It took some time and a lot of talk. But by the end he was doing everything. That's what made him such a well-rounded leader. He had a little bit of what everyone brought to the game and that brought us all together."

Perhaps not coincidentally, Donovan stepped completely

into who he could be in the run-up to the 2010 World Cup—after his difficult experience on loan to Bayern Munich and separating from his first wife. It was the end of structuring his life based on how others thought he should structure it. He decided to challenge the idea that the only way to prove he was a world-class player was to play for a world-class club. Donovan would have to do that himself, not only by the way he played, but by the way he connected with his coach and his teammates.

"The end of 2009 is when I really noticed a change," Mastroeni said. "And it was no shocker that he goes to have the World Cup that he had. He was comfortable being who he was versus what everyone else wanted him to be. Pseudo leaders are the ones that talk and have no actions behind it. Good leaders are ones that just show but don't vocalize. Great leaders do both."

Donovan led Team USA to a first-place finish in group play for the first time in eighty years by tying England and Slovenia and then defeating Algeria 1–0 when he netted the rebound of a Clint Dempsey shot in injury time. The goal against Algeria drew upon every element that made Donovan special. He sensed space for a counterattack and broke downfield as soon as an Algerian shot attempt hit goalkeeper Tim Howard's hands.

"Landon kind of knows me," Howard said afterward. "He breaks out when I get the ball, and it's kind of easy to find him."

Donovan then used his blazing speed to separate himself from the Desert Foxes' midfielders, his first touch putting the ball just far enough ahead to maintain maximum speed without risk of a defender swiping it. His next touch controlled it, followed by a perfectly weighted lead pass to Jozy Altidore on the wing, allowing Altidore to first-time a cross to Dempsey in the middle of the box.

Algerian goalkeeper Raïs M'Bolhi managed to block Dempsey's point-blank shot, but Donovan swooped in and slid the ball into the lower left corner.

Donovan also provided the lone U.S. goal against Ghana in the knockout round, glancing a shot off the inside of the right post to convert a penalty kick in the sixty-second minute, but an injury-time goal gave Ghana a 2–1 win. Despite the elimination, the team returned home feeling as if they had redeemed themselves after the 2006 debacle.

So how did Donovan hone his skills to world-class razor sharpness playing primarily in MLS? Well, he knew how fast and precise and immune to pressure he needed to be. So, in addition to whatever training was required by the Quakes or Galaxy, he put in extra work to meet that standard.

"His work rate and his desire to get better was unlike anyone I've ever seen," said Mastroeni, who became head coach of MLS's Real Salt Lake. "In real time today, our strikers, after training, will get on top of the eighteen-yard box and they'll have someone shove out a ball from the corner of the goalposts and they have two touches to finish in the top of the D at the top of the box. How many times do you get a ball at the top of the D coming from that angle? Almost never, especially if you're a striker. There's a big difference between that and what Landon did at the end of trainings to work on his finishing. Not only were his runs pertinent to real-game actions, but the amount of energy and effort he put into those actions mimicked high-level playing. He'd one-touch the ball from the top of the box, go wide, then make a dummy run to the near post and tap in the return pass. No player today wants to tap in a ball from six yards out for extra work because it's boring. It's lame. Not to mention he's got to do twenty-five yards of really hard running to complete the combination, get past the center back, and then tap it in. But he's training his brain, in small-group or two- or three-man settings, that mimic the game. And then, as with everything else in life, you could do these things, but if you don't create the type of pressure on yourself that those moments require, you're just doing it to do it. I think that's the way he was able to sidestep going to Europe to be a great player because of the amount of pressure and the way he committed to his work. It was unlike any other player I've seen."

Bruce Arena recognized that at the time.

"If we wanted to write out his program on how he was going to become an elite athlete, we may have failed," Arena said. "Not that he didn't fit into the rules of the team, but I let him have the leeway to do things the way he wanted to do them. If he did it our way all the time, I don't think he would've made it. He might've ended up writing poetry."

The vast majority of Donovan's success came with Arena as his coach, either on the national team or with the Galaxy. "You have to customize your actions with almost every player," Arena said. "I accepted him for what he is, for who he is."

The successful coaches I've met invariably have a high emotional quotient (EQ). If I owned a team or a company, an EQ test would be part of my CEO hiring process. Knowing the game, or the business, is not enough; knowing people is part of the deal.

"Bruce was able to push me while also knowing that I needed an arm around me a lot of times and we were able to achieve amazing things together," Donovan said.

MUCH LIKE DONOVAN, CAROLINE MARKS, at one point, lost the joy that her sport had always given her. The old-school answer: Keep going. You'll find it. Don't quit. Work harder. Work smarter. But. Don't. Give. Up.

If Marks had followed that advice, she wouldn't be surfing today. She certainly wouldn't be a World Surf League champion and Olympic gold medalist. And she might not even be alive.

Fortunately, neither her parents nor her coach peppered her with those standard-issue mantras after she went home empty-handed from the 2020 Tokyo Summer Olympics–pushed back to 2021 by the Covid pandemic–and then finished dead last five months later in the opening event of the 2022 Women's World Surf League Championship Tour.

Keep in mind, finishing fourth in surfing's debut as an Olympic sport and then failing to tame Oahu's tricky and treacherous Banzai Pipeline would not have been cause for alarm for most surfers. The sport is as fickle as they come, with unpredictable Mother Nature indiscriminately putting her thumb on the scales, and she did plenty of that in Tokyo. To the casual observer, Marks had simply noshed on her first real dose of reality after an unprecedented and nearly uninterrupted rise through the world surf rankings.

No one had ever risen as fast as she had. At thirteen she officially turned pro, winning her first of two Vans U.S. Open Pro Junior titles. At fifteen she became the youngest surfer ever to compete in a World Surf League Championship Tour event. She then won the first WSL event that featured equal prize money for men and women. At seventeen she finished second in the 2019 WSL standings and went to Tokyo as the youngest woman–and No. 2 seed–in a field of twenty.

The only thing rising faster were the expectations–both hers and the surfing world's.

"She went from 'Oh, we'll see how she does' to 'Wow, she's an actual top-five threat on the tour' just so fast," said her oldest brother, Luke. "At first she wasn't sure if she belonged. So she just surfed every wave, every heat, as hard as she could and whatever happened, happened. Then it changed to 'Okay, I belong here; now I should be winning these events.' It was such a dramatic shift from being on tour, doing way better than people expected, to 'I need to be in the top five.' And then she had a couple of bad events and it kind of messed with her head."

She was dealing with other by-products of her newfound celebrity. She was maturing from a girl into a young woman in the harsh and unforgiving glare of social media, introducing her to the ugly side of being successful and famous. Caroline's strong legs and athletic build were instrumental in her success, allowing her to respond to Luke's blunt directive to stop surfing with the hip swivels of a girl and corkscrew her entire body into every turn like a guy.

"As her big brother, I could tell her things most people couldn't," Luke said. "I could say, 'Hey, Sis, you need to stop that. Do this. Step it up.' I knew she could handle it because of her mentality."

But going from a young girl to a full-blown woman and then slipping from No. 2 in the WSL standings to No. 6 brought on critics of an entirely different kind: online gangsters who took shots at her on social media, critiquing her body and blaming her natural weight gain for her losses.

Those close to her first sensed something wrong midway through the 2021 WSL season, when she had back-to-back ninth-place finishes; two years earlier, as a rookie, she had been furious when she'd finished that low. Now she seemed strangely indifferent. Because surfing demands constant travel, family members were seeing more of her on webcams than in person, making it harder to recognize just how much her body was changing. She wasn't gaining weight now; she was losing it.

Caroline reassured everyone she was okay, but her trainer was concerned. Her cardio fitness had dropped off along with her overall strength.

"That's the problem when someone doesn't see what's happening," said her dad, Darren. "They'll say, 'I'm fine,' and we were saying, 'We don't think you're fine.'"

There is a tendency to forget, when young athletes appear physically advanced beyond their years, that they are still very much their age emotionally, psychologically, and socially. The sixteen-year-old six-foot-four basketball player may have the size and strength of an adult but all the natural insecurities, angst, and general goofiness of a teenager. The same applies to a teenage girl outdueling full-blown women, some of whom are already moms. In the water for a heat, all that mattered to Caroline was what the handful of contestant judges thought; walking up the beach, being online, recognized on the street, or making a public appearance, everyone became a judge.

"I just always wanted to make everybody happy and that's pretty much impossible, regardless of the position you're in," Caroline said. "Especially when you have a lot of eyes on you. Growing up on the tour and your body's changing in front of a camera–that's a lot of pressure."

While the Marks family of four boys and two girls–Luke, Zach, Caroline, Jack, Dawson, and Victoria–were raised in a Florida beach town in a house across the street from the Atlantic Ocean, there was no initial thought by Darren and Sarah Marks that they would raise professional athletes. Darren competed in motocross as a kid and earned a wrestling scholarship from the University of Florida, and Sarah is a triathlete, but they created a kid paradise in their Melbourne Beach backyard with a trampoline, a half-pipe for skateboarding, and a motocross track more for their sanity than anything else.

"Their biggest rule was we don't want you guys on your phones after school," Caroline said. "We want you guys playing and doing something active, doing something healthy. Don't just come home and sit in your room and play video games or whatever. You guys have too much energy; please tire yourselves out."

Caroline's first sport, thanks to a love for horses inherited from her mom, was barrel racing, but a desire to impress her older brothers led to more and more time in the water. She was nine years old when a neighbor organized a surf contest for the local kids who weren't already on the competition circuit, boys and girls all lumped together. Caroline walked away with the homemade first-place trophy.

"She got the itch for sure," Luke said. "She had the mindset where she didn't want to just beat the girls. She wanted to beat us, her brothers."

Three years later, the Marks family moved to San Clemente, California, home to San Onofre State Beach, which includes the world-famous surf break known as Trestles. The impetus for the move actually had more to do with her younger brother Zach, who had created a wildly successful supervised social platform for kids five to sixteen years old, Grom Social. Darren, an investment manager raised in Brooklyn who cut his teeth working on Wall Street, saw the oncoming proliferation of TV channels and other media outlets and purchased an old Hanna-Barbera animation studio to feed the need for content.

Grom Social caught the attention of renowned Los Angeles–based TV producer Eric Tannenbaum, and he reached out to Darren, prompting the move. But it did put Caroline to the test: after dominating in the smaller, mushier waves on the East Coast, what could she do against stiffer competition and proper overhead barreling waves?

"She went from winning everything locally and her first time out there she lost in the first or second round," Luke recalled. "She was super bummed."

Luke knew that winning at the national level required more than the ability to carve up a wave. He had already made the jump from regional to national competition—a career cut short by a severe foot injury on a motocross bike—so he knew the importance of strategy and ocean knowledge.

Caroline's first loss was so jarring and unexpected, she was ready to quit. "I don't know if I can do this," Caroline confided in Luke.

"I'm not saying you need to get used to losing," he told her, "but you're starting to get to a stage where you're not the big fish in the little pond anymore. At this level, if you're taking off on bad waves, there's a chance they're going to beat you just because the scoring potential is so much different."

Fortunately, Caroline had in Mike Parsons a coach who had built a legendary career off of those intangibles.

"I was the overachiever when I was on the tour," he said. "I was getting good results because I would try harder and study the system better. That was my deal. That translated into how I've coached."

Some of the greatest coach-player pairings have been between a less physically gifted coach who achieved personal success through execution and fundamentals and a naturally gifted athlete thirsty for that knowledge. Examples: Bob McKillop and Steve Kerr with Stephen Curry. Or Dean Smith/Phil Jackson with Michael Jordan. And, of course, Bill Belichick, who played center and tight end at Division III Wesleyan University primarily thanks to his film study, with Tom Brady.

Parsons recognized Caroline's raw potential the first time he saw her compete as a twelve-year-old in a Surfing America contest. She competed in the under-twelve, under-fourteen, and under-sixteen divisions and won all three.

"She had something crazy special," he said. "A really unique style, super low center of gravity. She never fell off her board. And she had this huge smile on her face, this glow about her, when she'd come in from her heats. I was like, 'That girl is really going somewhere.' It was way too obvious."

Parsons found her parents equally impressive. Darren knew

from his success as an investment manager the value of finding experts in a particular business and learning everything he could from them before sinking any money into it. He approached Parsons, a big-wave surfing legend and former WSL pro who already had established himself as one of the premier coaches, and admitted his surfing naïveté.

"He was the complete opposite of the overbearing mom or dad or parental surf coach type," said Parsons, who has turned down requests from parents giving off that attitude. "He was like, 'My daughter seems pretty good at this. I want to support her. You seem to know a fair bit about this game and how it works. How can we get involved and what are the next steps we take?' He was that dad that was ultra-supportive on every level but sat back and just gave her a big hug after a heat. It was never 'Why didn't you take that wave' or 'What were you thinking out there?' It was the complete opposite of probably 80 percent of the parents you see on the beach nowadays that are hoping their kids become the next Caroline or Kelly Slater. Caroline's mom was the same way, too. Caroline grew up with a really loving, supportive, and nurturing vibe."

Darren shaped his approach based on his experience as a kid competing in motocross.

"If I didn't do well, I had already beat myself up between the track and the pit," he said. "The last thing I wanted is my dad or anybody to be telling me, 'You should have done this or should have done that.' I know it's worked with her because when she doesn't do well, my wife or I are the first people she calls when she needs to hear, 'We love you; you're amazing. Go surf it off and let's get onto the next event.' We're a safe space for her. A lot of parents look at their kid's success and feel somehow that 'This is me, I'm responsible for this.' They're not. I've watched a lot of parents ruin their kid's career. My job is not to break down her surfing other than to be like, 'That was freaking sick. You crushed it.' Let the coach be the coach and the agent be the agent."

Darren took up surfing at forty years old primarily to spend time with his kids in the water, but when they started competing, he took a friend and former surf judge's advice and entered a few contests.

"I did two seasons," he said. "Most of the time I got smoked, going against guys that had surfed their entire lives. But it gave me an understanding about what my kids were going through with time pressure and managing a heat."

The Markses were in Brazil, where despite being thirteen competing in the U16 division of the Rip Curl GromSearch World Championship, Caroline was a heavy favorite. She lost in the semifinals when, after scoring an 8 on a rare quality left-breaking wave, her competitor caught the very next wave and scored an 8-plus to win. Caroline, sulking, walked right past her dad.

"Hey, you have to turn in your jersey," Darren said.

Caroline took off her jersey and held it out for him to take. Darren shook his head. "You're going to go up there and hand them the jersey," he said. "And then you're going to give that girl a hug and look her in the eye and tell her, 'Good job.' I get you lost. I know it stings. But you're thirteen years old and you're surfing in Brazil. You need to do this."

Caroline did as she was told but balked when Darren suggested they could learn something by staying to watch the final. In a fit of anger, he took her board and broke it over his knee.

"My whole thing with my kids was they needed to be grateful for the life that they had, that their parents were willing to sacrifice their time and people were coaching them and supporting them," he said. "If I could go back in time, I probably would've just taken her hand and walked her down the beach and let her vent."

The message, nevertheless, was delivered.

"I was being a brat," Caroline said. "To this day, if someone beats me really bad, I still have the courage to be like, 'All right, good job. I'll get you next time.' Moments like that were frustrating, but I'm grateful he made me do hard things like that. My parents' biggest thing was 'Regardless of whether you're really successful or really talented or whatever, we want to raise really good humans.'

"That was always their priority. Now I can look back and laugh, but those were character-building moments, for sure."

Parsons, meanwhile, impressed upon her that results were not always a reflection of how well she was surfing.

"There were some really close decisions that probably could have gone either way," he said. "When it's right on the bubble, the judges will give it to the higher-ranked surfer a lot. She had the raw skill, but then she'd make a small mistake, take the wrong wave in a key moment, all the little things you learn over the course of your first year or two."

Assuring her she was on the right track even if the results didn't suggest it required trust on Caroline's part.

"I kept telling her that this is the process, and she trusted me and believed in the things we were working on," Parsons said. "And obviously over time that really deep trust evolved."

Caroline appeared to be on an express elevator to the top by her fourth WSL season, finishing second to Carissa Moore in the standings and earning an automatic invitation with Moore to represent the United States in the 2020 Summer Olympics in Japan. The Covid pandemic prompted cancellation of the 2020 WSL season and pushed back the games to 2021.

"It was like someone pulled an airbrake and everything

stopped," Caroline said. "The beaches were closed. I couldn't even surf."

Whether it was the hyper scrutiny that comes with competing in a bikini and having life-sized ads promoting her sponsors or simply turning from a girl to a young woman in the public eye, Caroline became more conscious of her figure. Health restrictions limited her interaction with her family, so they weren't fully aware of her weight loss until Sarah Marks caught up with her in Japan shortly before the games were to begin. She was shocked by how slim Caroline looked and felt she was at 75 percent of her capability. Caroline refuted that, saying she had simply adopted a different training program and that she thought being lighter would help her, in spite of the evidence. Her trainer privately confided in Sarah and Darren that he did not agree.

Maintaining a clear perspective on what is most important can be challenging for an athlete, especially when they are showered by accolades and attention. "Keep the main thing the main thing," as Naismith Hall of Fame coach and executive Pat Riley liked to say. Stardom comes with unrelenting scrutiny on social media and amateur videographers, i.e., anyone with a smartphone. It is easy to suggest that all outside opinions should be ignored, but for those like Caroline who have grown up with TikTok and X and Instagram, those platforms are ingrained as forms of entertainment and information and social interaction. Eliminating them to escape the social media keyboard gangsters means cutting off their beneficial elements as well.

"My body changing and me just figuring myself out as a girl who was becoming a woman, I put a lot of pressure on myself," she said. "At some point that's going to get to you."

The impact on her surfing was immediately evident to her brother.

"Her picture is everywhere," Luke said, "and she was starting to think, 'Maybe I need to lose some weight, I need to turn my body up. She started losing muscle and it showed in her surfing. She wasn't as powerful or strong, and that played a factor into her not doing as well. And then it got into her head."

The perfect combination of circumstances led to her missing out on a medal in Japan. She reached the semifinals with a strong start in mushy, waist-high waves similar to the ones she grew up with in Boca Raton. Then Mother Nature showed her fickle ways.

"Caroline was definitely the best surfer going into the final day, even though she wasn't really mentally or physically at her best," Parsons said. "The last day the swell and conditions changed."

An ominous weather forecast prompted officials to move up the final rounds by a full day. The front edge of the incoming storm tripled the waves in size and frequency, bunching them together. A strong onshore wind also whitecapped them before they broke, making it infinitely harder to identify the waves worth riding, while the low tide intensified the rip currents and swirling eddies, making it a challenge to find the ideal takeoff spot and stay in it.

South Africa's Bianca Buitendag, eight years older and wiry strong at six-foot-one and 165 pounds, upset Caroline in the semifinal and advanced to face Moore for the gold. That put Caroline up against Japan's Amuro Tsuzuki. Despite being more diminutive and with far less overall competitive experience, Tsuzuki had a sizable advantage. She had surfed Tsurigasaki Beach countless times growing up, including in conditions just like these.

Familiarity with a surf break is particularly advantageous when conditions deteriorate; it's akin to knowing where the dead spots are on a basketball court or slippery footing on a soccer pitch or how wind affects a golf course. The difference in comfort level between Tsuzuki and Marks was evident. Marks once again struggled to get through the relentless procession of waves hitting the inside sandbars and pulling her back toward shore. Ten minutes into the thirty-five-minute heat, she had yet to take off on a wave, while Tsuzuki had already scored on two.

Tsuzuki knew that an otherwise innocuous wave coming in at the right angle could suddenly rear up on the inside sandbar and provide a canvas for maneuvers. Which is exactly what transpired eighteen minutes into the heat: she popped up with her board awash in white water, cruised practically standing up through a slow shoulder-high section, and then saw a second peak abruptly form in front of her.

Tsuzuki rocketed her board up the face and then quickly pivoted, aiming her board straight toward shore, and stayed on her feet as the wave closed out. Under normal conditions, the ride wouldn't have warranted anything more than a 3, but on low-tide, onshore-wind, typhoon-churned, and white-water veiny Tsurigasaki, the judges gave it a 5.0.

"The waves were super tricky that day," said Luke, who watched on a webcam from Florida. "It was super physically demanding. Caroline didn't have the power she once had, which played into it. But I really don't think her mindset or physical abilities would've changed the outcome."

With a minute left, Caroline made one last desperate attempt, taking off on a wave that instantly closed out around her. She dropped to her board and belly-rode it to shore as the final seconds ticked away.

"I came up one short of a medal and all of a sudden I'm like, 'Okay, what now?'" Marks recalled. "I struggled with that."

Concerns about Covid were still running fairly high as the 2022 season began five months later at Oahu's Pipeline, the first time the world-class, heart-palpitating wave was hosting men's and women's competition at the same time. With first-ever accomplishments being Caroline's trademark, it seemed like an ideal opportunity to re-stake her claim as the queen-in-waiting of women's surfing. But Caroline's funk continued.

"I just wasn't enjoying it anymore, straight up," she said. "I had always been like, 'Hey, I do this because I love it.' I lost that feeling. It felt like this pressure cooker, tick the box, be a certain way, look a certain way. Which was weird because I grew up in a very positive environment. My parents always had this amazing balance of pushing me, but not to the point where I hated surfing."

But her first heat at Pipeline confirmed she had lost her stoke. She was up against a promising sixteen-year-old rookie, Bettylou Sakura Johnson, and a close friend and fellow Parsons protégé, Lakey Peterson. What makes Pipeline tantalizing is that it peaks and breaks in both directions and on good days provides long, smooth right and left tubes big enough to stand up in and exit before the wave closes out. What makes it dangerous is that those tubes are created by a razor-sharp shallow reef that has delivered many a broken bone, concussion, or deep laceration to any surfer who falls or doesn't keep enough speed to stay in front of the wave as it closes. Having any of that happen when the waves are double overhead can be horrific, but smaller waves can be equally perilous because the barrels are smaller and more prone to collapsing on a rider and tomahawking them into the reef.

The direction of the swell can determine which side of the peak offers the potentially highest-scoring rides on any given day. When the right-breaking section, known as Backdoor, is working, it can be better than the more famous left-breaking section, but it also offers a greater risk of hitting the reef. Bettylou and Lakey chose to wear helmets, while Caroline did not. WSL announcer Makuakai Rothman, a big-wave rider and North Shore native, hinted at the start of the heat that Bettylou and Lakey would surf more confidently and therefore were making a smart tactical choice.

"Backdoor is one of the scariest, most shallow reefs there is," he said. "I like the choice of helmet here. Hesitation can be more dangerous than anything."

The pattern was set early: Bettylou and Lakey focused on Backdoor, while Caroline repeatedly went left–leaving her in last place with eight minutes left in the heat, prompting Rothman to say, "I think Caroline Marks has to start thinking about Backdoor right now."

Surfers in a heat can't hear the announcers' webcam analysis, but it seemed as if Caroline did. She almost immediately took off on a right-breaking wave–and almost immediately, and uncharacteristically, fell as the breaking wave clipped the rail of her board. Not only did it not improve her score, but Bettylou and Lakey had priority over her, which they used to run out the clock. Caroline's only chance now was to advance through the elimination bracket.

Strangely, she approached her next heat the same as the first with a similar result, losing to Bethany Hamilton, the one-armed surfer who inspired the movie *Soul Surfer*, and Brisa Hennessy, whom Caroline had trounced in the first round of the Tokyo Olympics.

"You learn from the mistakes you've made in earlier rounds," Rothman said halfway through the heat. "Move around, sit in a different position than last time. Caroline Marks is still opting to go on that left."

Parsons was stunned. Where was the joy that seemed to radiate from her as she effortlessly charged every wave, seemingly superglued to her board no matter how extreme the turn, finding the heartbeat of every section and having it pulse through the fiberglass under her feet? It was time, he decided, to step back and stay out of the water.

"My toughest conversation was telling her that she probably needed to take some time off," he said. "She knew that she wasn't surfing well and competing well and wasn't herself. That was a really challenging moment in time."

Unlike Tokyo, Luke couldn't attribute what he was seeing to the conditions. He thought long and hard about how to approach the subject before sending his sister this via text:

> Hey, listen, I think you are capable of winning multiple world titles. I think you are one of the best surfers to ever compete in women's surfing. You went from Caroline, Melbourne Beach little grom, to title contention, in such a short time. But I think you need a break from the spotlight and time to recharge and get back to that stoked grommet who just made the tour.

"The Pipe event, to me, was the biggest noticeable change," Luke said. "I'm like, 'She's letting go. She's half-paddling into waves. She looks frail, not powerful at all. Who am I watching right now?'"

Luke texted his dad: *Is she sick or something? Is there something going on?*

She looked even more fragile in person. As soon as Caroline and her mom landed back at LAX, Sarah took her directly to the UCLA Medical Center. The check-in nurse that took Caroline's pulse was stunned. The monitor read 29. A heartbeat below 60 is reason for concern. Anything lower than 40 generally requires immediate medical attention and is the sign of a weakened heart. Symptoms include shortness of breath, fatigue, and confusion or cognitive dissonance. Caroline had just been surfing Pipeline, making it hard for her to grasp the severity of her condition until the heart department's chief of staff visited her room.

"If you don't correct this," he said, "you're going to die."

That, Darren said, was a "holy shit moment" for Caroline. And everyone else. When Jessi Miley-Dyer, WSL vice president of competition, heard the test results, she supported Caroline dropping off the tour and assured the Marks family that there would be a wild card spot whenever she was ready to return.

The competitor in Caroline wanted to fight through it.

"You're not going to miss out on what you love to do," Darren told his daughter, "but if you don't take care of your health, you're not going to have a career. You're not going to be here anymore."

Caroline, of course, never would have intentionally set out on a course that would negatively affect her surfing. But what began as a desire to appease her critics resulted in an array of physical and mental dysfunction, including depression, anxiety, and bradycardia. She hadn't adopted some maniacal training regimen, but for someone who burns as many calories as a pro athlete, her body fat had dropped to an unhealthy level. Psychologists say any sort of nutritional disorder not only affects a person's physical appearance but their cognitive wiring as well, which may be why it took a very stark warning for Caroline to accept her condition.

"There's a good bit of research on aesthetic sports–i.e., judged sports such as gymnastics, diving, figure skating, and surfing–and the negative consequences for female athletes," said Kimberly Shaffer, the Barry University professor. "They are at higher risk of depression, burnout, eating disorders, anxiety, and low self-esteem, to name a few. Combined with Caroline being a people pleaser, what happened makes complete sense. There is research in team sports that shows for males to be successful, they only need task cohesion–to make sure everybody knows what the goal is and is working toward it.

Females need both task cohesion and social cohesion. They need to also be liked and like their teammates at some level. That doesn't mean having slumber parties and painting their nails, but there needs to be some level of respect and likability. So while she isn't in a team sport, feeling a need for that social cohesion with fans and people online would make sense."

The Markses, looking to raise their three youngest kids as they had their oldest three, moved back to the Florida coast. They convinced Caroline, once she was released from the UCLA Cardiovascular Center, to join them. They weren't suggesting she quit professional surfing; they merely wanted to shift her perspective on its importance so that she could make a healthy decision about continuing or not.

"Her parents had such a great mindset," said Shaffer. "She knew if she wanted to walk away from surfing, they would support her. That undoubtedly led her to have a high level of psychological safety with her decisions around the sport."

Once back in Florida, Caroline handed over her social media accounts to her brother Zach to monitor. She began seeing a therapist. "I just completely checked out," she said. "It was kind of weird at first, for sure. You're so used to doing something and then you just stop. But I felt in order to get in a good place and to really kind of find myself and why I was dealing with all these feelings, I had to really just focus on myself. And I feel like I learned so much."

She reconnected with her roots: fishing for snook and tarpon and hunting for wild boar and racing motocross bikes with her brothers.

"The stuff that Florida rednecks do," Darren said, laughing. "Her friends in San Clemente never knew what a little redneck that girl was. I told her, 'You have to come home and get your redneck on.' She got back to racing her brothers in motocross,

T-boning them on the berms. She was gnarly. I was like, 'That's the girl I remember.'"

Trying to live up to the illusory image of a surfing star, along with the pressure to climb the ladder of success as quickly as possible, had stolen her love for the sport. Caroline's voice gets thick with emotion recounting the early spring day spent in the water with her brothers when she got it back.

"We have a wave right out in front of our house," she said. "No one really surfs it. It's pretty low-key. Not many people around. The waves weren't very good: two-foot and windy, typical Florida waves. I was riding a little fish, a little fun board. The weather was nice and warm. I just remember being in the water and it being so therapeutic and being like, 'Oh my gosh, this is my happy place. This is my release.' My mom used to say when I got mad, 'Bring a bottle of salt water and spray her with it' because it makes me happy. But I'm also a big people person and I was with all the people I love."

When Caroline felt ready to move back to San Clemente and resume her career, Parsons stepped down as her coach to spend more time with his son, Grant, and recommended Luke Egan, a longtime friend and surfing peer, as his replacement. To make sure she and Egan were compatible, the two took a free-surfing trip to the Mentawai Islands off the coast of Sumatra.

"I never stepped away from supporting her, talking to her daily, all those things," Parsons said. "But it was time for a fresh person in her corner."

Five months after her visit to the UCLA Medical Center, Caroline returned to the WSL tour for the Surf City El Salvador Pro event with no expectations. In her first heat, Australia's Isabella Nichols beat both her and Brisa Hennessy, forcing the latter two to face off in an elimination heat. In a very close battle, Caroline won, 11.30 to 10.44. She then faced Moore, the gold medal winner in Tokyo and reigning WSL champion, in the quarterfinals—and won again, 14.03 to 11.56. The time off finally caught up with her in the semifinals, where she lost to Stephanie Gilmore.

She closed out the 2022 season with three consecutive fifth-place finishes. Prior to her hiatus, that might have frustrated her. Not now. She had regained the appreciation Darren tried to instill in her at thirteen years old on the beach in Brazil.

"I was initially disappointed in myself," Caroline said. "How did I even get in that position with all these amazing people around me and having everything I want? But, looking back now, I'm not that hard on myself. It was really good for me to hit rock bottom. I am very stubborn. To have to take time off and be like, 'Holy cow, everything that I love was taken away from me,' makes me appreciate it way more. I have a different perspective on everything."

The 2023 WSL season opened once again at Pipeline and this time she showed off her backside prowess, making two slashing turns on consecutive Backdoor runs for the best two waves of the heat to finish first and advance. She would get knocked out in the Round of 16 by Sakura Johnson, but her ninth-place finish would be the lowest of the season and she would end the year the WSL champion by beating Moore in a best-of-three heat format, 2–0, at Lower Trestles.

"She was a million percent back with confidence, with fitness, with training," Parsons said. "She had the attitude of 'I'm winning the world title this year and no one else has a chance.' She just smashed it."

The title earned her a return trip to the Olympics, this time hosted by France, with the surfing competition held at the French territory Tahiti's renowned big-wave spot, Teahupo'o. Just as she did in Tokyo, Caroline breezed through the opening rounds, this time reaching the semifinal to face yet another local favorite, France's Johanne Defay. Caroline trailed for most of the heat until in the final minutes she found a left-breaking wave, dropped into a barrel, came out of it, and added two more dynamic turns for the highest-scoring wave (7.0) of the heat, punctuating it with a fist pump as she looked toward the shore. With Covid protocol over, her family and friends were on the beach. The heat ended in a tie, Defay's and Marks's best two waves both adding up to a total of 12.17. But thanks to having the highest-scoring wave, Marks advanced to the final.

"When I won that heat, I got super emotional," she said. "I cried more than when I won the gold medal. I won that heat, and I was like, 'Oh, I'm guaranteed a medal!' Maybe if I didn't come up short in Tokyo, it wouldn't have felt so special in Tahiti. Looking back, I'm just so grateful. I won the world title at a break down the road from where I live. I rode my bike to it and took the world trophy back to my house. It literally was the biggest dream scenario ever. We couldn't have family in Tokyo, but at Tahiti we could. And it was this amazing wave. It feels like it really worked out."

The storybook ending, paradoxically, would not have happened had Caroline and her family made her comeback a priority. Caroline was given the time, latitude, and support to regain her physical and mental health by letting go of the demand to be great or the need to make up for what had happened in Tokyo. By moving back to Florida and discovering that she could be happy and the world would indeed keep turning if she wasn't a professional surfer recalibrated her perspective. The enjoyment of fishing and surfing with her family reminded her that staying in the moment and focusing on the work that needed to be done, not the results that needed to be achieved, is the secret to being happy and healthy.

"It was all energized to getting better and healing," Darren said. "I'm most proud of the way she handled that. She went into that same mode that she had when she was trying to be the best surfer she could be."

None of which could have happened without the constructive guidance of her parents and her coaches. She learned an invaluable nugget: When looking for a solution to a problem, step back and identify your motive. What is it that you're trying to do? And why do you want to do it?

Caroline and her parents can feel confident that whatever else she faces in her life, she knows the formula for making the right choice. In or out of the water.

"You can have the best people in your corner, the best trainers, nutritionists, the best everything," she said. "But self-belief is so incredibly important because I'm out in the middle of the ocean and I have to be the one performing."

ANY YOUNG PERSON HAS TO decide what part they want a passion of theirs to play in their lives, and they need the latitude to figure that out. Caroline lost her love for surfing when it stopped being about the sport and more about what she hoped to gain from it. The option to give up surfing and still be unconditionally loved by her family is what restored it.

"I will love it forever because my parents never made me feel like it was a job," she said. "I didn't realize how unique that was when I was younger."

Both Landon and Caroline had unprecedented success at a very early age, which can be a trap. A performer can begin to focus on what they're getting—popularity, free education, wealth, social status—and view that as the reason to perform. Their motivation morphs from "How good can I be?" to "How good do I have to be?"

"There is a study by Thomas Raedeke that identifies three factors as the antecedents of burnout: emotional and physical exhaustion, reduced sense of accomplishment, and sport devaluation," Shaffer said. "The algorithm in the athlete's brain is "Put in X and get out Y. If Y does not equal X, the investment, then the athlete creates separation. They put in less work or effort and that way they don't feel as shitty when the results aren't what they wanted. They can validate it in their minds by telling themselves, 'I didn't work that hard, so I don't care as much what the outcome is.'"

The goal can't be that of a coach or parent, either. "Don't you want to be great?" is not the question to ask the athlete. It is "What do you want to be?" or "What do you hope to achieve?" Sometimes an athlete will say they don't know, which is perfectly understandable at a young age. They are simply doing something that is fun. After thinking about it, their answer may not be what a parent or coach hopes to hear. It's okay to let them know you have higher hopes or a greater vision for them and you're there to help them achieve it but only if they want it. It's human nature for a young performer to say yes to all that out of wanting to please their parents or coach; save yourself some time and make sure that's not the *only* thing inspiring their answer. Imposing what you want for them will in no way make them capable of fulfilling your desire, but it will undermine your relationship. Darren Marks wanted what was best for his daughter; he didn't presume to know what that was. Motzkin took the same approach with Donovan. They prioritized their relationship over results.

Encouraged to step back, Caroline and Landon were able to make the simple shift from *This is what I have to do* to *This is what I get to do*, restoring the mindset that inspired their meteoric rises in the first place.

TRUTH 10

Tough Love Is Still Love: Richard Jefferson

RICHARD JEFFERSON MAY BE THE GREATEST EXAMPLE OF HOW being coachable can change someone's life. The charming, polished broadcaster who looks as if he spent his entire life, not just the last few years, preparing to hold a microphone is not the person anyone would have predicted he would become when he entered Moon Valley High School in Phoenix, Arizona.

And no one—including himself—would have described him as coachable. "Incorrigible" would have been a more apt description.

Considering how he came into the world, perhaps that shouldn't be a shock. As a kid, Jefferson was a fearsome bundle of undiagnosed hyperactivity with a fearlessness to fight, being the youngest of three boys who spent their formative years in

South Central LA and South Philadelphia. Because of growth spurts and his parents' limited means, his clothes often didn't fit, easy material for teasing and ridicule by his peers. But his parents were also hardworking, devout Christians and were not about to raise a bully or a juvenile delinquent. Richard, by nature, preferred cracking jokes over cracking heads and leaned into being a jokester to defuse or preempt situations that could become heated.

"It was really a defense mechanism," he said. "Where I came from, you had to be ready to defend yourself at all times. My stepdad taught me and my brothers to box. Anytime somebody said racial things to us, oh, we would pop 'em in their mouth so quick. He was like, 'You can't just be punching kids because they said something you don't like.' So I decided I'll just crack jokes. Don't make fun of the fact my shoes don't fit and I have mismatched socks and we're good. Don't mess with me and I will make sure no one else gets bullied."

Richard's mom, Wanda Marshall, decided there had to be something better than raising three boys on welfare in the midst of the LA crack cocaine epidemic. Paradise Valley, a suburb of Phoenix, Arizona, naturally caught her eye. They had barely settled in when Wanda got a call that she was needed back home in Philadelphia, so she and the three boys made the two-and-a-half-day ride on a Greyhound bus.

Richard's biological dad, a gang member who struggled with substance abuse issues, had stayed in LA. During the stint in Philadelphia, Wanda reconnected with a man she'd grown up with, John LeCato, and changed her name to Meekness. Wanda, John, and the three boys took a bus back to Phoenix and found work. With no car, John rode a bicycle in the Arizona heat to get from bagging groceries at a market to scrubbing floors at a resort. It wasn't exactly paradise, but there were no complaints. The LeCatos were grateful they could raise the boys in a relatively peaceful environment and, out of appreciation, became African missionaries to facilitate the same for others. John and Meekness offered Richard a grade-A example that he could shape his destiny if he was willing to seek guidance and do the work.

"The challenges Richard witnessed his mother go through in his early years provided him the grit to battle through the later difficulties in his athletic career," Shaffer said. "Research shows that it's a learned behavior. That's the good news. The downside is so much of it is fostered in those early fundamental years. Today's parents don't want to see their kids struggle. We think that we're doing them a service by saying, 'Here's this roof over your head, here's the food, here's everything. I never want you to lack for anything.' But at the end of the day, that actually does them a disservice. By the time that kid gets into sports, it can be too late. Now they struggle and the parent is like, 'Just rub some dirt on it. Push through it.' But that child has never had to do that before. That child has never had that modeled for them before. It can be trained, but so much of it comes from reinforcement by the coaches and the parents around them, i.e., modeling."

The challenge, for Richard as a student, was finding a willing guide. As a class clown with ADHD who already physically dwarfed his junior high teachers, he wasn't finding it in the classroom.

"I was always in trouble in junior high," he said. "My teachers passed me just because they wanted me out of there."

That size and frenetic energy hit a little different on a basketball court. John Boie, the Moon Valley varsity coach, was both surprised and thrilled to see a young, fresh face holding his own against returning varsity players in an open gym run.

"I didn't know who he was," Boie said. "He would've gone to a neighboring school, but they were the Demons. His mom is a Christian missionary and didn't want her son to be a Demon. He just showed up, a six-foot, two-inch freshman, and we didn't have many of those."

Boie had a rule that every ninth grader had to play at least half of a season with the freshman team before moving up to junior varsity or varsity. That was a problem on several fronts. One, Richard had never played organized sports before. He had all the necessary skills, but his knowledge of basketball was shaped strictly by pickup basketball, four-on-four, first to 11 points wins, a regular bucket counts as 1, a 3-pointer counts as 2. When the freshman coach introduced the team to a three-man weave, Richard thought it was dumb and said as much. He felt the same about his ninth-grade physical education class: if they weren't playing basketball, he refused to change into his gym clothes and wound up getting an F. "I was a fourteen-year-old," he said. "If I'm like this at forty-three, imagine me at fourteen!"

The freshman coach didn't have to imagine; he lived it firsthand.

"My freshman coach wanted Richard off the team because he just goofed around all the time," Boie said. "And since he was, at that point, already the best athlete we had, everybody followed him. The freshman coaches didn't want anything to do with him, and I understood."

Boie might have dropped Jefferson from the program had he not inadvertently seen something while watching tape of a varsity game. Moon Valley made a dramatic comeback behind one of his players hitting six fourth-quarter 3-pointers. In the background, Jefferson, watching from the stands, could be seen celebrating like a lunatic.

"You see Richard jump up and down and then he just doesn't know what else to do, so he runs down the sidelines and back," Boie said, chuckling. "Seeing him get that excited for a teammate was really a positive to me. Richard had the ability to play varsity as a freshman, and there's a lot of freshmen who would've put their heads down and have been upset, thinking 'That could have been me, should have been me.' But Richard was happy for his teammate, which was really big."

Told of Boie's description of his antics, Jefferson laughed. It wasn't just his teammate's electric performance that inspired his giddiness; simply attending an organized, official game was a brand-new and exhilarating experience. "I went to one NBA game when I was fifteen, so I just hadn't seen a lot of basketball in person," he said. "So when I see a guy I know hit all those 3s in person, it's like, 'Oh my God, this is amazing.'"

Boie provided Jefferson with another first-time experience: someone showing they believed in him. Not every coach would have interpreted Richard's histrionics as a positive, but Boie prided himself in looking for the redeeming value in every kid he came across. Jefferson's disruptive behavior, Boie suspected, wasn't inspired by malicious intent or disdain for authority as much as boredom—that he was essentially too smart and too athletic for his age and his own good.

"Richard's not the only one I ever sat down with," Boie said. "I always had an idea of how I wanted to coach, which wasn't like anybody that had ever coached me. I always thought that just getting to know players and telling them the truth was really important."

Boie decided to see if his hunch about Richard was right. He presented a rather unique plan: Richard wouldn't play in games or even get a uniform, but he would be allowed to practice with the varsity and prove he could take direction and be part of a team.

"It was the first time anyone had done that," Jefferson said of Boie's sit-down talk and specially designed course of action. "There is not a single more important person in my life who helped me navigate the start of my journey. He held me accountable as a freshman. I'm not a future NBA guy at that point in time. I'm not six-foot-seven. I'm just Richard Jefferson. There's a billion of me. But he's pleading with me to get good grades so I can be on the team. I never ever got the sense that he wanted something from me. He saw that I was a kid who had a chance to do something that you don't often see. That was always his message to me: 'You have a chance to do something that not a lot of people have a chance to do.' And he begged and pleaded with me to take it seriously."

Boie made it clear that Jefferson wasn't accountable just to him but to the rest of the team as well. Several of his players were two-sport athletes and actually better at football—including a future NFL backup quarterback, Travis Brown—and Boie enlisted them to keep Jefferson in line.

"I told my kids that for anything Richard had done or said before, they couldn't take anything out on him," Boie recounted. "But if he stepped out of line from this point on, they should kick his ass. Richard told me he was afraid to screw up. Those guys would've went and found him."

Richard returned to school as a sophomore, having grown three inches and spent another summer playing basketball every day, all day, in the park. Now he was throwing down reverse dunks and dominating the open gym runs. Boie made sure Jefferson understood that, for all his talent, making sure his grades were good enough to stay eligible was the first priority.

"I told him he could be the best JV player in the state, because if he didn't get his grades up, he couldn't play varsity," Boie said. "I had five seniors. We were going to be the No. 1 team in the state. I couldn't have him playing over seniors and one week he was eligible and the next week he wasn't."

Jefferson accepted the challenge. "To piss off everyone, I

went and got all A's and a B," he said. "People were like, 'This guy failed three classes his freshman year and now he has straight A's?' And my answer: 'Someone gave me the motivation to push myself because I love basketball.'"

As Jefferson's notoriety grew and the accolades arrived—McDonald's All-American selection, recruiting letters, TV interviews—the conversations between Boie and Jefferson became routine, with Boie often giving him a ride home from practice.

"We talked more about life and just what it meant for him at that point," Boie said of their car conversations. "I had to explain to him that his behavior had to be better than everybody else's because he was in a predominantly white school. 'You're six-foot-seven, you're African American. Everybody's going to know who you are, and half the people are probably looking for you to fail and would love it if you did.'"

Boie told Jefferson midway through his sophomore year that he had the potential to go to the NBA. "First and only player I've ever said that to," Boie said. Knowing that, though, created a challenge. The best interests for the high school team was to play their biggest, most athletic player at center, but Boie knew that for Jefferson to play in college and beyond he would need the skills to play on the perimeter. So he presented another plan: they would develop his post skills playing for Moon Valley and put in extra time to work on his perimeter skills and let him showcase those during the summer in AAU tournaments.

Jefferson's willingness to do that is why, when approached for this book, Boie endorsed Richard as an ideal example of someone who was coachable. Playing him in the post, at that time, served Moon Valley far more than it did Jefferson. Developing the footwork to operate around the basket is arduous; jump hooks and even lob dunks don't elicit the same oohs and ahs from the stands as draining a deep 3-pointer or blowing by a defender off the dribble. Playing in the post was never something Richard even considered all those years on the playground, and there wouldn't be much use for that skill in college or the pros. Someone unwilling to meet his coach halfway or who took for granted everything else Boie had done to fuel Richard's success might have transferred to a school that didn't ask for such a sacrifice. Jefferson knew that but stayed out of loyalty. And while those post skills weren't why he was recruited or drafted, that early exercise of adapting his game for the good of the team would prove valuable when the same request was made by his college coach and again in the NBA.

"Being coachable is being able to listen to outside sources and adjust your game to what is needed to win," Boie said. "It wasn't what was best for him if he was going to college, but it was what was best for Moon Valley. To put a six-foot-seven kid on the wing and have him shoot jumpers when he can grab the ball in the middle and just baby hook or dunk on people repeatedly, it wouldn't have made much sense."

Boie acknowledging the sacrifice he was asking Jefferson to make for the good of the team and finding ways to ameliorate that sacrifice certainly helped. The summer before Jefferson's senior year, they made the ten-and-a-half-hour drive to Salt Lake City so Richard could attend University of Utah coach Rick Majerus's "Big Man" camp, an annual invitation-only event that focused on skill work for power forwards and centers. Majerus famously welcomed any and all coaches interested in attending his practices. Boie had made the drive several times alone and struck up a friendship with Majerus, who died in 2012.

Boie also looked for any opportunity to showcase Jefferson's individual talent without letting it compromise his team-first principles. For example, the night before the first game of Jefferson's senior year, Boie told him to go after the school's single-game scoring record. Boie's purpose was twofold: he wanted Richard to realize just how special he could be and let him enjoy a game without restrictions. What he didn't tell him was that it would be his only shot, anticipating that Jefferson and the team would be so dominant that Richard wouldn't play in the fourth quarter of most games.

The school record was 43; Jefferson scored 46.

Even though–or maybe because–Moon Valley had been upset in the first round of the state tournament the previous two years, Boie told Jefferson his senior year would be a waste if he didn't walk away with a state title. The Rockets met the Greenway Demons, the school Richard was supposed to attend, in the championship game and came away with a 54–52 win.

"He held my hand for three years," Jefferson said. "He was putting incremental challenges in front of me, long-term goals and short-term goals. I learned in that space how important coaching is. It was learning and understanding."

Jefferson had offers from every major college program, including the closest one, the University of Arizona. Head coach Lute Olson had the same dual vision for Jefferson as Boie, developing him both as the player the Wildcats needed and the kind of player he'd need to be to make it as a pro.

"He was like your grandfather," Jefferson said. "He never screamed and yelled. He didn't cuss at you. He'd say, 'Richard, you won't get away with that against good teams. With your athleticism, you might drive baseline against a bad team and get away with it. But here at Arizona, we only prepare for good teams.' So, as a McDonald's All-American, am I going to let my ego jump in or am I going to listen to what this man who is winning championships and getting players to the NBA is saying?"

The idea of not listening to an accomplished coach may

sound absurd, but elite athletes often consider and sometimes indulge in it. Their physical superiority has allowed them to advance and possibly even excel without following protocol or directions, and some come to believe doing so is actually an essential part of their success. Many have never completely committed themselves to someone else's vision and, having gotten away with it, are convinced it's not necessary–until they reach a level where their innate talent isn't enough. And by then it's usually too late.

Even in a successful program such as Arizona, Jefferson's athleticism stood out. But rather than use that as license to skirt Olsen's principles, Jefferson realized that if he coupled his athleticism with the discipline necessary to fit within a system, he would be capable of not just meeting the demands of being a pro but excel as one.

"The pros that Coach Olson was churning out weren't McDonald's All-Americans," Jefferson said. "It was the Tom Tolberts, the Steve Kerrs, the Sean Rookses, the Luke Waltons. I don't want to be disrespectful, but those guys had nominal talent compared to myself. The minute they showed up at Arizona, no one would've thought they were pros. But they not only got to the NBA, they spent eight, nine, ten seasons there. After three years at Arizona, I was mentally prepared to compete every day and beat good teams. Which is how you stay in the NBA."

When Olson told Jefferson that for Arizona to win an NCAA title, he needed to focus on being a defensive stopper, Jefferson embraced it the same way he had Boie's idea of playing him in the post. The Wildcats made it all the way to the title game before losing to Duke despite 19 points and eight rebounds from Jefferson. (His four 3-pointers were also the only ones made out of Arizona's twenty-two attempts.)

Jefferson's demonstration of being coachable and willing

to sacrifice for the team produced an even bigger dividend. When the 2001 NBA Draft rolled around, the Wildcats' leading scorer, Gilbert Arenas, was the Golden State Warriors' second-round pick, thirty-first overall. Their second-leading scorer, Michael Wright, was taken eight picks later by the New York Knicks.

The New Jersey Nets, meanwhile, arranged a draft-night deal, agreeing to draft and send the seventh overall pick, Eddie Griffin, to the Houston Rockets in exchange for a package of first-round picks–the twenty-third, Brandon Armstrong; the eighteenth, Jason Collins; and the thirteenth pick, Jefferson.

Anyone who questioned the Nets for taking Arizona's third-leading scorer that high–and Arenas was one of them–were silenced by season's end when Jefferson played a vital role in the Nets' No. 1 defense and finished second in Rookie of the Year voting to future Hall of Fame forward Pau Gasol. His arrival also coincided with the Nets making back-to-back runs to the NBA Finals. By the time his rookie contract was set to expire, he had established himself as a solid two-way player, the team producing more points than they allowed whenever he was on the court. The Nets were eager to build around him, signing him to a six-year, $78 million extension. He rewarded them with a career-high 22.5 points per game average, but his overall game slipped; for the first time in his career, his defensive rating was lower than his offensive one. He knows exactly why: the ol' recalcitrant Richard reappeared, straining his relationship with head coach Lawrence Frank.

"I had a stretch where I wasn't coachable," he said. "It's like being in a relationship with a wife or a girlfriend. She's asking you to do the right thing; you just don't want to hear it."

Subsequently, the Nets were no longer interested in hearing–or seeing–Richard and traded him to the Milwaukee Bucks. The change of scenery didn't help. The Bucks, after finishing with a 26-56 record, let it be known around the league that Jefferson was on the trading block. Despite being twenty-eight years old and in his physical prime, his value in the eyes of many around the league had diminished.

San Antonio Spurs coach Gregg Popovich thought otherwise. He saw through Jefferson's blustery bravado and felt, just as Boie had, that to keep him engaged and focused he needed to be pushed.

"For a couple of years I thought, 'This is somebody that I think I can bring on,'" Popovich said recently. "The thing that intrigued me about him the most was I didn't think he was as confident as he was letting on. I thought he lacked a little bit of self-confidence. I thought he could be a better defender, given his physical skills, and I thought he was a talent that was not challenged–that he could get to a higher level."

The Spurs traded three players to the Bucks–Bruce Bowen, Fabricio Oberto, and Kurt Thomas–to find out, hoping Jefferson could be the piece that helped them capture their fifth championship and second in three years.

If Popovich could size up Jefferson from afar, it was because he not only tried to coach his players but also to learn from them. Much like Boie, he didn't stop at observing how someone he wanted to bring on board acted; he looked to find out why. It is surely why he has been able to win the trust of a wide assortment of personalities, from the stoic Tim Duncan to the human firecracker, Stephen Jackson. "Pop," as most in and around the NBA refer to him, is best known for his willingness to confront or chastise anyone he deems out of line, whether it be future Hall of Famers like Duncan, Manu Ginóbili, and Tony Parker, a United States president, or some hapless reporter who made the mistake of asking a trite question. What he asks of his players–or anyone who might incur his wrath–is that they take the message and ignore its delivery. He has learned to do the same when it comes to judging whether or not a player has received his message.

"What I've figured out is what I, as a coach, have to be aware of," he said. "Sometimes you think somebody didn't listen to you, but they did. A caveat for a coach would be: just because you don't get an immediate reaction or maybe somebody doesn't look you right in the eyes or somebody doesn't shake their head in approval to what you just said doesn't mean that they didn't hear you and that they don't agree with you or they're not going to employ what you're asking. Timmy [Duncan] would be a good example. I would say things to him, and sometimes I'd get zero reaction. He would just, well, *Timmy* a little bit. He's staring right at me, looking me in the eye. His lip does not quiver. His head does not shake. And, honest to God, many times I was thinking, 'Does he think I'm full of crap? Is he really buying this?' So if somebody doesn't react physically, you can't decide, 'Well, they're not coachable.' You have to make sure what your criteria is for being coachable. And for me, that's their actions. Some players will tell you exactly what you want to hear. They're good at it. I don't care what their words are. I care about how they employ what I've said on the practice court or in a game situation."

Manu Ginóbili taught Popovich that holding players to a certain standard doesn't mean holding them to a certain style. There is a right way to do anything but there is more than one way to do everything.

"I had to learn to zip my lip with Manu a little bit as time went along," Popovich said. "I couldn't put him in a box. I had to give him room to be Manu. He was such a mustang running through the hills and I was trying to get him to be a little bit more what I would call 'solid.' One and a half fewer turnovers per game, or trusting that Bruce Bowen is going to make the corner three, that just because Bruce doesn't dribble and doesn't pass, he can be trusted to make that open three. And I wanted him to appreciate Bruce, that he made life easier for all of us *because* he's not a one-on-one guy. So Manu listened, but I had to listen to Manu. I loosened the reins on him and realized that whatever mistakes he made were not as important as making sure he's free to play the game. We both allowed ourselves to be coached by each other, if that makes any sense."

Jefferson didn't know any of that about Pop when the Spurs acquired him. He was simply excited to be joining a storied franchise, led by a future Hall of Fame coach and a Hall of Fame nucleus. He also didn't know the role that Popovich had in store for him. His elation morphed into frustration when he found himself as little more than an emergency valve, asked to shoot only if Duncan, Ginóbili, and Parker were stymied and the shot clock was about to expire. Nor was he particularly adept at taking and making such shots. He had never been a spot-up shooter: if a defender didn't give him space to get off his long-range jump shot, it was an invitation to use his speed and hops to put the ball on the floor and go to the rim. But that wasn't an option in the Spurs system—at least, not his part in it.

"I was a 20-point-a-game scorer and then I went to San Antonio and I was standing in a lot of corners," Jefferson said. "Some of it was my doing, some of it was their doing, just the way they run their system. I was used to having the ball in my hands. But in San Antonio I would stand in the corner for three minutes, not get a shot, and all of a sudden the ball would end up coming to me with two seconds on the shot clock to knock down a three. That's never who I was in the first ten years of my career."

But Jefferson also wasn't a student who made the honor roll when he met Boie. Or a lockdown wing defender when he met Olson. Jefferson had to make a choice: cling to what he'd been or become the player the Spurs needed him to be.

"Athletes are inherently selfish," Jefferson said. "But if you can't change, that's when it becomes a problem. For me, it was like, 'Dude, I love to play this game. Am I going to only play it on my terms or am I going to play it in a manner in which I can be part of something?'"

Jefferson chose to pursue the latter. That meant forfeiting his downtime and spending a dry, dusty, 100-degree summer in San Antonio. Popovich, who loves to spend the offseason tracking down independent films, out-of-the-way bookstores, and little-known but exquisite restaurants, did the same. The two worked together, one-on-one, day after day, reconstructing Jefferson's long-range form. The most arduous drill consisted of a folding-chair obstacle course on the court, which Jefferson had to navigate as quickly as he could in a semi-crouch, getting him comfortable maintaining that posture so that when the ball was passed to him, he could immediately spring into his shot. Running in a more upright position meant catching the ball, coiling his body, and shooting, a slower process by only a half second or so, but a half second that could be the difference between a clean look at the basket and having a defender's hand in his face. The following season his usage rate plummeted to a career-low 15 percent–and his 3-point shooting percentage skyrocketed from 31.6 percent to a career-high 44 percent. It wasn't enough to get the Spurs another championship, but it extended Jefferson's career, which led to a championship ring as a vital part of the 2016 Cleveland Cavaliers.

"I had to become coachable again," he said. "It was 'Okay, Richard, you need to learn how to sit in a squatted position, how to be cocked and ready for one-second shots. If you can do that, we will be successful.' If I hadn't become a 40 percent 3-point shooter in year ten, I don't make it to year seventeen. The year we won the championship, I shot 39 percent from three in the postseason. If I don't have that skill, I'm not playing. I don't get to be a 3-and-D guy at thirty-six. I learned so much that proved to be transferable at a much later date. I would not have won a championship. Sometimes you have to be miserable to get where you want."

His summer of transformation still might not have happened had Jefferson been a miserable person, because Popovich would have been less inclined to spend a summer in a gym with him. It's one thing to invest that kind of time in a No. 1 pick such as Tim Duncan or Victor Wembanyama, players who clearly have the ability to transform a franchise; it's another to unearth the defensive skills and catch-and-shoot potential to create a "3-and-D player"—a 3-point shooter and defender—to complement the superstar.

"He didn't love it at the time, but he was always enjoyable," Popovich said of Jefferson. "I put a high priority on a player being coachable, and that's part of it. You might say, 'Well, what if the guy's got Kobe Bryant ability, but he doesn't want to hear your crap?' Well, then it gets into the ballpark of whether it's worth it. Is the rest of the team enjoying being with a guy that is just going to go his own way? A guy who doesn't allow the team camaraderie to come together, to allow players to fall in love with playing with each other? You have to gauge how willing you are to put up with someone who is not a very pleasant individual to be around. But that was never Richard."

In both sports and business, there is an unofficial metric that those in charge use to assess the value of an employee: production versus cost. It's not as simple as measuring what someone produces versus how much they're paid. Intangibles, such as the work atmosphere they inspire, and their trustworthiness, honesty, and punctuality, are all part of the equation. Pop invested in Richard because he enjoyed being around him as much as for what he hoped to get out of him.

Those early years defusing tense situations with deprecating humor rather than fists taught Jefferson how to forge relationships. During his years with the Nets, Jefferson befriended former New York Giants defensive end Michael Strahan. As successful as Strahan was on the gridiron–2001 NFL Defensive Player of the Year, XLII Super Bowl champion, four-time first-team All-Pro, two-time sack leader, 2014 Hall of Fame inductee–his broadcasting career might rank as more impressive. He not only has been part of Fox's NFL Sunday show for nearly two decades but won two Daytime Emmys as a cohost of the morning show *Live with Kelly and Michael.* He now cohosts ABC's *Good Morning America* as well as a game show, *Pyramid.*

When Jefferson retired from the NBA and decided to pursue a broadcasting career, he applied what he had learned about himself seeking success in basketball: he needed a mentor, of course, but he also needed to be challenged. Strahan provided the mentorship, outlining the rudimentary skills Jefferson needed to be on a TV studio show. Reading a prompter, when and how to address a camera, how to get in and out of a segment on time, taking cues and direction through an earpiece while simultaneously engaging in a conversation–much like in basketball, all that came rather easily to him. Too easily.

"I went into the studio and I was doing all that and I was like, 'This is boring; this is back to being in junior high,'" he said. "It wasn't what I needed."

Being a color commentator on live NBA games is much different. It requires the same basic skills, same preparation, same research, but the unpredictability and fluidity of a game, compared to the relatively static elements of the studio, make it far more challenging. It requires having both the confidence to give a strong opinion and the self-effacement to keep the game as the primary focus. The most talented know how to be good teammates but still authentic, alternately funny or serious, depending on what is appropriate in the moment. The competition for jobs is fierce because there are so few of them. Live national broadcast crews generally consist of one or at most two color commentators next to a play-by-play announcer. National networks generally carry two or three full-time broadcast teams and they are ranked. A network's No. 1 team works all the biggest matchups during the season. Only the No. 1 team for one network broadcasts the most visible and prestigious event, the NBA Finals.

At first, Jefferson was merely interested in being a broadcaster to show who he was: how funny, how smart, how knowledgeable. Mostly how funny, harkening back to his early teenage days as a jokester. The father of one of his closest friends and Arizona teammates, Luke Walton, proved to be an ideal model: UCLA and NBA legend Bill Walton.

The Waltons practically made Richard part of the family. He watched from their living room as the patriarch made the transition from player to broadcaster, trading in his tie-dyed Grateful Dead T-shirts for a sport coat and necktie and dialing back his stream-of-consciousness musings enough to be part of the two-man broadcast team for five NBA Finals. They included the 2002 Finals, in which Jefferson played.

When Richard first took the same player-to-broadcaster leap, he worked both lower-profile NBA and college men's basketball games, including a few of the latter with Bill. He fancied himself a court jester à la Walton in his latter years, who went back to wearing his tie-dyed T-shirts while working college games and dropping observations such as "I believe in science and evolution: I've been to the Grand Canyon," and "I had the only beard in the Western Hemisphere that made Bob Dylan's look good."

Being part of the NBA Finals broadcast, Richard thought, was reserved for legendary players like Bill and Magic Johnson or former head coaches like Doug Collins and Jeff Van Gundy, not journeymen who never so much as made an All-Star team.

Bill, of his own volition, routinely text messaged Richard critiques and encouragement before, during, and after his broadcasts, notes as simple as *Please speak up; Thanks, BW*; and *Great personal close; Excellent, we're so proud and happy; Happy anniversary to your mom.*

At the same time ESPN made Richard a fixture in their 2024 playoff coverage, he learned that Bill was battling cancer. The text messages, nevertheless, kept coming.

"I know he's sick but I can't tell anybody," Richard said. "Meanwhile, he's sending me messages–'Richard, you're going to be great. You're amazing. Keep killing it. Keep informing.' I would get this message literally before every game: 'I love you. I'm so proud of you.'"

Bill's passing just before the 2024 Finals and JJ Redick–another NBA journeyman–working them for ESPN/ABC as a broadcaster inspired Jefferson to aim higher and with a different purpose.

"I wanted it more for Bill versus my own ego of wanting to call the finals," he said. "It was more of wanting to have that connection to him."

To reach that goal, though, he had to turn back to the formula he had used with Boie, Olson, and Popovich. He had to synthesize who and what he wanted to be with someone else's vision of who and what he could be. Court jesters didn't work the finals for a network owned by Disney.

"I realized what my bosses were saying when I'd say funny shit and they'd say, 'We've got to trust you and the game's got to be the star,'" Jefferson said. "I didn't take it negatively. They were coaching me."

A month or so before the playoffs began, it was announced

that Jefferson would fill the seat left vacant by Redick's departure to coach the Los Angeles Lakers and partner with play-by-play man Mike Breen and incumbent analyst Doris Burke. That made Jefferson the first player to win a championship and broadcast the finals . . . since Walton.

The Indiana Pacers and Oklahoma City Thunder provided a thrilling seven-game series. Jefferson interacted with Burke and Breen seamlessly. His insight as someone who had played in the finals both as a young player and a veteran was invaluable, yet he had endearing moments of self-deprecation. ESPN opted over the summer to negotiate a new contract that would make him part of the finals team going forward.

None of which would've happened, he said, had he not been coachable.

"It's about finding your voice and that happy balance of what the company wants from you," he said. "What do they want from me and how can I, within what they want from me, find ways to be myself? It's learning how to be successful within the framework that you're given."

Motive is important as well. Speaking to an audience of millions when you're sharing the stage with two other people while the three of you are supposed to be the backdrop to the actual event is a balancing act that is far more delicate than most people realize. For someone doing it for the first time it could be particularly tricky. It would have been natural for Jefferson to want to prove to the audience, his colleagues, and his employers that he deserved to be there, which could lead to overdoing it or distracting from the game. It would be equally natural to overcompensate the other way and defer, fearful of rocking the boat.

Jefferson struck the perfect balance because of his motive: he wanted to honor Bill by adhering to all that text-messaged tutelage, by having the quiet confidence of all his encouragement, by being a good teammate. "The whole time he was on my heart and my mind," Richard said.

Jefferson is proof that finding Fulfillment and Victory aren't mutually exclusive. And, just maybe, there is another level to be reached by expanding the formula, by synthesizing our vision of who and what we want to be with someone else's vision of who and what we can be—in order to honor someone who inspired our vision in the first place.

YOUR GREATEST STRENGTH BEGETS *your greatest weakness.* Shakespeare is credited with being the first to say it, but the sentiment, phrased slightly different, is invoked by leaders in every industry all the time. (The late NBA head coach Flip Saunders was particularly fond of saying it.) For Jefferson, being funny served as a shield in his younger days and later opened the door to a career in broadcasting. But to advance, he had to evolve and realize that an asset, if leaned on too heavily, can also be inhibiting. The hidden value of being challenged to let go of what we do best—or we think we do best—is that it creates space to get good at something else. We don't lose the first talent; we complement it.

Every subject in this book grew by letting go of the idea that they had all the answers. They also had to temper or let go of an element that fueled their early success. Steve Young had to resist running with the ball. Steph Curry had to remake his jump shot. Brandi Chastain had to give up looking to score goals. John Staton IV had to dial down his white-hot competitive fire. Rose Zhang had to establish some independence from her father. Fred VanVleet had to reduce the boulder-sized chip on his shoulder. Landon Donovan had to be less malleable. Paolo Banchero had to be less strong-willed. Caroline Marks and Dirk Nowitzki had to be less self-critical.

There is one other common characteristic they all had: someone who believed they could make the necessary changes and be better for it. Someone who helped show them how. Not every coach or mentor is going to be as proactive or prescient as Popovich or the other coaches described here. Not everyone has the gift of recognizing potential and finding a way to extricate it. Sometimes the athlete has to be the one putting their proverbial cards on the table, both internally and externally. The conversation can start with the question, "What is it I'm not doing that would help if I did?" A coach or boss may or may not have the answer right away. Some may be satisfied with what they're getting, perhaps not seeing there is more to be given. (If that is the case, work on finding a different coach or boss.) Most will think about it and do some research, recognizing the benefit to them of facilitating an employee's or player's development.

When Jefferson arrived at Moon Valley, he said there were "a billion of me." At that point, maybe. But everyone has a unique gift waiting to be unearthed. Boie treated him as *one* in a billion, and Jefferson eventually saw himself in the same light. Whatever he does next, it won't be defined by what he can do now but what he believes he is capable of doing sometime in the future.

Even more valuable is the belief reflected in what he told his bosses as they evaluated whether to give him a shot at calling the NBA Finals. "As good as I am today, two years, five years, ten years from now, I'll be better," he said. "I put in the time and the work. Look at my track record."

His nine coachable compatriots all can say the same.

EPILOGUE

IF PLAYERS DON'T ALWAYS SEEM AS ELATED BY WINS OR CRUSHED BY losses the way fans or media sometimes are, it's because they learn not to be. That's particularly true in the NBA. An eighty-two-game season is too long and the energy players have to expend is too great to ride an emotional roller coaster. While joy releases an array of hormones that momentarily energize us and sadness or anxiety trigger hormones that sap us, in the end both consume more energy than we'd expend otherwise.

What I've never heard is how players actually stayed off that coaster. Another conversation with B. J. Armstrong provided the answer. "There aren't eighty-two games in a season; there is just one," he said. "The work isn't over after forty-eight minutes or when the buzzer sounds. You just stop playing. You assess what worked and what didn't and then the preparation for the next game begins. You just keep moving forward. You can't get wrapped up in how you played any one game until there are no more games to be played. Everything is about moving forward and where you are at the end. Every possession, every game, every practice, is just an opportunity to get better."

In other words, you might not end the season with a trophy but you will go home with a prize: all the lessons and information extracted from that season. Or that disappointing business quarter. Or that rejected manuscript. Play the long game. Nobody wins wire-to-wire in real life. Based on what I've learned from the legendary accomplishments of people in all fields, setbacks and disappointments are actually part of the formula, part of what drove them to previously unattainable heights. A loss isn't failure; it's fuel.

I was a *San Jose Mercury News* beat writer covering the Golden State Warriors when I met B.J., which meant I wrote on deadline on a daily basis, sometimes needing to turn in a game story minutes after the final buzzer. I often struggled, wanting my story to amplify what I had just witnessed. I'd get stuck in pursuit of perfection, searching for some sublime turn of phrase or poetic description, my heart hammering with one eye on the screen and the other on the clock. I'd send it in, then reread it and think, *It could have been so much better.* No matter what my editor said, I was rarely satisfied with the final product.

Applying the perspective B.J. shared didn't instantly solve my deadline angst, but it made it far more manageable and provided a lifetime blueprint for, well, everything. Whenever I'd stress over a particular story or assignment or TV segment, I'd simply tell myself, *This is just practice for the next one.* Afterward, I'd sit back and consider what I could've done differently to make it better, and then I'd apply it the next time.

Had I not adopted that perspective, I also might have not appreciated how much fun covering an NBA team as a job can be while keeping an eye on my real goal, which was to master long-form writing.

The overarching goal was to keep improving so I could stay in the game. Editors, bosses, and coaches alike appreciate growth. It has been more than thirty years and I'm still at it. That is my first piece of advice to those interested in pursuing a career similar to mine: Get in the game. Because if you're not, the chance to be coached is limited. That's why the drive to be part of a big-name enterprise right away—be it a company or an all-star travel team—is not necessarily the best scenario. Merely being on the staff or the roster offers precious little growth, personally or athletically.

My first job out of school was a one-year internship with New Hampshire–based Yankee Publishing, Inc. I was an editorial assistant but put in extra hours to pitch stories I could write for *The Old Farmer's Almanac* and *Yankee* magazine, along with submitting a few freelance memoir pieces for my hometown magazine, *Cincinnati*. I hoped that portfolio would land me a job with one of the New York–based national magazines—*Esquire*, *The New Yorker*, *GQ*, *Vanity Fair*—but the best I could get was a newspaper internship covering high school sports in San Diego. It was quite the letdown, but it turned out to be the best thing that could've happened to me. I was in the game every day, covering games and writing features. After a year, I spent a couple of months at a time writing for every section of the newspaper. Nobody in the community opened doors for me because of who I was or where I worked. I had to develop sources, cultivate relationships with coaches and administrators, and learn the history and rivalries of the local schools. Nobody told me what to write, only what passed for a story good enough to publish. Had I gone directly to a big-name enterprise as I had hoped, I would've always had the crutch of its renown and influence. Having to earn the confidence of those I wanted to write about on my own merit gave me the confidence that I could go anywhere and work for anyone.

My editors and fellow writers taught me a great deal, but my ambition, ego, and undisciplined lifestyle got in the way of developing close ties or accepting a mentor. One of my greatest regrets is that it took me as long as it did to realize this book's inherent message. For if you take anything away from the truths and the stories behind them, it should be that they are all rooted in and supported by relationships. When asked who I was writing this book for, I said, "The athlete–but it's as if the parents and coach are in the next room, listening." Because while it all starts with the athlete's willingness to be coached, the parents (or mentors) and coach play equally important roles in supporting the process. Being part of a healthy performer-parent-coach trifecta teaches the athlete how their personal and professional lives are intertwined and the importance of balancing them.

I didn't know all that–I just believed it, based on observation through my job covering sports–until I became a father and wanted to make certain that, if nothing else, my son and daughter were coachable. There were several reasons. One, I wanted to spare them the regret I have. Two, I knew from my work how vital it was to being successful. Three, I wanted to make sure that my role as a nationally recognized sports expert would not influence how they behaved or how they might be treated. I had seen too many young athletes who, frustrated by their role or their playing time, blamed the coach and looked to their parents to provide a solution, especially if they were influential parents. I wanted my kids to focus on what they could control, which was their effort and attention. I wanted them to believe that what they learned playing a sport was more important than what they accomplished. And four, I wanted to believe that being coachable would serve them beyond sports.

Did I hope they might go on to play beyond high school? Sure, if for no other reason than I love watching them compete. But I wanted it to be their choice. Besides, there are other ways to develop the skills—problem-solving, communication, discipline, teamwork—that I hoped they would get from playing. My priority was that their experience with sports, however long it lasted, would enrich and deepen *our* relationship, not damage it.

I am immensely fortunate that they are both now playing at the collegiate level. Both have distinguished themselves by the way in which they carry themselves, how they are as teammates; both have served as captains. What I am most grateful for is that my daughter, a basketball player, still asks me to work out with her and still considers me her shooting coach, and that my son, a football player, has enjoyed coaching me up on a sport I've studied and covered but never played. Even better, I've watched them build relationships with teammates and coaches alike that are sure to last long beyond their playing days.

You will find that, in every story in this book, the performers had someone relatively early in their lives who believed in their potential before anyone else. To anyone who has someone like that: Don't take them for granted and don't let them slip away. They can be ballast when your voyage gets rough and the greatest gift you can give them for that early faith is still being connected to you when it comes to fruition.

This book reveals the building blocks for success used by athletes, but I use the word "performers" often and interchangeably for a reason. We are all performers in one way or another and the view of obstacles, acceptance of criticism, approach to improvement, and overall principles herein can be applied by anyone, in any field, looking to realize the best version of themselves.

I have no doubt that most of you—performers, parents, coaches, and leaders—aspire to be versions of those I've written about and believe in some form of the truths they illustrated. This is my way of encouraging you to stick with it.

I'm reminded of what Grit Young taught his four sons: chasing a dream is fine, but make sure you have an attainable goal and a plan to reach it as a backup. My dream is that anyone who reads this book embraces the value of being coachable and experiences all that I—and my family—have. Or more. My plan simply was to provide the inspiration and the tools to make that happen.

Let me know if I was only dreaming.

ACKNOWLEDGMENTS

THE HARDEST PART OF THIS PROJECT WAS NOT BEING ABLE TO HONOR everyone who shared their stories and testimonies by including them in the final manuscript. They are represented in the book by way of having informed and bolstered my perspective, and I hope to find a forum for their stories at some point, but for now being mentioned here will have to suffice as recognition of their contributions. Along with all the performers, coaches, and parents who incrementally taught me about the value of being coachable over my thirty-year career, special thanks for their time and insight goes to Jalen Suggs, Larry Suggs, Mark Few, Roy Williams, Tyler Hansbrough, Diana Taurasi, Jerry Blevins, Chris Como, Brad Gilbert, Chuck Hayes, Nate Miller, Brandin Podziemski, Brendan Suhr, Zach Collins, and LeSean McCoy.

My great appreciation also goes to those who were instrumental in suggesting candidates for the book and/or connecting me with them: Craig Bestrom, Ray Ridder, Jon Wertheim, Ryan Tollner, Matt Rudy, Ben Zehnder, Paul Shirley, Joel Glass, Tom James, Steve Hawk, August Howell, Scott Tomlin, Lindsay Colas, Renee Felton, Aaron Heifetz, Brian Brownfield, Kevin Hopkins, and Bill Duffy.

This book might still be in the conceptual stage if not for the encouragement, enthusiasm, and prodding of my literary agent, Susan Canavan. Thanks to the entire Waxman Agency, most notably Ashley Lopez, for pitching the book to the entire globe.

I could not have found a better publishing house than Avery. The enthusiasm of the entire team, led by Tracy Behar and Lucia Watson, was inspiring. I also could not have asked for a more thoughtful and supportive editor than Jacob Surpin; he may have his down days but I have yet to see one.

Finally, to my wife, Corrine; our daughter, Chance; and our son, Mat: while you may (rightfully) see yourselves as athletes, you are the three most impactful coaches I've had in my life. Synthesizing who and what I want to be with who and what you think I can be has been the greatest and most deeply rewarding joy of my life. Honest, supportive, and trusting relationships are at the heart of being coachable, and no one has taught me more about what is required to cultivate and appreciate them than you.

A NOTE ON SOURCES

Almost all the interviews in this book were conducted by the author from 2023 to 2025. The few exceptions are noted and sourced in the text itself.

INDEX